KENT

A Chronicle of
The Century

Volume One: 1900-1924

by Bob Ogley

Kent journalist and historian, Bob Ogley, guides you through the highlights of the century — from those magnificent men in their flying machines to fashions of the day, from world wars to sporting victories, from archaeological discoveries to engineering achievements.
Here are the major scandals, the chilling disasters, the artistic triumphs and the dramatic moments of the most exciting and turbulent years Kent has ever known. The illustrations are evocative. They help to take you back in time, to re-live history as it happened. They help to capture the changing social and cultural life of a county that is also rich in folklore, and legend.
So vast is the subject that the book is to be published in four volumes. Here is the first.

  **Froglets Publications**

Publications Ltd

Brasted Chart,
Westerham,
Kent TN16 ILY

Tel: 01959 562972
Fax: 01959 565365

ISBN Hardback 1 872337 24 4
ISBN Paperback 1 872337 19 8

© Bob Ogley

Front cover illustration
shows
Shorts Biplane No 1 (FB1),
Dover Corporation tram,
Humberette Automobile,
Herbert Kitchener and
Marie Lloyd

This book was originated by
Froglets Publications Ltd and
printed and bound by Staples
Printers (Rochester) Ltd, Neptune
Close, Medway City Estate,
Rochester, Kent ME2 4LT.

Jacket design and additional
artwork by Alison Clarke

FOREWORD

To begin with a few defensive strokes I should explain that this is not a formal history of Kent in the 20th century. That would have required many more pages and photographs. This is a book of reportage rather than analysis — events of the first 25 years of this century written as though they had just happened. The project has been great fun, especially as it soon became clear that, in the first part of this century, no county has had a more dramatic story to tell than Kent.

It would not have been possible to complete this publication without the help and encouragement of many people. First and foremost is my partner Fern Flynn who helped with the research and worked long hours to help meet an impossible deadline. I am grateful also to Avril Oswald and Jill Goldsworthy who read and corrected the text and made many wise suggestions and to the printers, Staples of Rochester, whose professionalism I appreciate always.

This book has the support of Kent County Council's Arts and Libraries. Local history departments and heritage centres throughout the county have given me access to their photographic collections and reference files and I am grateful to all the librarians, in particular to the director, Mr Yinnon Ezra and Ms Hazel Halse of Thanet. I am also grateful to the librarians in the London boroughs whose boundaries were once in Kent and who are still strongly identified with the county.

I would also like to thank the staff of museums, editors and photographers of local newspapers and local history enthusiasts who have provided considerable help in my research. I am indebted also to the authors throughout the county, whose books I have scanned for relevant information and to members of the public who have responded to my appeal in newspapers for information. There are too many to name personally but they know I am grateful.

Finally, I would like to quote a passage from Arthur Mee's wonderful history of Kent. *"For those who love the past, Kent is incomparable within these islands. For those who love the present it has 1,432 square miles crammed with wonder and beauty. For those who look into the future it presents a bewildering problem of what will happen to this county now that thousands more residents are crowding in every year".*

Those words were written in November 1936 and they still apply today. Next year I will publish the second volume (1925 — 1949) and I will be delighted to hear from all those who may have a relevant photograph or story. I hope you will enjoy this volume well enough to place an order for the second and join our list of subscribers whose names are printed on page 197. The full details are on page 200.

Bob Ogley

PHOTOGRAPH CREDITS

Photographs in this book are the copyright of the following: **Kent County Council Arts and Libraries: Folkestone** (pages) 25, 31, 56 (bottom), 69, 76 (top), 85, 104, 110 (top), 115, 137, 141, 162 (top), 175, 178, 195. **Gravesend:** 10 (top), 16, 20, 196 (top). **Dartford:** 7, 30, 57, 164, 196 (bottom). **Deal:** 11, 60, 82 (top), 100, 102. **Ashford:** 13, 24 (bottom), 33 (bottom), 36, 44, 53, 92 (top), 132. **Tenterden:** 117, 121, 177, 184. **Dover:** 14, 18 (top), 46 (bottom), 48 (both), 78, 149, 193. **Tunbridge Wells:** 19, 72, 151, 186. **Heritage Services in Thanet:** 47 (both), 65, 87. **Sittingbourne:** 89 (both), 106, 126, 189. **Canterbury:** 63 (top), 76 (bottom) 181. **Gillingham:** 61, 62, 125, 150, 160. **Whitstable:** 182. **Rochester-upon-Medway Studies Centre:** 27 (bottom), 45 (top), 56 (top), 63, 70 (both). **London Borough of Bromley Library Services:** 22, 33 (top), 38 (bottom), 127, 172. **Bexley Library Service:** 9, 17, 50, 90 (top), 136, 148, 152, 171, 194. **Imperial War Museum:** 82 (bottom), 91, 98, 109, 111, 114, 118, 130, 139 (both), 142 (both), 147, 156, 161, 163 (top right), 166, 169, 170, 174. **Dover Museum:** 74-5, 122, 123,145, 159 (both). **Maidstone Museum:** 21, 64, 94. **Margate Museum:** 15, 24 (top), 90 (bottom), 93, 101, 168. **Topham Picture Point:** 10 (bottom), 18, 29, 52, 54 (top), 79 (both), 88, 108 (bottom), 154, 180, 185. **Tonbridge Historical Society:** 42, 49, 51, 73, 92 (bot), 140 (top). **Fleur de Lis Heritage Centre:** 128, 135, 144. **Philip Lane:** 4, 43, 55, 66-7, 110, 112. **Author's collection:** 5, 28, 32, 35, 40, 46 (top), 54 (bottom), 71, 80, 84, 86, 95, 97, 103, 124, 153, 163, 176, 183, 188, 190-1. **Mrs Phyllida Warner** 6 (top), 167. **Sport and General:** 107. **Salomons Centre:** 6 (bottom), 8, 119. **Hulton Deutsch:** 26. **Graham Edward-Smith** 27 (top), 37, 45 (bottom), 108 (top), 140 (bottom). **Lord Astor:** 34 (both), 187. **Fern Flynn:** 41, 186 (bottom). **Stone Collection of Birmingham:** 39. **Edwin Thompson** Collection: 99. **Gordon Anckorn:** 83: **Smallhythe Place (National Trust):** 105: **John Nelson:** 120. **Barry Wootton:** 38 (top). **MCC:** 129. **R.U.R.H.C:** 58-59. **Robert Opie Collection:** 23. **RAF Hendon:** 157. **John Williams Collection:** 192 (bottom). **Thomas Henry:** 192 (top). **Daily Mirror:** 194. **Daily Express:** 173

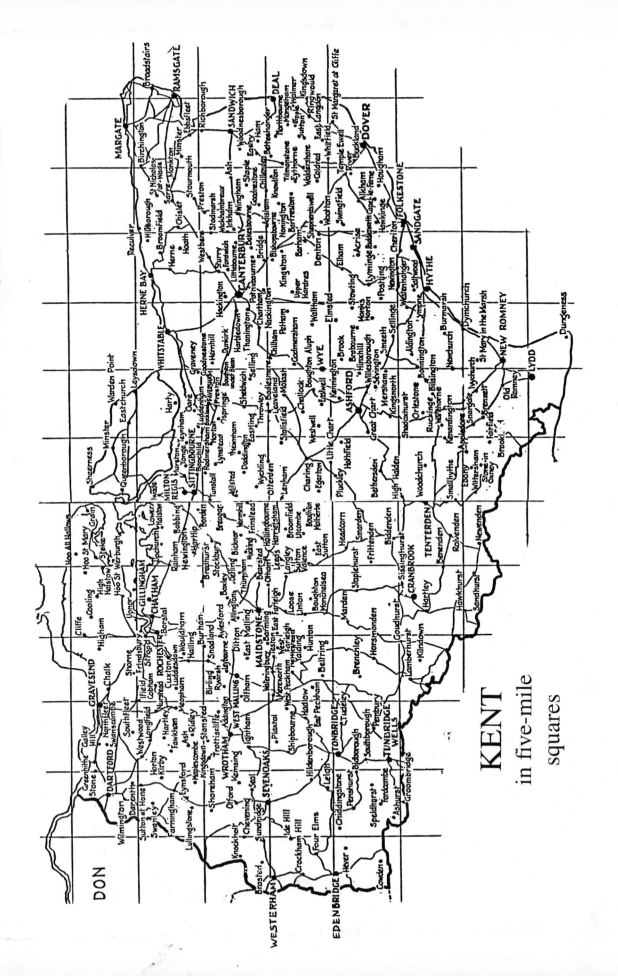

KENT
in five-mile squares

Railway gives Kent easy access to London

AS a new century dawns the Kent newspapers have been keen to review the old, looking back to the "grim old days of 1800" when the country was at war with Holland, Spain and France, America had only recently been lost and a man called Napoleon Bonaparte was just a threat on the horizon.

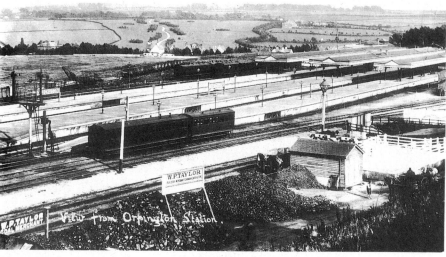

At the turn of the century the population of Orpington was 5,000 but the railway was changing all that — the surrounding countryside giving way to well-built unexceptional Victorian houses, the inhabitants delighted to live on the edge of lovely countryside

"But now, as we welcome the last century of the second millenium", says one Kent newspaper, "the extent of Britain's imperial powers has never been greater. The Empire stretches around the world. It has one heart, one head, one language and one policy."

In 1900, after a century of unparalleled success and expansion, there is peace in Europe with many nations contributing towards the World Exhibition in Paris. The financial outlook is buoyant and, in Kent, industrialisation is taking place at a fast pace. Great areas of the county are being transformed by modern industry and places like Deptford, Greenwich, Woolwich, Lewisham and Eltham are now part of Greater London. Industry is also creeping along the Thames Estuary making the huge maritime-industrial conurbation of Dartford-Gravesend-Rochester-Strood-Gillingham.

The railway, too, has changed the county. It provides easy access to the capital and makes the market towns of West Kent attractive areas for the homes of London businessmen. The first railway company to operate in Kent was the South Eastern which was an immediate a commercial success. The main line from Redhill to Ashford via Tonbridge was constructed in 1842. This had included the long straight track from Paddock Wood to Ashford. Extensions to Dover and Margate via Canterbury followed. The London, Chatham and Dover line reached Whitstable and Herne Bay in 1861 and, in 1868, the South Eastern opened its lines from London to Sevenoaks.

The railway is the making of the Kent towns. Large, expensive Victorian houses are springing up on the way to the station in every locality. Big mansions are making way for fashionable estates and desirable towns like

Sevenoaks have already become the haven of the first-class ticket holder. Briskly down to the station every morning in dignified procession go the top-hatted, frock-coated, white-cuffed businessmen.

Thanks to the railway, the most flourishing and highly developed industry is the holiday trade. Almost every coastal town from Sheerness on the north Kent coast round to New Romney and Littlestone on the south vies for a share in the expanding market. Entrepreneurs are investing huge sums of money in piers, promenades, hotels, theatres and entertainment facilities. Margate is fashionable for its regular hoy service from London. Folkestone is developing as a cross-Channel port, Ramsgate is "royal and respectable, restful and recuperating", Broadstairs "bourgeois".

There is one faraway skirmish that is causing some concern. Dutch settlers in South Africa have revolted against the just Sovereignty of the Queen but the Kent newspapers are certain that the Boer War, as it is known, will not last long despite the long sieges taking place in the garrison towns of Ladysmith and Mafeking.

Even so, the British cabinet have decided to send a further 10,000 men to defend Natal. A Kent contingent of Yeomanry and Volunteers is been raised for service in South Africa and Earl Stanhope, Lord Lieutenant of Kent, Colonel Lord Harris, commanding the Royal East Kent

'I intend to rid myself of the Kray stigma, start afresh and build a reputable career' — Charles Kray after his release from Maidstone Prison in January this year.

1975

January 1st: Richard Nixon's aides, Mitchell, Haldeman and Ehrlichman are convicted of trying to cover up Watergate.

January 2nd: Charlie Chaplin, expatriate Englishmen, who was born in South London, has been knighted in the New Year Honours. Arise Sir Charlie.

January 3rd: Charles Kray has been released after spending six years in the long-term wing of Maidstone Prison. His twin brothers Reggie and Ronald are serving 30-year sentences. Charles Kray intends to live with his friends Susan and George Dwyer at Amherst Drive, St Mary Cray.

January 27th: Five bombs exploded in London ending a long truce in the IRA's campaign of bombing and murder.

January 31st: Dr Donald Coggan has been enthroned as Archbishop of Canterbury in a glittering Christian pageant. The royal family was represented by Prince Charles and Princess Anne. Security was tight throughout Canterbury and more than 8,000 people attended the service.

February 4th: Mr Ted Heath is no longer leader of the Conservative Party. He telephoned his father in Broadstairs today with the news that Margaret Thatcher had won the first ballot. Mr Heath senior of Dumpton Gap Road said he 'was shocked'. It is now widely assumed throughout Kent that he will accept a peerage and be known as Lord Heath of Broadstairs.

February 25th: Miners have accepted pay rises of up to 35 per cent.

February: The Stour Centre, built on 20 acres of multi-purpose land between the East and Great Stour at Ashford, has finally opened. It includes a sports stadium, sauna suite, licensed bar, restaurant and snack bar.

Susan's murderer blames the devil

July 13th: **After a seven-day trial at Maidstone, Peter Stout has been jailed for life for the murder of Susan Stevenson at the Great Lines, Chatham, in September last year.**

Susan was hurrying to church when Stout pounced on her, pulled out a knife and rained blow after blow on the defenceless girl.

She dragged herself to the ornamental gardens next to Chatham police station but died later in Medway Accident Centre.

Her death sparked off the biggest murder hunt in the history of the Medway Towns. Stout, of Gillingham, eventually confessed but blamed the devil. "When he thinks I have one of my funny turns he does some extra poking and I give in."

March 1st: John Simpson, aged 26 of Seal Hollow Road, Sevenoaks, has been charged with the murder of 20-year-old Dawn Gregory of Pilgrims Way West, Otford.

March 7th: The body of Lesley Whittle, a young heiress who was kidnapped from her Shropshire home by a man known as the Black Panther, has been found in a 60-foot drain shaft. She was strangled.

March 25th: The mentally deranged Arab Prince Museid today assassinated his uncle, King Faisal of Saudi Arabia.

Rt Hon Eric Varley Minister of Energy opened Kingsnorth Power Station on the Isle of Grain. Costing £113 million it is the only oil and coal fired power station in Britain and is now the biggest in Europe. With an output of 2,000 megawatts, the station can produce sufficient electricity for a city of two million. The power is fed to the National Grid.

April 17th: After a brutal siege of 3½ months Cambodia has fallen under the control of the Communist Khmer Rouge forces.

Twenty-five miles of Kent's Thameside banks are being raised by five feet in readiness for the opening of the £200 million Thames flood barrier in 1979. The work is being carried out by the Southern Water Authority.

April 24th: The number of unemployed in Britain has passed the million mark.

April 31st: With the surrender of Saigon today the war in Vietnam is almost over.

June 6th: Referendum results tonight confirm that British people have voted overwhelmingly to stay in the Common Market with 67.2 per cent in favour.

June 21st: West Indies beat Australia by 17 runs today to win cricket's first World Cup.

July: St Mary's Hall at the King's School, Canterbury, has been opened by the Duchess of Kent.

August 24th: Today is the 100th anniversary of William Webb's historic cross-Channel swim which took him almost 22 hours and made him a hero throughout the land. Webb died in 1883 attempting to swim across the Niagara Falls rapids.

September 29th: Soldiers' local, The Hare and Hounds, Maidstone, was the target for IRA bombers. Thanks to the vigilance of the landlord and police in evacuating the area, no-one was killed. *See page 7.*

September 30th: Muhammad Ali beat Joe Frazier to retain his world heavyweight title.

November 3rd: A North Sea oil pipeline, which runs 110 miles on the seabed to a refinery on the mainland, has been opened by the Queen. Harold Wilson said today that he expects Britain to be self-sufficient in oil by 1980.

December 19th: Chrysler's closure of its components factory, Tilling Stevens in Maidstone, early next year will put more than 400 people out of work, it was announced today.

The £19,000 made by Mike Denness, captain of Kent and England cricket club, during his benefit year is a new county record.

GREAT HITS OF 1975

Sailing

Bye Bye Baby

I Can't Give You Anything

Heath 'beached' after clash with Thatcher

February 13th: Last year Sir Edward Heath's troubled three-and-a-half year reign as Prime Minister ran onto the rocks of an oil crisis and miners' strike. This week, Kent's best-known sailor-politician is well and truly beached after a head-on collision for the leadership of the Tory Party with Margaret Thatcher.

The MP for Finchley, who has lived with her husband Denis at Lamberhurst for nine years, won by 130-119 in the first ballot of Tory MPs and forced Ted Heath to resign. She then went on to become the first woman leader of a British political party by defeating four male rivals.

Mr Heath's supporters, shocked by the election of "an outsider to the mantle of Peel, Disraeli and Churchill" are speaking of her as a stop-gap or temporary aberration which in due course will be corrected.

Mrs Thatcher, aged 49, who has 17-year-old twins Mark and Carol, was ecstatic. "I just beat four chaps", she said. "Now let's get down to work."

Until recently the family lived in The Mount, Lamberhurst, an eight-bedroom centuries old house which snuggles against a small hill and has magnificent views of Goudhurst beyond. The family moved there in 1966 and it served as a successful retreat during holidays and weekends but this year the Thatchers decided to move into a comfortable flat at Scotney Castle.

Her election as Conservative Party leader has left most of her friends and supporters breathless for she is considered both a dissident and an outsider. More extraordinary is the fact that this 'dissident outsider' is a woman.

Yesterday, on the morning after the result had been declared, Mrs Thatcher went round to Mr Heath's house in Wilton Street in an attempt to preserve the spirit and appearance of party unity. No-one knows what was said although there are various, dramatic versions. The meeting was over within seconds.

Many believe the former Prime Minister will now accept a peerage and be known as Lord Heath of Broadstairs and others say he will not join the Shadow Cabinet, even if invited. He will go to the back benches where he will be free to express his personal views. The rift with Margaret Thatcher, say friends, will heal in time.

See page 13

Mrs Thatcher with her twin children, Carol and Mark, seen here when she lived at Farnborough, Kent, before the family moved to Lamberhurst.

The horrors of Moorgate

February 29th: Kent commuters today described the horrors at Moorgate when 33 passengers died in the worst-ever tragedy on the London Underground. Among them was trainee accountant Charles Gale, 23, from Seal who was en route to his city office.

Frank Gaunt, a print designer from Hythe, said the train was whizzing along and then suddenly there was a bang. He found himself sitting on someone else's seat surrounded by a tangle of bodies, choking soot, darkness and complete silence.

The driver, Leslie Newton, apparently accelerated into the blind tunnel when his 8.37 am commuter train from Drayton Park should have been braking. It crashed through sand, over the buffers and embedded itself in a wall.

Mr Gaunt said that many people were pinned to the roof of the carriage by a seat. It had ridden up a wall. "My shoulder was feeling stiff but I managed to free myself and prayed. Then the screaming started."

A doctor on the scene was Mrs Margaret Haig from Ide Hill, Sevenoaks, who crawled among survivors giving them pain-killing gas and injections. "There were bodies up above us and on the side but we ignored them because there was nothing else we could do. Another doctor told me that he had often wondered what hell was like. Now he knew."

Charles Kray released from Maidstone

January 3rd: Charles Kray, pictured here in the centre with his twin brothers, Reggie (left) and Ronnie, has been released after spending six years in the long-term wing of Maidstone Prison. He intends to live with his friends Susan and George Dwyer at Amherst Drive, St Mary Cray, until he is able to buy a new home.

Reggie and Ronnie, who are also in Maidstone Prison, will have a longer wait for their release. The gangland bosses who gained a reputation for violence while also commanding a cult following received life sentences in 1969 for murder. It is believed the brothers still have control of many properties, including pubs, hotels and nightclubs in South London and Kent.

See page 170

Maidstone pub blasted by IRA bombers

September 27th: The IRA bombing campaign on the British mainland moved to Maidstone last night when an explosion outside the Hare and Hounds pub on the Lower Boxley Road rocked the centre of the town and injured two policemen.

The pub, a popular meeting place for servicemen from the Royal Engineers Invicta Barracks, had been deliberately targeted by terrorists who hoped to inflict the kind of carnage caused by recent London and Birmingham pub bombs.

The policemen had been called to the road after a suspicious package was found four feet from the wall of the Hare and Hounds. The landlord, Mr Brian Wooster said: "I realised immediately it was a bomb and cleared the pub of customers. The police arrived and were in the process of evacuating the area when the explosion

occurred." He added: "We have a lot of soldiers in the pub and with the recent wave of bombings I knew it must happen locally, sooner or later."

One family who had a lucky escape were Mrs Christine Greenaway and her four children who lived in the house opposite the Hare and Hounds. The two policemen knocked on her door and said: "You've got four minutes to get out." Mrs Greenaway was just preparing to run with her children when an enormous bang threw them across the room. The family escaped serious injury but the house is badly damaged.

Kent police, led by Chief Constable Barry Pain, set up road blocks immediately and put a well-rehearsed emergency plan into operation. All pubs nearby were evacuated and suspicious packages investigated. *See page 32*

The county is losing its stately elms

October 30th: The countryside of Kent is being ravaged by Dutch elm disease. Thousands of these stately trees — in woods and parks, around cricket grounds and alongside river banks — are dying because of a suffocating fungus, spread by beetles, and growing beneath the bark.

The disease, first identified some years ago, has been particularly virulent in the past few months.

In Hythe, it is not so much a rural calamity as an urban disfigurement. Hundreds of magnificent elms planted along the banks of the Royal Military Canal, dug as part of the defences against Napoleon's army, are dead or dying.

According to a report by the Forestry Commission, 6.6 million elms have now been destroyed. The disease started in southern England and appears to be advancing northwards. Some trees are 200 years old.

Local authorities are now working closely alongside conservation groups in a bid to plant replacement trees. The Civic Society in Hythe estimates that 2,000 will be required.

Elizabeth Taylor and her mother Sara. With her brother, Howard she lived with her parents at Little Swallows, Cranbrook.

Happy days in Cranbrook for little Liz Taylor

October 10th: As Elizabeth Taylor and Richard Burton were remarrying today in a remote Botswana village, older people in Cranbrook were recalling the time that "little Liz" lived with her parents in a cottage on the Great Swifts estate, within sight of the famous village windmill.

Mr and Mrs Taylor were offered the cottage by Major Victor Cazalet. They called it Little Swallows and enjoyed several happy years in the village.

One lady who remembers the family well is Mrs May Ealding who worked for the Taylor family and looked after Liz. "She learned to ride in Cranbrook and on occasions we used to hitch the pony to the trap and go shopping in the village. She was a lovely child but very vain."

The family went to America on the outbreak of war and Elizabeth grew into a violet-eyed beauty, making four films by the time she was 12 including

Lassie Come Home and *National Velvet*. She has gone on to make many fine films and won an Oscar for her performance in *Who's Afraid of Virginia Woolf?* (1966).

Today she is celebrated for her glamorous personal life and eight marriages — most notably to Richard Burton in 1964. They were divorced last year after a stormy ten years but, to the delight of villagers in Cranbook, are making another attempt.

Graham Hill with two of his three children, Brigette and Damon.

Channel Tunnel plan abandoned

January 20th: The concept of a fixed crossing across the Channel, independent of wind or tide, which has been an engineer's dream since the beginning of the 19th century, has foundered yet again.

The scheme, approved by both governments in 1973 for a 32-mile tunnel costing an estimated £468 million, has now been abandoned.

Kent County Council chairman, Mr Robin Leigh-Pemberton, said he was surprised and concerned that the decision was taken without any consultation with the KCC. *See P 82*

July: Work has begun on building the largest on-river flood storage system in Britain at Hayesden, near Tonbridge, in an effort to prevent the kind of disastrous floods which devastated the intensively-farmed flood plain between Tonbridge and Yalding in 1968 and 1974.

The Medway Flood Relief Scheme is unique. The idea is to throttle back flood water in the channel behind a 1,300 metre long barrier, and to release it under control, so that the river level downstream will never rise above "bank-full" condition.

September 22nd: Firemen with turntable ladders rescued several nurses, trapped by fire in their rooms at Oakwood Hospital, Barming, last night. Other nurses, dressed only in night clothes, fled in panic as the blaze spread rapidly through their nurses' home.

The bravery shown by the firemen was extraordinary. Wearing breathing apparatus they fought their way into the blazing building and when the roof collapsed two were seriously injured. More than 100 rooms were badly damaged and many nurses lost all their clothes and belongings.

Kent racing ace Tony Brise dies alongside Graham Hill

November 30th: Graham Hill, twice world motor racing champion and the sport's number one ambassador, died today along with five members of the Lotus Grand Prix team when the light aircraft he was piloting crashed in freezing fog near Elstree Airport yesterday evening.

Among those who died was Tony Brise of Bexley, one of Kent's best-loved and most promising Grand Prix racing drivers who was tipped as a future world champion.

A funeral service for Tony, 24, will be held at St Michael's Church, Wilmington next week. Among the mourners will be his widow Jackie and Bette Hill.

Graham Hill's interest in motor racing began at Brands Hatch in 1953 when he paid six guineas, completed four laps and gave up his free time to work there as an unpaid mechanic.

A year later he joined Colin Chapman and Team Lotus. Hill is the only Formula One champion to have won the other major events, Indianapolis (1966) and Le Mans (1972).

See page 59

The Union Windmill, Cranbrook, the finest smock mill in the country. In 1960 it was taken over by Kent County Council which, with assistance from the Society for the Protection of Ancient Buildings, restored it as a working mill. Built by Henry Doubell in 1814 it is the tallest in Kent and the largest in England. It dominates the centre of the 'capital' of the Weald.

75 for 75: The best buildings in Kent

September: Kent's richness in architectural heritage is well known. It has more than 16,000 listed buildings and 250 conservation areas — figures which exceed those of any other county apart from the Greater London Council area. In celebration of European Architectural Heritage Year, the county is holding an exhibition of photographs of 75 buildings of special excellence for 1975. They are:

82 High Street, Dartford (15th century), **Cobham Hall** (16th - 19th), **Cobham College** (14th), **Meopham Windmill** (19th), **Quebec House,** Westerham (16th), **Squerryes Court,** Westerham (17th), **Chevening House** (17th), **Sevenoaks School** (18th), **Knole** (15th), **Archbishop's Palace,** Otford (16th), **Ightham Mote** (14th), **Old Soar,** Plaxtol (14th), **Yotes Court,** Mereworth (17th), **St Lawrence Church,** Mereworth (18th), **Mereworth Castle** (18th).

Hadlow Castle (19th), **Whitbread Hop Farm**, Beltring, **Hever Castle** (14th), **Penshurst Place** (14th), **Somerhill**, Tonbridge (17th), **Groombridge Place** (17th), **The Pantiles**, Tunbridge Wells (17th), **Church of King Charles the Martyr,** Tunbridge Wells (17th), **Finchcocks,** Goudhurst (18th), **Union Windmill,** Cranbrook (19th), **Corn Exchange,** Rochester (18th), **Eastgate House**, Rochester (16th), **The Guildhall,** Rochester (17th), **Restoration House,** Rochester (16th), **Rochester Castle** (12th).

Cathedral Church, Rochester (13th), **Gibraltar Terrace**, Chatham (18th), **Town Hall**, Chatham (19th), **The Quadrangle Storehouse**, Sheerness Dockyard (19th), **The Old Court Hall**, Milton Regis (15th), **80 Abbey Street**, Faversham (15th), **Gillett's Granaries**, Faversham, **The Guildhall**, Faversham (19th), **Lees Court**, Sheldwich (rebuilt after fire in 1910), **Tithe Barn**, Boxley (14th), **All Saints**, Maidstone (14th), **The Archbishop's Palace**, Maidstone (14th), **The Chequers Inn**, Loose, **Estate Cottages**, Linton (19th), **Synyards**, Otham (15th).

Leeds Castle (13th), **Quested Almshouses**, Harrietsham (rebuilt 18th), **Archbishop's Palace**, Charing (14th), **Estate Cottages**, Pluckley (17th), **The Old Cloth Hall**, Biddenden (16th), **Clock Tower, Marine Terrace**, Margate (19th), **Farmhouse and barns**, Sevenscore, Minster-in-Thanet (18th), **Christchurch Cathedral**, Canterbury (from 11th), **The Norman Staircase, King's School,** Canterbury (12th), **Greyfriars**, Canterbury (12th), **Eastbridge Hospital,** Canterbury (12-14th), **St Martin's Church**, Canterbury (14th), **Barns and Oasts, The Manor House**, Littlebourne (18th), **113 and 114 High Street**, Wingham (17th), **Richborough Castle** (3rd).

Manwood Court, Sandwich (16th), **22 High Street**, Sandwich (15th), **The Salutation**, Sandwich (1912), **Chillenden Windmill**, (1868), **St Nicholas Church**, Barfreston (11th), **Betteshanger House** (1886), **13 Middle Street**, Deal (18th), **Deal Castle** (1540), **Dover Castle** (1185), **Roman Pharos Lighthouse**, Dover Castle (1st AD), **Waterloo Crescent**, Dover (1838), **Maison Dieu Hall**, Dover (1221), **Swanton Mill**, near Mersham (17th), **Barns at Westernhanger Manor**, near Stanford (16th), **St Augustine's Church**, Brookland (14th).

'Unless consumption is cut by a half all over Britain, the country will face water rationing until Christmas' — Dennis Howell, Minister of Drought, after the "summer of the century".

January 2nd: It was announced today that the High Court made 1,875 winding-up orders last year, making 1975 the worst year for financial failures in Britain's history.

January 7th: Troops from the Special Air Services have been ordered into South Armagh where 15 Protestants and Catholics have died in sectarian murders in one week.

January 13th: Dame Agatha Christie, Britain's wealthiest author, died today just after completing her latest Poirot story. She was 85 and renowned as Queen of the Detective Story.

January 21st: Two Concorde aircraft took off simultaneously today from London and Paris on their maiden commercial flights.

February 11th: John Curry has won the men's figure skating gold medal at the Innsbruck Winter Olympics with a display of athletic agility.

February 24th: L.S. Lowry, the northern industrial townscape artist, famous for his matchstick characters, died today.

March 16th: Harold Wilson, leader of the Labour Party for 13 years, today resigned as Prime Minister. In a surprise announcement he instructed his press secretary: "Tell lobby correspondents I have a little story that might interest them."

March 19th: Princess Margaret and her husband, the Earl of Snowdon, are to separate after 15 years of marriage.

March 24th: President Isabel Peron has been deposed by Argentina's military leaders in a bloodless coup.

April 5th: James Callaghan, 64, defeated Michael Foot, leader of the left wing, by 176 to 137 in the latest ballot for the job of Britain's Prime Minister.

April 26th: Actor Sid James collapsed and died on stage at Sunderland.

May 1st: Second Division Sunderland has beaten Manchester United 1-0 in the Cup Final.

May 10th: Jeremy Thorpe has resigned from the Liberal Party after claims by a male model, Norman Scott, that they once had a homosexual relationahip.

June 2nd: Lester Piggott today won the Derby at Epsom for a record seventh time.

June 18th: More than 100 are dead and a 1,000 injured after three days of looting, rioting and burning in South Africa's black townships.

July 3rd: The blond long-haired Swede, Bjorn Borg, today became the youngest Wimbledon champion for 45 years by beating Ilie Nastase in the final.

July 4th: In a brilliant military operation Israeli commandos rescued 100 hostages held by pro-

The people of Kent have found many ways of raising money but how about this for a novel idea? Peter Brown, 35, lived in a 135-gallon cider barrel suspended above the village green and raised £1,300 for the All Saints, Biddenden Church Roof Appeal and the building of a sports pavilion and squash courts. For seven days he ate, slept and watched television.

Palestinian skyjackers at Entebbe airport today.

Iron railings, cast in Lamberhurst in the early 1700s for St Paul's Cathedral, have been returned to the village and placed outside the village hall. Lamberhurst was once the centre of the Wealden iron-smelting industry, the water to operate the hammers provided by the nearby River Teise. The iron railings stood at St Pauls for more than 200 years and it was a decision by the Dean and Chapter to return them to Lamberhurst.

July 7th: David Steele was today elected leader of the Liberal Party.

July 30th: Richard Ingrams, editor of *Private Eye* is sent to trial on criminal libel charges brought by James Goldsmith.

New wheels and cogs for Big Ben have been cast at the works of MJ Allen in Ashford following the breakdown of Westminster's famous clock

August 1st: In her new book *And The Morrow Is Theirs*, Sue Ryder, wife of wartime fighter pilot Group Captain Leonard Cheshire, says she wants to open a home in Kent, similar to the Cheshire Homes her husband is opening all over the country. Sue, who worked for Special Operations during the war, went to school at Benenden.

Kent's gipsy population is now the largest in the country, but the KCC is still looking for official sites to house the growing number of itinerants. At the moment there are seven which cost the county more than £100,000 per site per year.

August 13th: Winnie Mandela, wife of the jailed African black leader, has been arrested following the recent township riots.

Viv Richards, the West Indian batting sensation from Antigua, today hammered 291 in his team's total of 687-8 against England.

September 9th: Mao Tse Tung, leader of Communist China, died today aged 82.

September 29th: Britain has applied to borrow $3.9 billion from the International Monetary Fund to prop up the pound.

October 24th: Britain's James Hunt has won the Formula One championship from Niki Lauda by a single point.

October 26th: The National Theatre on the South Bank was opened by the Queen today.

November 2nd: Jimmy Carter of Plains, Georgia, is the new President of the United States.

November 29th: The Grant of Arms, recognising Ashford's status as a borough, has been presented by Lord Astor of Hever, Lord Lieutenant of Kent. It was received by the Mayor of Ashford, Cllr Harry Watts.

GREAT HITS OF 1976

Mississippi

Save Your Kisses For Me

1976

Jim Swanton retires — but promises to carry on writing

January: E.W. (Jim) Swanton, well-known in Sandwich, his home town since 1963, has recently retired as the *Daily Telegraph* cricket correspondent after a journalistic career which began in 1927.

One of the most celebrated and prolific members of the press corps and certainly the longest serving, Jim has followed the MCC (and later England) all over the cricketing world, reporting many of the greatest Test matches ever played.

In 1937-38 he had one season with Middlesex and then spent most of the war years as a POW in the Far East, having been captured when Singapore fell.

Jim, who has twice taken his own touring team to the West Indies and once to Malaya, is currently president of Kent Cricket Club, a founder member of I Zingari, a member of the Cricket Society and the MCC. He is a regular BBC broadcaster and has written scores of books about the game.

His latest, *Swanton in Australia,* follows the fortunes of five England tours "down under". On most of these he has been accompanied by his wife Ann, a pianist, painter and former championship golfer, whom he married in 1958.

Jim and Ann Swanton after their wedding in 1958.

Gravesend psychopath charged with five murders

September 12th: An unbridled two-year climax of terror came to an end today when Patrick Mackay, a former Gravesend school caretaker, gardener and odd job man, was sentenced to life imprisonment for the manslaughter of three people. Among his victims was Father Anthony Crean, a retired chaplain, who was brutally stabbed to death in his home at Shorne.

Mackay, who appeared in court charged with five murders, was described as a "cold, psychopathic killer" who was obsessed by Nazi propaganda and the brutalities of the Third Reich.

As a Gravesend schoolboy he was a bully and torturer of pet animals. At the age of 16 he tried to strangle his mother and threatened his sisters. He spent three years in mental wards where he committed violent assaults on nurses and other patients. In 1974 he absconded from a mental hospital and embarked on his rampage of terror.

Father Crean, who had once befriended and tried to help Mackay, was his last victim — killed with a knife and axe in his home near the Rose and Crown pub in Shorne.

Mr Michael Parker QC who defended Mackay at his trial said that in everyday life his client appeared to be normal. He was a classic psychopathic type and admitted the present state of medical science held out no immediate hope for his condition.

The judge said: "You knew what you were doing and you knew it was wrong therefore you are not insane." Mackay was sentenced to life, not for murder, but manslaughter. Two cases were left on file and another five required police investigation.

'Kent is the most alluring of counties — from the nightingale in the bluebell woods to the music of the roundabout on Margate Sands' — Dorothy Gardiner.

1800-1899

Toys Hill — the summit of Kent. It was here that Octavia Hill sank a well 96 feet deep which yielded an unfailing supply of pure water. It took two people some minutes to wind up the buckets.

Mounted Rifles and Major Cornwallis on behalf of the West Kent Yeomanry have opened a subscription fund in aid of funds for equipment.

The good news far outweighs the bad. The county is ecstatically celebrating the long reign of Queen Victoria and the many advances of scientific knowledge since she ascended the throne; the advent of the steam engine and its many uses; the railway, steam ships, the introduction of the telephone and the telegram, the coming of electricity, the bicycle and even the great automobile craze, which may be here to stay. More incredibly there is talk of "moving pictures" and men are even trying to fly!

Already one aeronautical pioneer has lost his life. Percy Pilcher, who built Hawk gliders in a shed near Lower Austin Farm, Eynsford and once glided through the air at Magpie Bottom, was killed near Rugby in September 1899 — the first Briton to die in a gliding accident.

The use of gas for lighting, heating and cooking has also spreading rapidly. Some Kent towns have electric tramcars. In Dover the tramway is three years old, setting the standard for this new form of transport and rivalling both the train and the horse-bus — perhaps soon to be in competition with the motor bus.

In this first year of the new century there are many important industrial centres; shipbuilding at Chatham, Rochester, Gillingham and Sheerness, electrical manufacturers at Erith on the banks of the Thames, railway coach and waggon builders at Ashford, gunpowder manufacturers at Sittingbourne, Milton and Faversham, all giving employment to a large number of men. Almost 5,000 Kent people are engaged in the manufacture of paper. There are scores of breweries as befits a hop-producing county. Agriculture is still the staple rural occupation but, among a few far-sighted people, there is anxiety over the future of the countryside and Britain's wonderful heritage.

One of those most concerned is Miss Octavia Hill who lives at Crockham Hill, near Edenbridge and has recently helped to form an organisation called the National Trust. Already the people of Kent are donating buildings and land to the Trust including Mr and Mrs Richardson Evans of Toys Hill, 700 feet high on the Greensand Ridge above Westerham, who have given three cottages and a small terrace which contains a well. Octavia Hill has sunk the well and the people of Toys Hill are drawing up water for the first time. It revolutionises their lives.

As the county congratulates itself on a century of achievement, the people of Kent know the age of discovery is far from over. Every town is attracting or producing an abundance of inventive individual genius. Tunbridge Wells has David Salomons, the automobile pioneer, Gillingham's great scientific innovator is Louis Brennan, Crayford has an enterprising mechanical draftsman in Hiram Maxim and Broadstairs boasts a budding newspaper tycoon in Alfred Harmsworth.

Those who want to get away from the towns and the cutting edge of technological development can climb the North Downs and sit on top of the world between fields of blue and gold, surrounded by wild flowers, listening to nothing but the song of the birds while looking at God's own canvas stretched out below. This is the real Kent.

Guy Lubbock of Emmetts, Ide Hill driving Via Pym of Foxwold, Brasted Chart in his smart new Rexette.

Sir David Salomons in his Peugeot, the first car seen in Kent — which had been a sensation at Tunbridge Wells in 1895

Mr Edward Waterman of Dartford with his chauffeur, Mr Martin in a 1900 Humberette.

Wonderful invention — but only for the rich

1899: More and more people in Kent — but usually the very rich or very sporty — are buying their own private automobiles. The great motor craze which swept through America and Europe may have been slow to reach Britain, but there is no doubt now that it is probably here to stay and Kent is showing the way.

The first to own an automobile in Dartford was Dr James Hamilton who swapped a Locimoto steam engine for a Brock. He was soon joined by Alexander Marcet, a director of Halls who bought a Benz while Everard Hesketh chose a Clement-Talbot and Edwin Sharp an 8hp Speedwell.

In Sevenoaks the honour of being the town's first automobile car owner falls to a local doctor, Dr Brown who drove a Benz Ideal supplied by Mr Bywater of London Road. The *Sevenoaks Chronicle* wrote: "Upon enquiring we learn that Dr Brown is very pleased with the performance of his new carriage. He has now had it for two months during which time he has experienced no trouble whatsoever and pronounces it quite a success. It does the work of two horses and climbs any hill with ease, being fitted with a special gear for this purpose."

The first owner in Tonbridge is Mr Alfred Cornell, a watchmaker and jeweller, who occupies premises at the lower end of the High Street. Another is Harry Beckett, pharmacist, dentist and inventor of Quarry Hill Road.

Both these men campaigned to end of tyranny of the man with the red flag who had to precede every motor-powered vehicle to warn horse drivers. They were joined by William Arnold of East Peckham who was actually prosecuted for "proceeding at a speed greater than four miles an hour."

The Red Flag Act was eventually repealed. It had been introduced to control steam-driven tractors and then applied to motor vehicles. In 1896, however, the restriction requiring vehicles to be preceded by a man carrying a red flag was lifted and then the speed limit raised from four miles an hour to a more reasonable 20mph.

Today horse-drawn transport still rules the road but there are now powered vehicles in the ownership of professional men who keep their motor car in the stable yard and a chauffeur in livery in addition to the stable man. The cost of motoring is high so it will never be as popular as the railway or tram but it will be interesting to see how many people find the money to invest in automobiles during the early years of the new century.

One man has three automobiles, which he keeps in his stables. He is Sir David Salomons of Broomhill, Southborough.

Sir David Salomons, mayor of Tunbridge Wells and owner of Kent's first motor car.

When Sir David defied the Red Flag law

SIR David Salomons of Broomhill, Southborough is the man who first saw the enormous potential in the horseless carriage and then made endless journeys to the Continent to see how such vehicles were developing. In fact his enthusiasm was so great that he actually bought a single-cylinder Peugeot to England and — at his own expense — held an exhibition at the Agricultural Showground in Tunbridge Wells. That was in October 1895.

At that time probably not more than one person in a million had ever seen an automobile but Sir David entered his own Peugeot and found three more — a twin-cylinder Panhard et Levassor, owned by the Hon Evelyn Ellis, a small but rather under-powered de Dion Bouton tricycle and a fire pump powered by a Daimler engine.

The exhibition was attended by 5,000 people, fascinated by this unprecedented spectacle of carriages moving without horses. They saw a hill-climbing demonstration by the Peugeot and the Panhard and learned that the Peugeot could travel about 180 miles on one charge of petroleum. Finally, Sir David defied the law of the land, the local police and the mayor by driving his car for a short distance along a road near the showground without the necessary pedestrian walking in front. He didn't worry too much. He was the mayor!

Sir David realised that such laws would have to be changed if the automobile was to stay and campaigned furiously for the repeal of the four-mile-an-hour limit and the Red Flag law. To his delight it was amended in 1896.

Hiram Maxim and friends with their flying machine.

The Flying Machine — will it ever get off the ground?

IS this a vision of the future? Will man ever be able to fly? Hiram Maxim, Crayford's eccentric inventor thinks so and here is the man himself, with his full white beard, among those who share his great dream. They are sitting on a "flying machine".

It was more than 16 years ago that Mr Maxim, an American by birth, relocated his works in Crayford and then prepared his first drawings of a prototype flying machine, estimating that it would take £5,000 and five years of careful preparatory work to realise his great pioneering ambitions. It would take a further three years, he guessed, to build an engine light enough to power the machine.

Maxim began to work on his idea in 1891. He obtained permission to erect a large hangar in Baldwyns Park between Bexley and Dartford where he could experiment with the development of engines and propellers. He then laid 1,800 feet of track on which the flying machine could be run and tested.

By 1894 the machine was ready for testing. It was composed of a four-wheel platform to which was attached a boiler, fired by naphtha, which produced steam to a pressure of 320 lbs per square inch. The steam was fed to two engines, fitted to the tubular steel framework supporting the flying surfaces. Two twin-bladed propellers were fitted. The whole machine weighed 8,000 lbs with a flying surface 120 feet long by 104 feet wide.

Various initial trials were conducted and, on the third, the flying machine sped along the track and flew 100 feet before structural failure brought it down with a thud. It had attained a height of only two feet but Hiram Maxim had become the first person to design a machine that could lift itself off the ground.

The great man is continuing with his experiments and we wish him luck. Is it beyond the realms of possibility to imagine that, by the turn of the next century, flying machines will carry passengers around the skies, perhaps even to foreign lands.

Only time will tell.

January: The old boathouse on the banks of the canal, near Gravesend looking very much as it did when Charles Dickens strode across the marshes from his home in Chalk soon after he was married. This was the inspiration for "Peggoty's boathouse" in David Copperfield. Dickens wrote: "We turned down lanes bestrewn with bits of chips and little hillocks of sand and went past gas-works, rope walks, boat-builder's yards, ship-wrights' yards, ship-breakers' yards, caulkers' yards, riggers' lofts, smiths' forges....until we came out upon the dull waste....I looked in all directions, as far as I could stare over the wilderness and away at the sea, and away at the river, but no house could I make out.....only a black barge, or some other kind of superannuated boat...high and dry on the ground...and smoking very cosily."

THE PROPHECIES OF H.G.WELLS ARE CAUSING QUITE A STIR

'People of today take the railways for granted as they take the sea and sky; they were born in a railway age and they expect to die in one'

May: The novelist H.G.Wells, who once lived with his parents above a small shop in Bromley High Street, has moved with his wife Jane into a new home, Spade House, Sandgate, Folkestone. There he will continue with his writing and entertaining. Wells has already won wide repute as a prophet of what science may one day bring to pass. His latest fantasy is called *War of the Worlds*. It follows *The Time Machine*, written while he lived in a small flat in Sevenoaks, *The Island of Dr Moreau* and *The Invisible Man*.

Wells was originally apprenticed to a draper but, after attending T.H.Huxley's lectures at the Royal College of Science, he decided to be a teacher. Then his health broke down so he starting writing, promoting the theory that scientific progress can bring about a glorious millennium if man-

kind can only act in a rational way.

His fantasies are causing a great stir and so are his prophecies. In a series of articles, called *Anticipations,* which he is writing for the *Fortnightly Review*, Wells questions whether the railway will remain the predominant method of land locomotion in the future. He

writes: "The abounding presence of numerous experimental motors is so stimulating the imagination that it is difficult to believe the obvious impossibility of them, their convulsiveness, clumsiness and exasperating trail of stench will not be rapidly fined away."

He says that "trucks" will one day be used to distribute goods and parcels, that automobiles will be capable of a day's journey of 300 miles or more and that the horse and pedestrian will be segregated from the high road. "When that segregation sets in", he says, "higher, profitable, longer routes will be joined up...and the quiet English citizen will read with surprise in the violently illustrated magazines of 1910 that there are many thousands of miles of these roads. And thereupon, after some patriotic meditations, he may pull himself together."

'I know not whether laws be right, or whether laws be wrong. All that we know who be in gaol is that the wall is strong' — Oscar Wilde, The Ballad of Reading Gaol.

January: John Lubbock of High Elms, Downe is among those ennobled by the Queen in her New Year's honours list — and no award has been more popular. In 1871 Lubbock, then a Liberal MP for Maidstone, introduced an act which provided the public with four extra holidays; Boxing Day, Easter Monday, Whit Monday and the first Monday in August. The August Bank Holiday is now known throughout Kent as St Lubbock's Day.

Margate councillors have accused their dashing fire brigade of "showing off". The criticism follows an accident when the engine, on its way to a fire, was involved in a crash with the carriage of the local doctor. The council have had to find £50 for damages.

Chatham Town Hall opens to great acclaim.

The typhoid outbreak in Kent has reached epidemic proportions and hospitals are having difficulty in coping with the great demand for beds.

February: Units from The Buffs (East Kent Regiment) and the Queen's Own Royal West Kent Regiment sail to South Africa as the Boer War intensifies.

They are followed by the 36th (West Kent) Squadron Yeomanry. Each soldier is providing his own horse, uniform and arms and has paid his own fare to South Africa.

Tonbridge Urban Council has bought the Norman castle at Tonbridge from the trustees of Emma Lady Stafford and moved their staff into the new quarters. The cost was £10,000. The first meeting was held on March 7th and the 14 acres of grounds were formally opened by Lord Stanhope of Chevening, Lord Lieutenant of Kent.

March: Headley Brothers of Ashford has become only the third firm of printers in Europe to install a Monotype printing press.

Beckenham has joined the age of electricity. The power station at Arthur Road uses water from a nearby stream and domestic

1900

The Deal Lifeboat off an another life saving mission to the Goodwin Sands which have been associated with shipwrecks since men first ventured to sea.

rubbish as part of the fuel.

April: The Rother Valley Railway has opened between Tenterden and Robertsbridge. Work is still in progress on the Headcorn extension.

Navy House, Chatham has opened for the sailors of the port.

May 15th: The Theatre Royal, Chatham is completely destroyed by fire despite the hurried arrival of military and civic fire fighters.

June: Welcome to Kent. The urban district of Penge has transferred from Surrey to Kent.

Summer 1900: The friendship of actress Lillie Langtry and Edward Prince of Wales is causing much critical gossip throughout the country.

St John's Recreation ground has opened and a new bandstand has been erected on the Pantiles, both at Tunbridge Wells.

Oscar Wilde dies in poverty

November: Oscar Wilde, once renowned for his wit and humour and later convicted of homosexual offences, has died in Paris, aged 44. In 1895 Wilde was sentenced to two years' imprisonment with hard labour and his experiences led to the anonymous publication of *The Ballad of Reading Gaol*.

In reporting his death the Kent newspapers have explained that he has been living in Paris since his release under the name of Sebastian Melmoth and his ballad written under the pseudonym C33, his prison number. Because of the "terrible disgrace" no theatre company in the county has performed any of his stage plays and are unlikely to do so ever again. Wilde died in poverty, dependent on the charity of his friends.

During the summer the Prince of Wales has been a guest player at the recently-opened St George's golf club, Sandwich — laid out by Dr Laidlaw Purves a distinguished surgeon from Guy's Hospital. A few years ago Purves, decided that the marshes between Sandwich and the sea were the perfect place for new links. Now his dream has become a reality.

July: The name of Halstead railway station, near Sevenoaks, has been changed to 'Knockholt' to avoid confusion with Halstead, Essex.

Dover Grammar School for boys is founded.

July 22nd: The second Olympic Games of the modern era closed in Paris today. Britain gained four gold medals all of which were won by middle distance runners. The United States topped the medal winners with 16 golds.

August 1900: The first weekly long-distance bus service begins; the journey between London and Leeds takes two days.

An isolation hospital is built in Beaver, Ashford for £400.

A new drink from America, Coca Cola, is on sale in Kent for the first time.

In his first full season for Kent, Colin Blythe, the county's new left-arm bowler, has captured 114 wickets and helped Kent secure third place in the championship.

Erith Yacht Club is formed. The club hopes to attract hundreds of members.

October 25th: Prince Ernest Albert, Duke of Kent dies.

December: The Theatre Royal, Chatham is re-opened with seating for 3,000.

GREAT HITS OF 1900

I'm only a bird in a gilded cage.
Goodbye Dolly Gray

Mafeking relieved — and so is Tunbridge Wells!

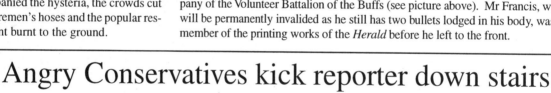

May 17th: There has been a spontaneous outburst of joy in Kent at the news that Mafeking, the small town on the railway line to Rhodesia which has been under siege for seven months, is now relieved. Reuters brought the glad tidings yesterday and immediately newspapers planned special editions and singing crowds surged into town centres. Patriotism has reached fever pitch.

The attention of the nation has been following the confused events at Mafeking ever since the relief of Ladysmith on February 28th. Interest has been intense particularly in Tunbridge Wells, for the British commander in the sieged town, Colonel Robert Baden-Powell, is a former pupil at Rose Hill School, London Road.

The commander is a national hero and the celebrations have been very boisterous. At Gravesend, the Bell Vue restaurant on top of Windmill Hill was set on fire and firemen raced to the scene. Enjoying the flames which accompanied the hysteria, the crowds cut the firemen's hoses and the popular restaurant burnt to the ground.

During his 217-day defence of Mafeking which cost the British 168 casualties, Baden-Powell must have had time to think about his schooldays in Tunbridge Wells and the eight-mile walk he made each day from his aunt's home in Speldhurst. He is an expert in military scouting techniques and has already published a manual called *Aids to Scouting 1899*, which is now acquiring an unexpectedly wide readership.

The relief of the town on the evening of May 6th was effected by a flying column from Kimberley, joining forces with Canadians and pressing south. Although resistance was broken it is clear the war is far from over — for the Boers are repeatedly turning to guerilla tactics in their bid to resist the ambitions of Britain in South Africa.

July: A hero of Mafeking has returned home to Tunbridge Wells — not Baden-Powell but William Gilbert of Little Mount Sion who was one of the few West Kent men to take part in the siege. A great reception has been held for him on The Pantiles and many speeches made.

Another soldier home is Lance-Corporal W. Francis of the Folkestone Company of the Volunteer Battalion of the Buffs (see picture above). Mr Francis, who will be permanently invalided as he still has two bullets lodged in his body, was a member of the printing works of the *Herald* before he left to the front.

Angry Conservatives kick reporter down stairs

October: After more than 20 years of Tory domination, Maidstone has returned a Liberal member to Westminster. John Barker won a majority of just 38 votes over Fiennes Cornwallis but, nationally, Lord Salisbury's Conservative Party has returned to power with little trouble.

Tory popularity plummeted when the war in South Africa opened badly but the tide has turned with the relief of Ladysmith and now Mafeking and the government seized the opportunity to call a quick election.

The surprise events at Maidstone were soured by an extraordinary incident in which a *Kent Messenger* reporter, seeking comments, wandered into the local Conservative Club and was attacked by an angry member of the Association. He accused the reporter of being pro-Boer and threatened to throw him down the stairs.

The *Messenger* wrote: "The said bully proceeded to put his threat into execution amid the tacit approval of those present and our representative would have had a bad fall had it not been for the crowd coming up the stairs."

The following week's newspaper contained another report about the incident. "Our reporter Mr A.W.Reader has been in bed since his arrival home from the Conservative Club prostrate with weakness and unable to eat solid food. He was set upon and mauled for no reason whatsover and not a word of regret has been expressed by any member of the Conservative Association."

The election controversy is not over. Electoral corruption has always been suspected by Maidstone Conservatives who have lodged a petition against John Barker on the grounds of widespread bribery. The hearing, before two judges of the High Court, will be held in the Sessions House, Maidstone in a few months time. *(see page 17)*

Little has been heard of the new political party which was formed just prior to the 1900 elections. Trade Union leaders resolved to abandon their alliance with the Liberal party and sponsor their own candidates with James Ramsay MacDonald as secretary. Their leader is Keir Hardy who wants to develop "a distinct Labour group in parliament."

Horse bus on the Ashford to Willesborough run. The Union Jack signifies a special occasion.

Pioneer motor buses threaten the horse

1900: Despite the advent of self-propelled carriages or motor buses which are gradually being introduced on certain routes in Kent, the reliable horse bus is still providing a regular and efficient long and short distance service throughout the county. They operate one or two journeys a day along the main routes in the county and are particularly popular on market days and between towns without a direct railway link. The country services certainly retain a stage-coach image and the owners are taking little notice of the mechanical competition. But, as this new century dawns, there is no doubt that the era of the motor bus has arrived.

In April last year two demonstration motor buses ran for a week at Tunbridge Wells in connection with the motor show in that town. Then, in the same month, a twice-a-day service was introduced between Canterbury and Herne Bay with a Daimler waggonette and, later in the year, two buses were laid on to take spectators to the St Lawrence cricket ground at Canterbury.

Today motor buses can be seen regularly in East Kent. The Dover and East Kent Omnibus Company runs a steam-bus service to St Margaret's-at-Cliffe, Folkestone Motors Ltd operates a service to Hythe via Cheriton using a Coventry waggonette and J.W.Cann is planning a timetable of services between Hythe and Folkestone.

More will follow. In five or six years time every town in Kent may have its own motor bus. Meanwhile the horse plods on but for how long we wonder.

Queen offers to be godmother to unborn child of Boer War hero

June 7th: Two days after the fall of Pretoria an angry mob has attacked the home of Mr Lawson Dodd, a social democrat, Fabian and councillor of Tunbridge Wells because they believe him to be a pro-Boer. It is not true. Mr Dodd strongly disapproves of General Kitchener's decision to intern all families in South Africa whose men are still fighting for the Boers and has written letters to the newspapers denouncing this "method of barbarism". He is not alone. As the army begin to sweep women and children into camps, scores of people are objecting, including Sir Henry Campbell-Bannerman, the Liberal leader.

There have been more Kent casualties in South Africa. One of them is Major Henry William Denne of the Gordon Highlanders who lived at Elbridge House, Littlebourne and is a member of a well-known landowning family. Major Denne was killed in the Battle of Elandslaagte, leaving behind a pregnant wife and two young children at Littlebourne.

Queen Victoria has heard of the tragedy and generously given Mrs Denne an apartment in Hampton Court. She has also offered to be Godmother to the baby who was born just two months after her father's death.

Trains, motor cars, motor buses and now electric trams. The great transport revolution has moved into another gear as tramlines begin to appear in many Kent towns. This tram belongs to the Dover Corporation and it is carefully inching its way through the crowds in the Old Fish Market at Crosswall where catches are sold daily by auction. Dover is the first town in Kent to introduce the tram. The lines were built in 1897 on two routes from the pier to Buckland Bridge and from Biggin Street to Maxton. An extension to River is now being planned.

August: *The Jetty at Margate, built in 1853 to give large steamers a better landing place, is attracting hundreds of visitors in this first summer of the new century. The Jetty extension was opened recently.*

Cricket's famous 'ashes' are from Ivo's grate!

The Hon. Ivo Bligh, who took the English cricket side to Australia in 1882-3, has become the 8th Earl Darnley on the death of his uncle. His many friends in the Rochester area will recall how Ivo Bligh became the central figure in one of cricket's most romantic and enduring stories. Before the tour of Australia, England had been beaten at the Oval and an "obituary" appeared in the *Sporting Times*. The memorial ended: "The body will be cremated and the ashes taken to Australia". Bligh's team actually won the series "down under" and two Melbourne ladies cremated a bail and presented the "ashes" to Ivo Bligh in a small urn. He kept the prize at Cobham Hall, Rochester, the seat of the Darnley family.

Now we hear that the "ashes" may no longer be the remains of that bail. A few years ago a parlourmaid accidently knocked the urn from the mantlepiece of the drawing room at Cobham and the famous contents scattered over the floor. According to local gossip, she quickly took a handful of ash from the fireplace, filled the urn and replaced the lid.

Today, the ashes from Melbourne, or perhaps Lord Darnley's fireplace, are kept at Lords. They remain a disembodied concept of one of cricket's greatest prizes.

132 die in typhoid epidemic

January: The epidemic of typhoid fever which swept through mid Kent, and Maidstone in particular in the last few years, is now under control. No-one will need reminding how rapidly the disease spreads. Schools in the area were closed , emergency hospitals improvised, teams of nurses brought in and relief stations set up for the poor. In just a few months 1,847 cases of typhoid were notified, with 132 deaths.

The health authorities now know that the cause of this epidemic was the contamination of a spring at Farleigh caused by the primitive sanitary arrangements at a hop-pickers' camp. The medical officer warned the local council that surface water was being contaminated but nothing was done. A government inspector confirmed the Farleigh fears and the supply was shut down.

The typhoid outbreak has led to prolonged anxiety about other contagious diseases. It is known that tuberculosis in Kent is responsible for 37 per cent of all deaths among young people under 35. Influenza is widespread, measles consistently claims the highest number of deaths followed by whooping cough, scarlet fever and diphtheria. Smallpox is no longer such a threat because a vaccination is available but some doctors believe the disease will continue to afflict many people.

March: *Another hard day's work is over and the men of Bevan's Cement Works, Northfleet pose for a photograph, wondering what their new employer will be like. The Bevan brothers, Robert, Wilfred and Edmund, along with 23 other local firms have joined forces to create the Associated Portland Cement Manufacturers Ltd. Known locally as 'the combine' APCM is now a world leader and should be able to raise the capital required to invest in new rotary kilns and other sophisticated plant. It was on the Bevan site many years ago that William Aspdin discovered Portland cement and revolutionised the building industry. Today more than 1,000 bottle kilns are clustered along the estuaries of the Thames and Medway, the rivers are alive with sailing barges and, in the chalk quarries, work continues at a relentless pace.*

Cobham Hall, near Gravesend, the seat of the Darnley family.

Tragedy in Tonbridge as four die in fire

September 7th: A man and his three daughters were burned to death yesterday in their small flat above Harris' draper's shop in Tonbridge High Street. The fire broke out in the night and Mr Tatham, manager of the shop, his wife and four children were trapped because the town's only escape ladder was locked behind gates in the Castle grounds — the headquarters of Tonbridge Urban Council — and no-one could get to it.

Mr Tatham's son Tommy was saved because he jumped into the arms of people waiting below and his mother, outlined on the roof of the flaming building, was about to jump when a ladder was found and she was saved. For the rest of the family there was no escape.

The people of Tonbridge are shocked. Already demands are being made for a professionally-led fire brigade to replace the group of volunteers who have been manfully attending fires with woeful equipment.

January: An extraordinary era in British history has ended with the death of Queen Victoria who has died peacefully in her sleep at Osborne House, Cowes. She was 81. Victoria became Queen of England at the age of 18 and ruled for 63 years, almost 40 of them as a widow.

High Court judges have declared the Maidstone general election void on account of widespread bribery by leading members of the Liberal Party. The MP John Barker has been unseated, prominent Liberals disenfranchised and one sent to jail. Barker cannot stand again for seven years.

Maidstone's electricity works have now opened at the Fair Meadow adjacent to the baths. This will enable the works to have the benefit of a riverside wharf for coal supplies.

April 4th: An electric tramway service between Ramsgate, Broadstairs and Margate was opened today by the Isle of Thanet Electric Tramways and Lighting Company Ltd. A second service between Margate and Ramsgate via Dumpton is due to open in July.

May: The census of 1901 reveals that the population of Britain has reached a new peak of 41.5 million, overtaking France for the first time. The population of Kent in 1901 is approaching one million; more than two thirds, 667,170, live in the towns and the proportion is increasing.

July 16th: There has been a fatal accident on the pier tramway at Herne Bay. A luggage trailer left the tracks, the driver and conductor panicked, jumped off and the carriage plunged through railings into the sea. An elderly passenger was killed.

July 19th: The West Kent Yeomanry have returned from the Boer War, to an overwhelming welcome in Maidstone and they have accepted the addition to their title of the word 'Imperial'.

The first motor buses in Gravesend, two small 12-seaters operated by Messrs Smith and Day between Gravesend and Northfleet have been inaugurated, while a tramway is being re-laid for electric operation.

Summer: The Sheppey Light Railway has opened from Sheerness to Leysdown.

A county cricket match has been played on the Nevill ground, Tunbridge Wells, for the first time. There are plans afoot for a cricket week next summer.

September: A decision in the House of Lords that employers can sue for damages arising out of strike action has outraged Trade Union leaders and given fuel to a campaigning issue by the newly formed Labour Representation Committee.

Sir Edward Watkin, Liberal MP for Hythe (1874-1895), has died aged 82. As a promoter of great enterprises Sir Edward was known for his proposal to build a tower at Wembley 150 feet higher than the Eiffel. His grandest scheme, however, was a tunnel under the Channel which he costed at £3.5million. He thought that military objections to his tunnel idea were absurd.

GREAT HIT OF 1901
Mighty like a rose

Sir Hiram Maxim, Crayford's great inventor

Arise Sir Hiram — our knight of flight!

January: Shortly after becoming a naturalised British subject, Hiram Maxim, Crayford's eccentric inventor, has been knighted. And he plans to celebrate by constructing a new flying machine which, this time, he is confident will actually get off the ground.

Sir Hiram is a remarkable man. He was born in Maine, USA and went on to become chief engineer of the first electric light company in America before coming to England to organise electricity services in this country. In 1881 he began to work on an automatic machine gun and he carried out his experiments in a small factory in Hatton Garden, London. Maxim perfected a single-barrelled gun which could fire 666 rounds a minute and received a visit from the Prince of Wales who was intrigued by this new weapon.

By this time Maxim had relocated his works at Crayford, bought a house nearby called Stoneyhurst and eventually amalgamated with an Erith-based firm of gunmakers which, in time, became known as Vickers and Son and Maxim. In 1891 the British army adopted Maxim's gun and it was used in the Matabele War and is currently used by both sides in the Boer War.

Sir Hiram's knighthood has delighted the people of Dartford and district. Few will forget the day a few years ago when his flying machine actually flew for 100 yards and how he put it on display at Baldwyns Park to raise money for the Bexley Cottage Hospital.

Some people actually paid five shillings for the privilege of hurtling down the trackway. They didn't take off. That privilege is for people of the future.

The Prince of Wales becomes Edward VII of England. The mayor of Dover reads the proclamation.

Kent mourns the death of Queen Victoria

January 25th: The news that Queen Victoria, Queen of England and Empress of India has died in her sleep has been received with great sorrow throughout Kent. It was announced from Osborne House at the weekend that Her Majesty would not live much longer and this was followed by the cancellation of social and civic functions throughout the county. On Tuesday morning Victoria's three physicians indicated that she was sinking and the sad news finally came at 6.45 pm.

The *Kent Messenger*, with heavy black borders down each column, below a pen and ink portrait of the Queen and accompanied by a large solemn headline in today's paper says: "Intelligence of the Queen's death reached Maidstone shortly before half past seven on Tuesday evening when the streets were thronged with people sadly awaiting the melancholy news. Within a short time a crepe bordered flag was run up half mast on the Town Hall and between eight and nine o'clock the bells of All Saints, Holy Trinity, St Philip's, St Michael's, St Luke's and other churches were tolled. On Wednesday the Mayor issued a notice requesting the inhabitants to adopt some suitable method of displaying their grief and suggested that mourning attire should be worn..."

Similar requests were made by other Kent mayors. In Ashford all social functions were postponed including the Conservative smoking concert but it was too late to stop a Band of Hope meeting at which the Rev O.R.Dawson conveyed the sad news and the children present burst into tears. At Canterbury the Cathedral tower "Bell Harry", rung every evening for the eight o'clock curfew but otherwise only used to indicate the death of a Sovereign or Archbishop, tolled until 10 o'clock — accompanied by the bells of other churches in the city.

Victoria, the daughter of the impoverished Duke of Kent was only 18

when she ascended to the throne. In 1840 she married Prince Albert from the German Duchy of Saxe-Coburg-Gotha. Of the couples' nine children, several have married into other royal families. She was known as the grandmother of Europe.

The Queen was devoted to Albert and devastated by his death in 1861 of typhoid.

Tunbridge Wells — home of the first municipal telephone company

January: To the surprise of many sceptics the Tunbridge Wells Municipal Telephone Company has successfully completed its first great challenge by installing telephone links from the council offices to the High Street, the sewage works and the isolation hospital — not in Tunbridge Wells, but neighbouring Tonbridge. It is the first independent company in the country to achieve such a technical feat and it happened because of a tragedy.

A few years ago there was an accident in Tonbridge and a call was made immediately to the local doctor in East Street. Contact could not be made, however, because the telephone wire had been broken, so a note was taken by hand to the doctor. He went quickly to the scene of the accident but too late — the man had died.

The National Telephone System was bombarded by angry letters from people who considered the conditions of telephonic communication in both Tonbridge and Tunbridge Wells to be almost intolerable. As a result of this and other pressures the Government introduced legislation enabling local authorities to set up their own telephone services.

Tunbridge Wells was the first to apply and obtain a licence. In fact the new company decided to open exchanges in 49 locations covering 180 square miles, but it was Tonbridge who made the first request. "Fix up our town offices and departments by January 1901, or we will not join your system", wrote the Town Clerk. The target has now been met, the inaugural celebrations held and the two towns have a place in the history of telephonic communication.

This new company has some catching up to do for the National Telephone Company has already more than 100 subscribers in Tunbridge Wells, 30 in Tonbridge and 48 in Sevenoaks. Nearly all the entries in the local directories are commercial customers but there are some exceptions. For example the honour of holding the number Sevenoaks 1 belongs to Mr Alfred J. St George McAdam Laurie of Rockdale. In Tonbridge, the numbers have three digits, starting with a 2; Baltic Saw Mills is Tonbridge 201.

Tunbridge Wells has the first municipal telephone company in the country. This is the borough's principal telephone.

The installation of tall masts to carry the dozen or so crossbars supporting the telephone wires and the introduction of public call offices where "anyone can use the telephone", continues to intrigue many people. The Sevenoaks mast has been erected in the Market Place outside Messrs Quinnell's shop and the first public call office in Tonbridge is on the premises of C.A.Woolley, cycle agent at 76 High Street.

In these three West Kent towns Alexander Graham Bell's wonderful invention is certainly showing its enormous potential and the signs are that it will be a huge success. In fact all over the county masts are being erected and exchanges opened. A submarine cable has even been laid

August: The heroes are home from South Africa and the new King is soon to be crowned. With plenty to celebrate the customers of the Rising Sun, Northfleet set off for an outing to Tunbridge Wells.

Yeomen return to an imperial welcome

July 20th: The remains of the 120-strong company of the West Kent Yeomanry, who left Liverpool in February 1900 for the long voyage to South Africa, returned home yesterday. The heroes received an ecstatic welcome in Maidstone and for the people of the town it was a day to remember.

Thousands turned out to meet them: time is too brief to detail their exploits whilst at the seat of war but we learn that they have seen much fighting and only 27 of the total number of men in the Company have gone unscathed. They had the honour of remaining in the firing line throughout, while their comrades were disabled, some temporarily and others more permanently either by the bullet of the enemy or the even more deadly enteric fever. In fact the roll of the Company on its return is 43 NCOs and men and one officer. Captain Potts remained with his men throughout the conflict. Although many were wounded, and several died from disease, not one Yeoman was killed in action.

Yesterday's reception at Maidstone contained speeches and toasts to the "glorious heroes, the Yeoman from the Front". The men were given the freedom of the town and the word Imperial was added to their title. It was ex-

plained how the volunteers each with his own horse, uniform and arms, had responded to Field Marshal Kitchener's rallying call for more men. By the time their tour of duty ended, the supreme commander had a force approaching 240,000 with one third mounted — and that was five times the strength of the Boer army.

The Yeoman fighters at the Maidstone party were aware that many regular Kent soldiers had suffered badly in South Africa and some were coming home, terribly wounded — the lucky ones. Scores died in the fierce fighting which preceded the fall of Pretoria and some succumbed later to their wounds. Among them was Private A. Brewer of Fordwich (Cameron Highlanders), Private Goodsmark who had played football for Ashford and Kent (2nd Army Service Corps), Colour Sergeant W.J.Fountain of Buckland, Dover (Northumberland Fusiliers), Trooper Isaac Wildash of Faversham (33rd East Kent Yeomanry) and Trooper A.T. Beeching who was the son of the manager of Lloyd's Bank, Tonbridge.

Illness in the form of enteric fever and dysentery had claimed the lives of many West Kents and Buffs, one of them — Private William Huckstepp dying on the way home

continued page 21

Maidstone welcomes the West Kent Yeomanry as they march over the Medway bridge. Not one Yeoman died in action but of the regular soldiers 114 lost their lives in South Africa.

to his wife and children in Ashford. He had a relapse of enteric fever on board the *Idaho* and his body was consigned to the waves.

It hasn't all been bad news. Early in March Lieutenant Quartermaster William Parker arrived in Romney Marsh to visit his aged father, the venerable rector of St Mary's. The whole parish turned out and on the arrival of the carriage, sturdy hands yoked themselves to the vehicle and drew their gallant lieutenant to the rectory where a glad welcome awaited him. Three triumphal arches had been erected and the school children, drawn up in line, sang *Soldiers of the King* right cheerily.

Back in South Africa the war continues but Boer numbers are falling rapidly in the face of Kitchener's tactics and their morale is being steadily worn down. It could soon be over.

Horse-drawn traffic is still dominant in Beckenham, now known as "the last parish in Kent". May's national census shows this to be a desirable area for the Edwardian businessman, for here are the better houses. The growing residential development now threatens to merge Beckenham without distinction into Penge on the west, Bromley on the east and the suburbs of Lewisham and Catford to the north.

London swallows N.W. Kent— and the trend may continue

May 9th: Kent's population is growing faster than ever. Last month's national census which was published today shows that more and more people are moving into the north western area of the county which is in danger of being totally enveloped by London. There are fears that the vast tracks of countryside around Bromley and Beckenham will be transformed into one enormous dormitory, from which workers are sucked into the City at daybreak and scattered again as night falls.

GREATEST AREAS OF POPULATION

Gillingham MB	42,745	Gravesend MB	27,196
Dover MB	42,672	Beckenham UD	26,288
Dartford RD	37,532	Erith UD	25,296
Chatham MB	37,057	Canterbury CB	24,899
Maidstone MB	33,516	Malling RD	24,724
Tunbridge Wells MB	33,373	Margate MB	23,118
Folkestone MB	30,650	Sevenoaks RD	22,687
Rochester MB	30,590	Penge UD	22,465
Ramsgate MB	27,733	Bromley RD	18,808
Bromley MB	27,396	Dartford UD	18,644

The population boom is due entirely to the industrial revolution, the availability of employment and now the amazing fast railway services to London. In 1800, four-fifths of the inhabitants of Kent lived in the country and, in 1850, the equation between the town and country was roughly equal. This year's census shows that urban districts have grown and rural parishes are in decline. The trend is almost certain to continue for some years.

The biggest areas of industrialisation are west of the Medway valley, along the Thames and in the lower valleys of the Cray and Dart where the paper-making, engineering and cement industries are also transforming the countryside.

'Tobacco — a lone man's companion, a bachelor's friend, a hungry man's food, a sad man's cordial, a wakeful man's sleep and a chilly man's fire' — Charles Kingsley, *Westward Ho,* 1855.

January: Gravesend Grammar School for boys has been opened in Pelham Road.

An outbreak of smallpox in London and north Kent has prompted doctors to warn that only public support for a vaccination programme will halt the epidemic. The number of victims has risen to 2,273.

February: A petition signed by 37,000 women textile workers has been presented to Parliament demanding votes for women.

The Royal Sailors' Home has been opened in Upper Barrier Road, Chatham and partly financed by the Admiralty. The large military presence in Chatham is influencing the way in which the town is developing. A large number of clubs and institutions are being opened — all designed to meet the off-duty needs of both "Tommy Atkins" and "Jack Tar".

March 18th: Harold Apted has been hanged at Maidstone Prison for the murder of Frances O'Rourke, aged seven of Vauxhall Road, Tonbridge.

April: North Kent fire-fighters have been called to the City of London to help quell a massive blaze which threatens to destroy more than 30 factories, warehouses and shops in the Barbican.

June 1st: The Boer War has ended. At midnight last night the Boer leaders signed the terms of surrender in the presence of Lord Kitchener.

June 10: The Chatham and District Light Railway Company has opened its tram service with routes to Chatham Cemetery, Chatham Dockyard and Gillingham (Victoria Bridge/Pier Road via Brompton or Jeezrels).

June 24th: King Edward has been admitted to hospital for an appendix operation. The Coronation, due to take place at Westminster Abbey in two days time has been postponed.

June: The floating dock built in Sheerness dockyard has been suc-

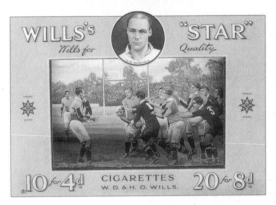

The habit of smoking cigarettes, introduced many years ago but popularised in recent months by the King is becoming a fashion accessory throughout Kent where smoking concerts are regularly held in most towns. In London a new company, The British-American Tobacco Company Ltd has been created. A packet of 20 of the better cigarettes costs 8d.

cessfully towed non-stop to Bermuda by two tugs. The journey took more than a month and the average speed was four knots an hour.

August: An electric tramway has opened in Gravesend and Northfleet. Until very recently the borough has been served with horse trams. The trams have been supplied by the Electric Railway and Tramway Carriage Works, Preston and there are 20 for Gravesend. Extensions are planned to Swanscombe, Denton and Pelham Road.

August 9th: King Edward VII has been crowned at Westminster Abbey before most of the monarchs of Europe. Our new King is aged 59 and a grandfather.

The Prince of Wales Pier has been opened at Dover, in honour of Prince George.

August 12th: The Ramsgate fishing smack *Idalia* has been lost on the Kentish Knocke sands in a fearful gale.

October 4th: Kitchener has visited Chatham and been presented with the Freedom of the Borough. He dined with the officers of the Royal Engineers at the Mess, be-

fore his departure to India the next day.

October 30th: A tram, out of control, ran down Westcourt Street, Chatham and into the Police Quarters where it turned over. The tram has been in operation for just four months and was carrying 70 men from Old Brompton to the dockyard. One person died and several were injured.

A gifted young Rochester girl, destined for a glittering career as a concert pianist, has been forced to retire at the age of 20 because of pains in her wrists when playing. Young Sybil Thorndike has been encouraged by her father, vicar of St Margaret's Church, Rochester, and may now turn to the theatre for a career in the arts. Her mother is an enthusiastic performer in amateur theatricals.

The Tales of Peter Rabbit, a charming book for young children, has been published this year. The author is Beatrix Potter who has also painted the watercolour illustrations.

This year there has been a threat to close a number of beds in West Kent hospital. The *Kent Messenger* has asked its readers for 10,000 shillings in an appeal that is set to continue until sufficient money has been raised.

FASHIONS OF 1902
Straight-laced corsets and stiff bustles are being replaced, hemlines are creeping above the ankle and the knickerbocker seems set to replace the skirt.

GREAT HITS OF 1902
*In the good old summer time.
Bill Bailey, won't you please
come home?*

October 29th: The old viaduct over Railway Street, Chatham has now been demolished to make way for the fine new viaduct, opened today amid much acclamation. It took a year to complete and, thanks to the use of iron girders, a much greater span has been created. The greatest beneficiary will be the newly-opened Chatham and District Light Rail Company whose trams will shortly pass underneath. The old viaduct contained massive brick archways which had formed part of the line of fortifications built during the preparations for war with France 100 years ago.

May: *Uncle Bones and his Margate Minstrels will soon be entertaining the masses on the sands this summer. Bones (real name Alfred Bourne) is one of the most popular seaside entertainers in the country. He worked for some years as a carpenter but then he bought a straw hat, learned to play the banjo and decided to sing Negro Spirituals for a living. And what a huge success he has been. Adored by children, he is able to marshal them into rows and can even make them sneeze in unison at a given signal. He will then polish their noses with his hanky as they sit in perfect order, tell jokes and sing. Last summer the children not only greeted him with howls of delight but frequently followed him into town like the Pied Piper.*

Heroic Fisher's scouts at Dover camp, newly returned from their exploits in the Boer War. Sir Robert Baden-Powell, hero of the defence of Mafeking, was so impressed by the skills shown by the army scouts during his tours of duty in India and Africa that he is considering setting up a similar movement for boys in England as a way of encouraging a sense of discipline and duty.

May 15th: *There was a joyful reception in Folkestone for Boer War heroes who landed at the harbour today. Already there have been numerous civic receptions. In Tenterden the mayor, Mr E.H.Hardcastle, welcomed home Private Albert Millen and Private Arthur George Watson, members of G.Coy, 2nd Volunteer Batt. East Kent Regiment (The Buffs). The decorated coach was pulled by the local fire brigade. The two soldiers were presented with a silver key, watch and money contributed by 300 residents.*

A message of peace as the people pray

June 1st: The Boer War is over. After two years and seven months of intense fighting the Boer leaders arrived in Pretoria to meet Lord Milner, the High Commissioner and Lord Kitchener, the Commander-in-Chief, just before the midnight deadline last night. Here they signed the terms of surrender.

The news did not reach the county town until this morning when a telegram addressed to the station master at Maidstone was delivered to the mayor. It was signed by Francis Evans, MP. As many people were in church the mayor was able to distribute the information to those already praying for peace. Impromptu demonstrations of joy then continued until well past midnight.

During the wild rejoicing several buildings in Mill Street caught fire and above the shouts of the crowd and the roar of the waters of the Len could be heard the rattle of the hose cart and the cries of the firemen as they rushed down the narrow streets to deal with the blaze.

Sevenoaks also heard the news this morning as did Bexleyheath and Bromley but it will be Monday before the messages of peace arrive via railway telegrams at most Kent towns. The Boer commanders have voted to accept British colonial rule with a promise of self-government later plus a £3 million British grant to assist reconstruction.

Many of Kent's heroic soldiers have already been welcomed home. They include Lieutenant John Norwood from East Peckham who distinguished himself at Ladysmith when, under heavy fire, he picked up a wounded colleague, placed him across his horse and then led the horse to safety. Norwood, born at Pembury Lodge, Beckenham has been recommended for the VC. Among those who will not be coming home are the three Hamilton brothers from Hythe. One was killed by lightning at Machadodorp, the second died of enteric fever at Bloemfontein and the third was killed in action at Sheepers Nek. Local newspapers throughout the county will be producing special Peace editions on sale at around 6d.

Kent schools taken over by county education committee

October: Despite a large demonstration in London and massive opposition from Liberals and non-conformists, the sweeping new powers contained in the Education Act — introduced in the House of Commons on March 23rd — are now being implemented.

School boards have been abolished, local councils are taking reponsibility for primary and secondary schools and, in Kent, the county council has created an education committee.

The KEC has taken responsibility for secondary education throughout the county, with just one exception. Canterbury remains in the hands of the city council. One problem which faces the new authority is how to redress the balance between boys and girls. It is estimated that 2,348 boys are receiving education in the grammar schools, established since the previous Education Act, but only 1,726 girls are attending similar schools. Many consider this anomaly to be a great scandal.

As far as elementary education is concerned the KEC is responsible for only about half the county area as 16 of the larger towns remain independent. Also, more than two thirds of the elementary schools are controlled by denominational bodies which retain statutory powers including the appointment of teachers.

In the few months it has been established the KEC has grown to be the fourth largest education authority in the country and, through its technical education committee, has already made considerable advances, awarding grants to 32 technical institutions across the county. It has also set up three new institutions including a horticultural college for women at Swanley, an agricultural college at Wye and a school of domestic economy at Maidstone.

W.G.Grace, immediately recognisable by his beard takes to the road with four friends. Grace lives near Eltham and now plays a lot of cricket in Kent.

Slow but steady for the great doctor

September 1st: Dr W.G.Grace, the great England cricketer, was among those taking part in the Automobile Club's reliability trials from Crystal Palace to Folkestone and back to prove that the motor car is almost as reliable as the railway as a means of transport.

All the cars were laden with passengers and the idea is to see how each performs over the 139-mile route. The legal limit is 12 miles an hour in the country and eight mph in the towns. Most managed to complete the course although there were a few unfortunate mishaps.

The *Kentish Express* writes: "The leading car was a Panhard Lovasson driven by Mr Jarrod which arrived at Folkestone at 12.30 o'clock (sic). Not far behind was Baron Rothschild's car which was proceeding within the regulation rate when it was met by a very nervous horse harnessed to an American trotting buggy. The horse dashed for the hedge and leapt into a clover field taking the buggy and the driver with it. Neither were hurt. A car belonging to the Motoring Manufacturing Co collided with a cart near Maidstone and one of the occupants was thrown out onto the route."

Triumphal arch and hardy oaks in honour of our new King

Here's a toast unto His Majesty. Sailors at Chatham celebrate in the Long Bar in the High Street.

August 9th: Before most of the monarchs of Europe, King Edward VII has been crowned today at Westminster Abbey. The coronation service was conducted by the Archbishops of Canterbury and York. The new Sovereign is in his sixtieth year.

Hundreds of people from Kent travelled to London on a bright sunny day to see the royal procession and those who were left behind celebrated this "gayest of occasions" with special church services in the morning, processions in the afternoon and firework festivities in the evening. Bands played, bells rang, children paraded, volunteers marched, mayors spoke, buildings were illuminated and the National Anthem has been sung everywhere on dozens of occasions. "Long live the King."

The quietest celebrations have been on the Isle of Thanet. "At Margate, Ramsgate and Broadstairs

This picture shows the specially erected celebration arch on Rochester bridge.

the decorations are extremely effective", writes the *Kentish Express*, "but as it is the height of the holiday season, business has not been suspended and there is an absence of festivities". A Coronation holiday for the people of Thanet is now planned for later in the year.

One novel feature of the day has been the presentation of Coronation mugs to Kent children and a special feast for the inmates of many workhouses. At Sevenoaks, in a special ceremony on the Vine cricket ground, seven sapling oak trees have been planted. A large gathering was told they would grow big and strong — guarding the town of Sevenoaks for many centuries to come.

At Rochester, in honour of the coronation, a special triumphal arch has been erected at the eastern end of the bridge across the River Medway. It will not be a permanent feature, but adds to the air of general festivity.

The Sevenoaks Ready, a fine fire engine which has been controversially confiscated by the local council.

The Sevenoaks Ready — pride of the town

September: To the great consternation of the people of Sevenoaks, the local fire brigade — affectionately known throughout the district as *The Ready Volunteer Brigade* — has been disbanded after a massive row with the local council.

The trouble first began a few months ago when the town's only fire engine was secretly sold to the council, without any consultation with the officers and men of the brigade. The money to buy the engine, a fine steamer called *"The Ready"*, was raised by public subscription in 1882 and for 20 years it has been the pride of Sevenoaks; in fact the volunteer firefighters with 12 officers and men have dealt with hundreds of fires and won prizes for good work throughout the district.

Why Sevenoaks Urban Council want to buy the old steamer is not known but it has certainly divided the town and many letters have already appeared in the *Sevenoaks Chronicle*.

One of them is signed by the men of the *Ready Brigade*. "Sir, we the superintendent, engineer and firemen of the *Ready Volunteer Brigade* having heard indirectly that our engine has been sold to Sevenoaks UDC, and not having heard anything from our captain, decided to have a meeting in the engine house. Greatly to our disappointment and sorrow we found a new padlock on the door which prevented us from entering. As we are all still willing to volunteer our services we think we are justified in asking for an explanation."

Still no explanation has been received and it is likely now that the *Sevenoaks Ready Volunteer Brigade* will be consigned to history.

A rather similar fate has overtaken the gallant men of Maidstone Volunteer Brigade. In the last two years the Kent Fire Office Brigade has been taken over by the Royal Insurance and their steamer presented to the Maidstone Borough Corporation. Long discussions have been held over the formation of a Borough Fire Brigade but no-one has bothered to ask the volunteers for their expert opinion.

The Maidstone Borough Brigade is now in existence and all the Volunteers' appliances have become the property of the Corporation. The Volunteers have been invited to apply to join the new brigade — but all have refused!

'Kent, sir — everyone knows Kent — apples, cherries, hops and women'
Charles Dickens in Pickwick Papers.

February 12th: Randall Thomas Davidson, Bishop of Winchester has been appointed Archbishop of Canterbury.

February 14th: Maidstone has created a record among towns of a similar size for obtaining more than 200 customers and a maximum load of 223 kilowatts. Behind them in the first year of the "electricity league" are Leicester, Brighton and Worcester.

February 20th: An unusual phenomenon over much of Kent. A great fall of dust mixed with light rain has adorned shrubs and trees with a thick murky covering. At Edenbridge the fall is exceptional.

May 15: King Edward inaugurates London's first electric trams.

May 21st: Chatham's Royal Naval Barracks is completed with accommodation for 5,000 sailors. Prior to the erection of the barracks the sailors have been occupying a series of old "wooden walls" which collectively functioned as HMS Pembroke.

Trams are running at Bexley for the first time. The tramway depot is situated behind the council offices in Watling Street.

June 11th: King Alexander and Queen Draga of Serbia have been murdered in their bedroom in the early hours of the morning.

A second cliff lift has opened at Folkestone between Lower Sandgate Road and The Leas near the Metropole Hotel. The lift works by a sea water pump from the lower station. A flag will be flown when the lift is operating.

July 6th: President Loubet of France landed at Dover.

June 16th: American motor pioneer, Henry Ford of Detroit has formed the Ford Motor Company.

August 17th: Bromley and Gillingham have both been incorporated by Royal Charter. The first mayor of Bromley is Cr T.C.Dewey, and of Gillingham Cr J.R.Featherby.

Dr Randall Thomas Davidson preaching in the King's private chapel at Windsor following the confirmation that he is to be the new Archbishop of Canterbury. The enthronement takes place in February when the new Primate will receive a magnificent welcome.

August: Sheerness Tramway Service starts with just eight cars.

Sylvester's New Hippodrome theatre has opened in Lock's Meadow, Maidstone. It is built of corrugated iron and wood and "possesses inner comfort, commodiousness and convenience with stage and galleries in the style of a London music hall". The theatre can seat 1,500. Seats in stalls are 1s.6d and gallery 4d.

August 28th: The Great Wild West Show which has enjoyed a tumultuous run at Earls Court has given the inhabitants of New Brompton "a day they will never forget". Buffalow Bill (alias William Fred Cody) and his colleagues gave an exhibition of sharp shooting, rough riding, bronco busting and even staged a hold- up.

September 10th: a great storm in the south of England has caused many deaths and widespread damage.

October 10th: A number of women met in Manchester to form a new militant movement to gain the vote for their sex. The leader is Emily Pankhurst.

October 11th: Olantigh Tow-ers, Wye has been severely damaged by fire.

November 5th: Texan Sam Cody has designed a special war kite which he believes will provide an unrivalled aerial observation post in wartime. To advertise his invention he has built a special boat, attached one of his kites and today completed a dramatic crossing of the Channel from Calais to Dover with the kite towing the boat.

November 11th: Lord Selborne, First Lord of the Admiralty has presented a gunnery trophy and scoring album to *HMS Kent* on behalf of the County Society. The Captain is D.A.Gamble.

The American millionaire Mr William Waldorf Astor has purchased Hever Castle near Edenbridge with ambitious plans to restore it.

SS Queen, the first cross-Channel turbine steamer has gone into service.

December 17th: Two inventors from Dayton, Ohio, Wilbur and Orville Wright have flown a heavier-than-air machine over the beach at Kitty Hawk, North Carolina.

Boxing Day: A variety programme at St Margaret's Hall, Canterbury includes animated colour pictures. The audience are fascinated as these "cinematograph" images flicker into life.

New church:
St Andrew's, Catford.
Church rebuilt:
St George's, Beckenham

GREAT HITS OF 1903

Ida
Sweet Adeline

HOUSE FOR SALE

£1,600 north of Edenbridge, capital residence on high ground. South aspect containing three reception rooms, six bedrooms, bathroom, stabling, inexpensive grounds. Good hunting. Guy Ewing and Co.

Matron Wacher and some of her nurses of the newly-opened Joyce Green Hospital, Dartford. They are pictured on the Long Reach tennis court.

River hospitals open as smallpox epidemic grows

January: Although there are now more than 800 patients receiving regular treatment aboard the three hospital ships anchored in the Thames Estuary, the worst smallpox epidemic in British medical history continues to claim more and more victims. The ships are the *Endymion,* the *Atlas* and *Castalia* which accommodate, in addition to the patients, a staff of more than 200.

Treatment centres on the remote banks of the River Thames in north Kent have also been opened including the Orchard, the River and the Joyce Green hospitals, Dartford. In addition, health authorities are opening vaccination clinics and ordering suspect cases to undergo further tests.

Those people who live in towns alongside the sewage-polluted Thames and other riverside communities in Kent are particularly threatened. Maidstone is vulnerable due to the presence of the barracks and neighbouring mills, for these were the sources of infection for the outbreak 20 years ago.

However, there is a vaccination available for smallpox and doctors are warning that only public support for an enforcement programme will halt the epidemic. But in Maidstone, Dartford and many other Kent towns the public are totally indifferent to the idea of vaccination, so the disease continues to spread.

By the end of the month the number of smallpox cases has risen to 2,273, which includes 873 patients on the Thames hospital quarantine ship.

June 18th: Fifteen people have been killed and 17 seriously injured in an explosion on "the island" at Woolwich Arsenal today. The tragedy occurred in the high risk building where lyddite and cordite shells are manufactured.

The building has been blown to pieces and bodies mutilated beyond recognition. In fact the explosion was so enormous that many limbs were found in the Thames and on the other side of the river. Police and firemen have had the gruesome task of collecting all the parts together in buckets.

Apparently 30 ten-inch lyddite shells had been filled overnight and the men had gone to work early for a special firing. It is believed that seven of the shells exploded prematurely.

The War Office will award all the widows a grant equal to three years of their husbands' wages, averaging about £200 per family. A relief fund has also been set up by the mayor.

FROM THE PIER FOLKESTONE.

August Bank Holiday: There has been a record attendance for the annual Folkestone Regatta which was held in brilliant sunshine. It is estimated that 30,000 people witnessed the various events either from the Leas, the beach or the Lower Sandgate Road. A feature of the Regatta was the blowing up of a wrecked ship by the Whitstable Salvage Company. Rigged up as a man of war, the wreck was moored opposite the boathouse and then blown into tiny pieces as the spectators cheered.

All Ramsgate is "thrilled with horror"

February 25: Samuel Henson, a 58-year-old foreman ganger who tried to murder his wife by blowing up the family home, has instead killed his 20-year-old son and seriously injured himself, his wife and a lodger. The house at 14 Flora Road, Ramsgate was demolished in the blast which was caused by a mixture of gun cotton and cordite.

According to the local newspaper the town is "thrilled with horror" by the tragedy. The victim, William Henson was a well-known local footballer and a bricklayer by trade. His mother has been badly injured by the explosion and also has a deep cut on the throat which the police are convinced was made by a knife.

At the trial last week Samuel Henson admitted that he took the explosive into the family home but had no idea that it was fitted with a fuse and detonator. He had also been injured in the blast and then twice attempted suicide, once by banging his head against the wall of his cell.

Henson was found guilty and ordered to be hanged but a petition for leniency has been launched by a number of local people on the grounds that he was insane when he committed the dreadful act.

The season is over and London hop pickers and their families are homeward bound via the railway station at Paddock Wood.

Cockneys say that 'opping's good for 'ealth

September 3rd: Despite the misgivings about their unhygienic living conditions it is estimated that more than 80,000 "hoppers" are now in Kent and the county should produce this year almost two-thirds of the entire national crop of what is widely known as "the Englishman's wine".

The first hop-pickers arrived at the end of August from the East End of London, complaining as usual about the "miserable huts and converted pig-sties". They poured into the areas which lacked sufficient local supplies of labour. To the Weald, especially around Paddock Wood, Yalding, Marden, Hunton, Horsmonden and Goudhurst and the hop-growing belt between Faversham and Canterbury.

They arrived in any way they could. Some walked, some brought their horses and carts but this year the railways have laid on more chartered hopping trains. One family who arrived complete with grandma and grandad said they are not worried by the conditions "cos 'opping's good for owr 'ealth. It gives us marvellous appetites. We eat like 'orses. We go back, brarne as berries with enough 'ops for owr winter pillars."

This year the famers are paying 1s 4d for five bushels picked, which means that a woman and her children can hope to earn £6 to £8 over the six week period. Many of the Londoners are working alongside women and children from local villages and those who walk out daily from neighbouring towns. At one farm near Tonbridge a group of "respectable ladies" are picking for church funds and in the same field are some gipsies and didikais who are expert pickers but feared for their violent tempers.

Working in the hop gardens was socially acceptable for women from the middle and upper classes — if they picked for a charitable cause or for church funds. Here is a young mother with her small child.

September 2nd: *With a population of almost 30,000 inhabitants and 5,000 houses, Bromley has at last received, from the Crown, its Charter of Incorporation. Yesterday, this large Kent town, with its crowded streets (see picture), celebrated in style with a procession whose splendour has rarely been seen before and a lunch for civic dignitaries in the Drill Hall. The Charter Mayor, Thomas C. Dewey told his guests that the Corporation of Bromley has now assumed a status which befits its rapid development. The scroll itself was brought down by train to Bromley South station by a Charter Deputation in a special saloon carriage from London, a sumptuous vehicle laid on by the London and Chatham Railway. From there Councillor Dewey led mounted police, trumpeters of the Royal Horse Artillery, a Bromley volunteer band, Bromley postmen and messengers, a collection of red fire engines and fine carriages carrying sheriffs and mayors from London and Kent on a journey through the streets. It was a procession that easily rivalled the Lord Mayor's Show of London.*

American millionaire buys Hever Castle

July 27th: Hever, a dilapidated 13th century castle where Henry VIII once courted Anne Boleyn, has been purchased by Mr William Waldorf Astor, a 55-year-old American millionaire who came to settle in England more than 10 years ago.

The Castle and 630 acres of surrounding land has suffered centuries of gradual decay. The last owner, Mr Edmund Meade Waldo, who resided at Stonewall Park some two miles away, had leased the property to a succession of tenant farmers.

Mr Astor, whose wife died some years ago, already owns a grand house at Cliveden in Buckinghamshire and others in New York, Rome and London. He has gained practical experience of building construction, interior decoration and garden design. More important, he has a keen appreciation of quality and a true respect for history. He was devastated to find the oak panels whitewashed, large rooms partitioned off, windows filled in (to avoid window tax) and the garden totally neglected.

The American plans to restore the Castle, construct a Tudor-style village beyond the moat as an annexe for his house guests and domestic staff, create a lake, restore the gardens, perhaps in an Italian style, and furnish the house with rare and beautiful works of art.

William Waldorf Astor is also the owner of the elegant Waldorf Hotel in Fifth Avenue, New York. He became a naturalized British subject in 1899 and last year entered the newspaper business by buying the Pall Mall Gazette.

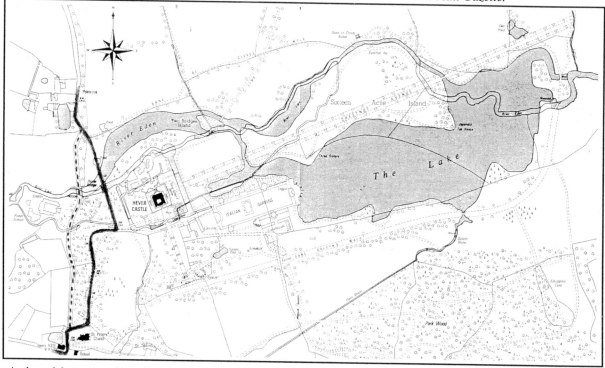

A plan of the proposals for Hever Castle and gardens. The solid line north from Hever shows the route of the road as it is now. The dotted line shows the proposed diversions. Also shown is the natural course of the river running through the shaded areas which are the planned lakes and water works. Hever was the home in the 16th century of Thomas Bullen.

'If some beneficent friend would rebuild the pettitfogging steeple, Rochester Cathedral would be one of the most impressive buildings in the land' — Arthur Mee, The King's England.

1904

January 8th: Kent's elegant Catholic society ladies have been stunned by the news from the Vatican that no woman should wear a low-cut evening gown, particularly when Cardinals or other church dignitaries are present. Pope Pius X's controversial ruling means that diplomatic wives will have to find other ways of maintaining their allure.

February 3rd: A freak tidal wave has swept up the Channel leaving a trail of devastation in East Kent coastal areas. Elsewhere in the county, gale force winds and heavy rain have caused considerable damage to property and widespread flooding has brought work to a standstill.

March: A plan to build two parallel railway tunnels under the English Channel, first suggested by the eminent British engineer William Lowe in the last century, has been re-examined by Albert Sartiaux and Sir Francis Fox who are encouraged by the advent of electric traction.

May 4th: The Hon Charles Stewart Rolls, whose company sells and repairs cars from Conduit Street, London, and Henry Royce, who runs a firm of electrical engineers from Manchester, have merged to sell cars under the trade name of Rolls-Royce. In the Thousand Mile Trial of 1900 which helped to popularise motoring in Britain, Rolls was the winner in a 12 hp Panhard. His new partner, Royce has established a reputation for perfection in engineering and is planning to produce cars from his workshop in Manchester.

July: Four people have died in a fire at Cliffe. When the outbreak was discovered a villager rode on horseback to Rochester to alert the nearest fire brigade but by the time they were in attendance four had died and their house had been completely gutted.

July 14th: The first tram line has been opened in Maidstone. It runs from the town centre to the borough boundary at Barming and is powered by electricity from the borough works. Further tram lines are planned but will not be ready for some years. Alongside the new tram service is the steam-driven omnibus owned by Maidstone and District Motor Services Ltd which operates from the county town to Sutton Valence.

September: Reliable light motor cars are now on the market through Kent's automobile manufacturers at prices between £150 and £200. Many of the county's businessmen now believe that these machines are an improvement on the horse, the tram and the railway. In town centres they are faster and for going out into the country they save all the usual waiting time. They are also more reliable with fewer breakdowns.

October 3rd: Dartford Grammar School for Girls opened. It is to be followed, next week, by Sittingbourne Grammar School for girls. More girls' grammar schools are being built in Kent.

October 21st: Edward VII visits the Royal Engineers at Maidstone.

The old military prison at Borstal has been opened for young offenders only. By separating boys from men it is hoped the new institution will "cure" as well as punish.

November 29th: Figures published show that 520,000 people in England and Wales are now on poor relief, more than at any time since 1888. A further 250,000 are in workhouses.

Dec 13th: The first train operated by electric power left Baker Street station today bound for Uxbridge. The new train is quieter than its predecessors and moves much more quickly. The operating company is the Metropolitan Railway and all their trains will eventually be converted.

A new church at Sevenoaks has been consecrated. It is called St Luke's and is situated in Eardley Road, one of the newer residential roads near the railway station.

The appeal for leniency against Samuel Henson of Ramsgate, who killed his son in a bungled attempt to murder his wife, has been successful. The appeal court decided he was insane and would be sent to an asylum rather than the gallows.

GREAT HITS OF 1904
Meet me in St Louis
Give my regards to Broadway

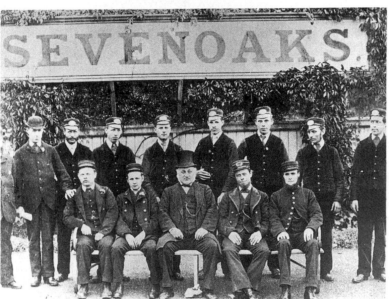

The Sevenoaks station master in top hat and frock coat sits proudly in the centre surrounded by his staff. The two men on the left, wearing curly brimmed bowlers are carters. The station staff consists of signalmen, pointsmen, switchmen and gatemen. They work a 12-hour day, seven days a week.

> Arthur Till of Eynsford, teetotaller and a great local benefactor has bought the Harrow Inn in the village centre, renamed it the Castle Hotel and decreed that the landlord should serve only one alcoholic drink per person per day. The brewery freeholders who understandably want to increase sales are furious about this eccentric ruling and plan to take Till to the High Court.

July: This happy picture taken on the steps of Eastwell House near Ashford shows King Edward and his friends during his recent visit to the house where his sailor brother, the Duke of Edinburgh, lived for many years. The royal party enjoyed a splendid meal and took a summer stroll in Eastwell Park which is one of the largest in the country. Left to right (back row): Lady Norreys, Hon Mrs George Keppel, Mr L de Rothschild. Hon H Milner, Hon H Legge, Sir Ernest Cassel.
Second row: Mrs L de Rothschild, Lord Herard, Marquis de Soveril, Countess Mar Kellie, Earl Mar Kellie, Hon Mrs Lowther. Third row: Baroness de Forest, H M King Edward VII, Lady Gerard, Lord Charles Montagu. Fourth row: Baron de Forest, Master A Lowther, Master Edmonstone, Miss Goosclin, Count Mensdorff and Lady Maud Warrender. This was a great occasion for the people of Ashford who turned out in force to see if they could catch a glimpse of the royal party as they travelled through the park. Queen Victoria once visited Eastwell and a few inhabitants of Boughton and Kennington retain pleasant recollections of her visit.

Rudyard Kipling and the marshmen

August: One character often seen in recent weeks wandering on his own in the southern corner of Kent is the author of the best-selling *Jungle Book*. Rudyard Kipling lives with his wife Carrie at Bateman's, Burwash — a house he bought on September 3, 1902 — which is set in the valley of the River Dudwell, a not insubstantial tributary of the Rother. In this pleasant environment he intends to continue with his writing.

Kipling's friends have said how much he loves the villages to the east of Burwash and he how he understands the marsh and the marshmen. He blames the "diks" for the puzzling, winding roads. "They twists the roads about as ravelly as witchyard on the spindles, so ye get all turned round in broad daylight". He has also found peace in the area: "O Romney level and Brenzett reeds, I reckon you know all my mind needs".

Rudyard Kipling was born in Bombay and spent many years travelling in the Far East and America. In fact he wrote *The Jungle Book* while living in Vermont. He then lived briefly at Rottingdean before moving to Burwash. "We had seen an advertisement for Batemans", he wrote, "and we reached her down an enlarged rabbit-hole of a lane. At first the Committee of Ways and Means said: 'That's her! The only She! Make an honest woman of her — quick' We entered and felt her spirit — her Feng Shui — to be good."

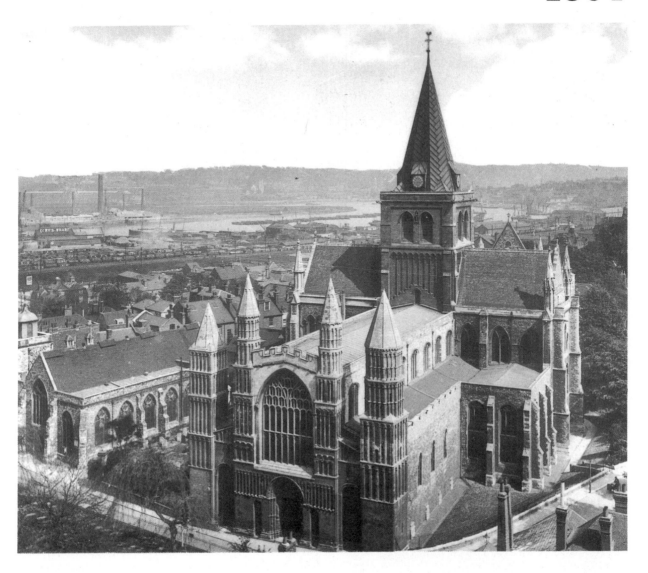

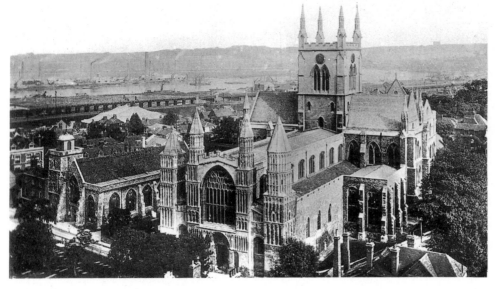

October: A postcard view of the reconstruction of Rochester Cathedral tower which has just been completed. Instead of four pinnacles on the tower a spire has been erected, conforming with the original design of Bishop Hamo de Hythe in 1343. The work has been undertaken at the expense of Mr Thomas Hellyar Foord.

37

The Thatched House at Elmwood Avenue

Mr Harmsworth's thatched house 'the ideal home'

Summer: Alfred Harmsworth, the popular owner of the North Foreland Golf Course at Kingsgate, which he founded a few years ago, has been deeply involved lately in his other great passion — newspapers and, in particular, the *Daily Mirror.* This week the newspaper, which was launched last year exclusively for women, used a photograph in colour on the front page and intends to pioneer this revolutionary kind of illustrated journalism.

The newspaper tycoon, now a millionaire and very popular in the Thanet area, introduced the era of popular journalism when he founded the, now well established, *Daily Mail* in 1896. At the time he was living in a small cottage opposite Trinity Church near the gas works in Broadstairs.

Mr Harmsworth's other ambitious idea has been the launching of the successful *Ideal Home Exhibition* at Olympia which he hopes will become an annual affair. A feature of the exhibition was the Thatched House, which he designed and then entered into a competition for the ideal home in England. No-one was surprised when it won the first prize as a 'pioneer in residential building'.

The Thatched House has now been dismantled at Olympia and re-erected at Elmwood Avenue, Kingsgate, adjoining the North Foreland Golf Course as "an ideal home for the golf secretary".

May 17th: Mafeking Day — and the celebrations in Kent once again mark the great occasion in 1900 when this South African garrison town was finally relieved. The girl with the decorated bicycle entered the procession at Chislehurst where Boer War veterans also took part. Not all of them were involved in the siege of Mafeking but the occasion remains the popular memory of the war.

Easter Sunday at Biddenden and the queue outside the Old Workhouse stretches into the distance. The occasion is the distribution of the Biddenden Charity set up in the name of the Siamese Twins, Eliza and Mary Chalkhurst, born many centuries ago. The charity is drawn from the revenue of 18 acres of land to be spent in "bread and beer for the poor of the village" and (with exception of the beer) has actually been given every year for more than 300 years! Originally the poor queued outside the church to receive their gift, now they wait by the Old Workhouse.

Sunday dinner for the workhouse inmates

November 29th: Figures just released show there has been a dramatic increase in the number of people receiving poor relief. At the end of last month there were about 250,000 in workhouses in England and Wales and more than 520,000 getting outdoor relief.

Despite the sudden increase in the figures there is little doubt that, in Kent at least, the workhouse is finally showing signs of throwing off its terrifying image as a place of the last refuge and the unions are displaying numerous acts of compassion. Maidstone's elderly inmates, for example, are now awarded a weekly ounce of tobacco, New Romney has placed boxes in the railway station asking for the receipt of books and newspapers for their inmates, Sevenoaks has modified the workhouse dress so the residents will not be identifiable outside the house, Faversham's tea and sugar allowance has been doubled and Tonbridge is to substitute a Sunday meat dinner for bread and cheese.

Although humanity is reasserting itself the public hatred for the workhouse is expressed in frequent calls to scrap the system which was first established under the Poor Law of 1601 when parishioners were made responsible for the well being of the poor. Then workhouses were built throughout Kent and, in them the poor were provided with work of a kind that was useful to the parish.

In the mid-nineteenth century they were redefined as institutions with discipline and hard work to reinforce the message. The workhouse inmates included "paupers, idiots and lunatics, orphaned and deserted children, widows and the deaf, dumb and blind". A Board of Guardians was responsible for their welfare.

The twentieth century has seen considerable changes. Workhouse girls are now sent into service, children are placed with cottagers for a weekly sum and men are working on farms. With the imminent introduction of industrial training there is a growing view that "pauper places", are not needed especially as the possible advent of Old Age Pensions, which some Kent boards have discussed, would also considerably alleviate the situation.

July 14th, 1904.

Another new lighthouse as the sea recedes even further

June: To the delight of sailors and to the great satisfaction of Trinity House, the new Dungeness lighthouse has now been completed and will soon be beaming its warning messages across the Channel. It stands some 136 feet high and 38 feet in diameter at the base and is nearer to the sea, which continues to recede at an extraordinary pace.

Since one tragic year early in the seventeenth century when more than a thousand lifeless bodies of shipwreck victims were collected at and near the Ness, there has been a succession of lighthouses on the point. The first was in 1615, but as time passed by and the shingle built up, seamen complained of the distance of the lighthouse from the sea so the tower was pulled down and a new one erected with a coal fire on top. This continued to light Dungeness for 100 years but the sea receded further leaving the tower once again far from the water's edge.

In 1792 Samuel Wyatt's tower was built to the same design as the Eddystone Lighthouse. Eighteen sperm-oil lamps took the place of coal until 1862 when an electric light was installed and Dungeness became one of the first lighthouses in Britain to be lit by this means. Nevertheless candle power was found to be even more effective and a huge oil lamp of 850 candle power surrounded by glass prisms which increased the illuminating power by a hundredfold was installed.

By 1890 the lighthouse was some 500 yards from the high water mark so Trinity House place a small revolving light near the water's edge and commissioned yet another new lighthouse. With the shingle growing at the rate of about 18 inches a year the day will come when this lighthouse too will have to be replaced.

July 14th: Great excitement in Maidstone today as the tramway is opened. Here the crowds gather in Week Street. Below: a tram advertising Colman's Mustard makes its way down the High Street

'The good, the gentle, high-gifted, ever-friendly, noble Dickens — every inch of him a gentleman' — Thomas Carlyle, 1870

A memorial to Charles Dickens in the form of a bronze bust has been placed on the wall of Bleak House, Broadstairs where the great writer lived for many years.

January 24th: Four new grammar schools for girls have been opened in Kent within a week. They are at Erith, Tunbridge Wells, Folkestone and Tonbridge.

March 6th: George, Prince of Wales has been elected Lord Warden of the Cinque Ports.

May 12th: A bill to give women the vote has been "talked out" by MPs. Under the rules of Westminster, if MPs are talking when the House is due to adjourn, a bill is automatically lost and this was the case. Many MPs consider that it will "not be safe" to give women the vote.

"Lord" George Sanger's' English circus at Margate, the largest in England, has closed In its place Sanger has set up an amusement park which includes an Italian gardens, zoo, roller skating, ball room, concert hall and restaurant.

June: The plan to build two railway tunnels under the English Channel has been rejected by the British military who are concerned about the possibility of French troops marching through the tunnel.

July: The controversial Jezreelites tower alongside the A2 at Gillingham, home of a strange religious sect, has been repossessed. There are plans to turn the unfinished buildings into a factory.

July 20th: John Reginald Harmer has been enthroned as Bishop of Rochester. The boundaries of the Diocese of Rochester have also been altered. East and mid-Surrey (added in 1877), are now to accompany the Metropolitan boroughs of Deptford, Greenwich, Lewisham and Woolwich into the new diocese of Southwark. The Rural deaneries of Shoreham and Dartford are to transfer from the Canterbury diocese to Rochester which now retains its original mediaeval boundaries.

July 25th: King Edward arrived at Rochester station, drove to Chatham and unveiled a memorial arch erected for the last Royal Engineer to die in the Boer War. The King then opened the new Naval Hospital in Windmill Road, New Brompton.

August 1st: General William Booth, founder of the Salvation Army has visited Dover to begin the first stage of his country-wide crusade. The streets were packed to see the General standing in the back of a motor car addressing his eager followers. The crusade will last a month and the aim is to encourage the troops and spark a new fire of religious enthusiasm throughout the land.

August 4th: A tram driver and his six passengers had a lucky escape when a Ramsgate tram (No 41) ran out of control, descended Madeira Walk in pouring rain, crashed through a fence and fell onto waste ground some 30 feet below. This is the second major tram accident in Ramsgate this year. On May 26th No 47 ran into a shop when the brakes failed. There is much concern in the town over the efficiency of the Isle of Thanet Tramways service.

Harry Houdini, the great escapologist, was a visitor to Barnards Rochester. He performed many astounding acts including one in which he invited the police at Rochester to lock him in the cell for "the night". Watched by a huge crowd he managed to escape in two minutes flat.

September 11th: Dover Grammar School for Boys has been opened by George, Prince of Wales.

September 28th: Thanks to a gift from the Scottish-born US philanthropist, Andrew Carnegie who believes that " a man who dies rich dies in disgrace", Gravesend has a new public library. Built of Ancaster stone and red brick it was opened by the mayor. Mr Carnegie's benefactions in Britain include libraries at Dartford, Ramsgate and many others

WA Stevens of Stevens and Barker a firm of mechanical and electrical engineers of St Peter Street, Maidstone has converted a motor car to electric power and plans to collaborate with the Tilling bus company of London to provide an electric drive bus. The chassis and engines will be made at the Maidstone works.

October: Sir Martin Conway has bought Allington Castle near Maidstone. It is largely a ruin but he intends to restore it.

November: A railway line has been built down the complete length of the Prince of Wales pier at Dover for the benefit of the boat trains. One of the biggest to enter service is the *SS Amerika* which carries almost 4,000 passengers.

William Parrett, who broke into the world of newspaper ownership in 1865 when he created the *East Kent Gazette* has died. Parrett also acquired the *Chatham News* in 1885 and installed his colleague George Neves as editor. Neves is now the chairman of the company.

A library has been opened at The Drive, Sevenoaks thanks to a gift from local benefactor, Mr Henry Swaffield.

New churches: St Pauls Northumberland Heath; Ascension, Plumstead, St Martin's Plumstead.

GREAT HITS OF 1905:

Wait 'till the sun shines, Nellie...

The Harrow Inn at Eynsford is at last allowed to serve more than one alcoholic drink per day to each customer. After last year's eccentric ruling to the contrary the brewers, who supply the pub, took the owner Arthur Till to the High Court. They lost the case but have won on appeal. The drinking fraternity of Eynsford is mightily relieved.

At last — Kent opens more grammar schools for girls

January 24th: It has been a great week in the short history of Kent Education Committee with the opening of three new grammar schools for girls at Tunbridge Wells, Tonbridge and Folkestone. Similar schools were opened at Dartford and Sittingbourne last year and others are being built at Chatham, Dover, Ashford, Gravesend, Ramsgate and Bromley. Soon the balance between the provision of secondary schools in Kent, which has been so greatly in the boys' favour, will be redressed — to the delight of many campaigners.

The formation of the Kent Education Committee which followed the Education Act of 1902 led to the provision of numerous grammar schools in the county and by the start of 1905 an estimated 2,348 boys and 1,726 girls were attending. This great anomaly, however, has prompted many letters of complaint to the education authority and to local newspapers and the provision of more grammar schools for girls has been a top priority. The Government now plans to award a grant to these schools to offer free places provided they admit at least a quarter of their children from elementary schools.

January 24th: Tonbridge Grammar School for Girls has opened with 21 pupils and Miss J.R.Taylor as the headmistress. Some years ago the Skinners' Company were approached with a proposal that they should fund the building of a girls' school in Tonbridge but, while they were in agreement, lack of funds made it impossible to help. The Skinners' Company had already established two purpose-built boys' schools— Skinners at Tunbridge Wells (1887) and Judd at Tonbridge (1888) and as Tonbridge School, founded by Sir Andrew Judde in 1553, was also under their auspices, money from their educational fund was exhausted. The town turned to the KEC and, thanks to them, a Girls' School has finally opened in the Technical Insitute.The young pupils of the national school pictured, may later move on to the Grammar School.

With the opening of the Headcorn to Tenterden line, the Weald of Kent is now well-served with railways. Here is a reminder of an earlier occasion — at Goudhurst on the Hawkhurst to Paddock Wood line, completed in 1893.

Railways change the landscape of Kent

April: The final link in the great railway network of Kent has been completed with the opening of the line from Headcorn to Tenterden. In just 75 years, hundreds of miles of railway track have been laid across the county — at first a novelty but now seen as a catalyst for social and economic change.

Despite the introduction of the motor car, the tram and the bus, "railway mania" still exists in most communities. Trains are accessible to everyone and only a few people have objected to the impact they have made on town and village life, and on the landscape. Right across the county there are enormous cuttings and embankments, spectacular viaducts and many long tunnels. It is now possible to travel on a train from London to every major town in Kent, and via Dover to the Continent.

Some months ago the two major rival railway companies responsible for the key routes across the county amalgamated. The South Eastern Railway and the London, Chatham, Dover forgot the fierce competition of Victorian days and now exist as the South Eastern and Chatham Railway Company.

The amalgamation has prompted many observers to look back nostalgically to 1830 when the first railway line in Britain to carry passengers in a train drawn by a locomotive was opened in Kent. This was from Canterbury to Whitstable and it was difficult to construct and even more difficult to

work. The locomotive was called *The Invicta* and was similar to *The Rocket* built by Robert Stevenson. But, sadly, it proved so unsatisfactory that it was replaced by horses.

In 1841, the newly-formed South Eastern Railway Company built its first line from London to Brighton via Redhill — where it struck off eastward to Tonbridge to Ashford in 1842 and to Folkestone and Dover by 1844. It included 45 miles that ran straight and level through the heart of Kent. A tunnel was constructed at Sandling and the extension of the line to Dover necessitated a viaduct at Ford, Folkestone which had 19 arches.

Other lines soon followed, from Paddock Wood to Maidstone(1844), from Tonbridge to Tunbridge Wells(1845), from Ashford to Canterbury, Ramsgate, Broadstairs and Margate (1846) with a branch line from Minster via Sandwich to Deal (1847).

Various links were made with London and the Medway towns and, in 1858, the East Kent Railway Company built a line from Strood to Faversham, via Rochester and Chatham and Sittingbourne. The effect on the landscape was dramatic. In two years the line was extended to Canterbury (1860), Dover (1861), from Sittingbourne to Sheerness (1860), Whitstable(1860), to Herne Bay (1861), and Margate (1863).

The East Kent Railway changed its name to the London,

continued

Work in the great Ashford railway factory briefly grinds to a halt for the visit of the man with the magic box. Here, in the wheel room, workers stand motionless for a few seconds until the cameraman moves on. Ashford has completely changed in character ever since the South Eastern Railway Company decided to establish its main workshops in the town. The population — 3,000 in the mid-19th century — is now in excess of 13,000 and growing rapidly as more people depend on the railway for their livelihood. The company has completed the building of shops, school and a public house and contributed towards the cost of a church.

continued

Chatham and Dover and, following a few minor accidents, earned the title of "London, Smashem and Turnover". Competition between them and the South Eastern was now keen. Having completed the link to the industrial Medway towns, the bucket and spade resorts of Thanet and to the Continent via Dover, the race was on to service the more difficult towns beyond the North Downs. The LCD were first to Sevenoaks via Swanley but not to be outdone the SER took the more difficult route through the North Downs to Sevenoaks and then through the Greensand Ridge to Tonbridge. Two long tunnels, both more than a mile long were constructed.

Between 1868 and 1895 more branch lines were built — some by smaller companies such as the Sheppey Light Railway Company in 1901 and finally the Kent and East Sussex Light Railway this year. The great Kent railway network is now almost complete with the railway works conveniently situated in the town of Ashford.

UNPLEASANT POLICE ARE 'HOSTILE TO MOTORISTS'

June 29th: An Automobile Association has been formed to help motorists avoid the increasingly widespread speed traps in which policemen use conventional stop-watches to estimate speeds over 20 mph which is the legal limit. Kent car owners claim the tests are wildly inaccurate and they also say that the police in many towns are unpleasant and hostile.

The new association's objectives are "the protection and advancement of the legitimate interests of motorists and opposition to restriction on the use of roads".

All members at the meeting at the Trocadero Restaurant in London agreed to pay an annual subscription of two guineas to support the association.

May 20th: The 457 ft HMS Africa in the water at Chatham. She is heavily armed, weighs 16,350 tons and has a maximum speed in excess of 18 knots an hour.

Chatham launches its greatest battleship

May 20th: The world's biggest battleship, *HMS Africa* slipped gracefully down the slipway at Chatham accompanied by a military band, a heartening rendition of 'Rule Britannia' and tumultuous cheering from local inhabitants. It has been one of the greatest occasions since *HMS Victory* triumphantly left Chatham in 1769 for her inaugural trials.

July 26th: This has been a red-letter year for Chatham. Today His Majesty King Edward VII unveiled the South African war memorial in the Royal Engineer Barracks and then opened the Royal Naval Hospital which covers an area of 39 acres on the edge of the Chatham Lines and overlooks the town from a height of 223 feet above sea level. The buildings have been erected at a cost of £800,000. Chatham now boasts the biggest dockyard in the world, refitting the largest ships in the Navy. As on the occasion of the launch of the *Africa*, a special train was laid on to bring dignitaries from London.

HIS MAJESTY'S 1st CLASS BATTLESHIP
"AFRICA"
WILL BE
LAUNCHED AT CHATHAM
ON SATURDAY, 20th MAY, 1905,
At 1.0 p.m.

Admit Bearer to Port Platform **C.**

R. W. CRAIGIE,

Carriages to Enter and leave by the Alexandra Gate.

Admiral Superintendent

Admit bearer to Port Platform. A valued invitation to the launch of the battleship HMS Africa by the Marchioness of Londonderry.

The Prince of Wales Pier showing the first American liner to call.

A welcome in Dover for biggest liner

August: Dover is now officially a trans-Atlantic port. The huge liner, *SS Amerika,* sailed into the harbour, berthed at the seaward end of the recently-completed Prince of Wales Pier and took aboard 4,000 passengers bound for the United States.

The arrival of the liner follows the successful trial berthing last year when the Hamburg-Amerika Company made its decision to transfer the Southampton call to Dover with four boats in each direction a week. The first large ship was the *Deutschland,* new in 1900 and able to carry 2,000 passengers. Then came the *Prinz Sigismund* and finally the *SS Amerika* which has just

entered service.

The completion of the Prince of Wales Pier and the railway line which runs the complete length — mainly for the benefit of the boat trains across the Channel — has been accompanied by the extension of the western arm on the Admiralty Pier. The next project in Dover Harbour will be the construction of the southern breakwater.

This is the Admiralty Pier, taken a few years ago, with the larger paddle steamers which could cross the Channel in less than two hours. This pier has now been extended.

The picture above, taken last year, shows a tram negotiating the steep descent of Madeira Walk on an identical journey to that which ended in disaster yesterday. The picture on the right shows the final resting place of the ill-fated vehicle. That there were no serious injuries to passengers seems quite miraculous.

Ramsgate tram plunges over the cliff

August 4th: In an extraordinary and chilling accident at Ramsgate yesterday an electric tramcar carrying five passengers and a conductor left the rails on the East Cliff, crashed through a fence and plunged 35 feet onto unoccupied land at the rear of the Queen's Head public house.

The driver, Mr L.W. Lloyd was hurled onto the roof of a disued building. He sustained severe injuries but the passengers and conductor miraculously escaped with little more than bruises and shock.

An eye witness said it was an Isle of Thanet Company electric tramcar, no 41, on the Broadstairs loop-line and had turned out of Wellington Crescent at the start of the steep descent of Madeira Walk towards the harbour. "It was just after 11 am", he said. "It gathered speed, seemingly unchecked and crashed down the cliff. I ran to where the ruined car lay and expected to see everyone killed but to my amazement the injuries were only slight. It was the height of the holiday season but as it was a wet day there were few people about and therefore few passengers on the tram."

For a time after the accident great excitement prevailed as hundreds of people flocked to the scene with the fear that their friends might be among the injured. The police, however, kept the crowds back until the doctors arrived.

Ramsgate Corporation is certain now to demand a Board of Trade inquiry. No-one has been to Ramsgate in recent years without being struck by the dangerous character of the spot where the accident occurred. The gradient, almost as steep as the side of a house, with a curve at the very worst point, has made many passengers shudder. The rails must be re-aligned.

The first two trams loaded with civic dignitaries is about to start on its maiden run. Right: One of the loyal Dover tram conductors with his boy.

A new route to River for the Dover trams

October 2nd: The Right Hon George Wyndham, MP for Dover today drove the first tram from the town hall to the River crossing following the opening of this long-awaited extension. It was a red-letter day for Dover. Several trams made the maiden run to River and Mr Wyndham in his speech reminded the many spectators that Dover was the first town in Kent to invest in an electric tram system.

It was in 1897 that Dover Corporation opened two routes to Buckland and Maxton and the initial fleet was ten trams built by Brush of Loughborough. In 1902 the Electric Railway and Tramway Carriage Works built a modern tram with the upper deck extended over the platforms. This carried 26 passengers outside and 22 inside.

'I cannot imagine what an English summer can be like without playing cricket for Kent' — Frank Woolley in his autobiography.

February 7th: The Liberals have won the General Election with a victory of landslide proportions. They have 399 seats in the new Parliament compared with 183 elected in 1900. The Tory seats have gone down from 401 to 156. Equally remarkable is the success of the Labour Representation Committee led by James Keir Hardy with 29 seats. This party has trebled its share of the total vote.

February 10th: *HMS Dreadnought*, the largest, fastest battleship ever known has been launched by the King. She is the most powerful warship in the world placing the Royal Navy ahead of all its potential adversaries.

February 14th: Dartford Council have decorated their trams for the opening day of the service from Bexleyheath to Horns Cross with a branch service from Victoria Road to Wilmington. The fleet consists of 12 United Electric Tram cars. The branch service from Victoria to Wilmington has a single deck car.

February 23rd: Workmen excavating in a quarry near St Peter's Cement Works, Wouldham have discovered the tusk of a male mammoth with some teeth. The tusk is 10 ft five inches long.

March 6th: 80 people have been thrown out of work by a disastrous fire at Eynsford. The paper mill owned by Messrs Arnold and Foster has been partially destroyed and it will be at least six months before the machinery can be reconstructed.

March 22nd: England have won the first rugby international against France in Paris by 35 points to eight.

The archdeaconry of Tonbridge has been formed in the diocese of Rochester. and A.T.Stott has been appointed first Archdeacon.

April 12th: The first motor bus service between Canterbury and Herne Bay has begun, and Dartford has a new electric tram service.

All England is talking about an exciting new cricketer who made his debut for Kent this season. Frank Woolley, who was born in Tonbridge, is an all-rounder with tremendous potential, He has played 16 matches, scored 779 runs and taken 42 wickets.

April 25th: Noisy protests by a group of women who shouted "give us votes" and "justice for women", has halted a debate in the House of Commons. The women were ejected from the building.

June: Florrie Ford, the great Australian chorus singer, is appearing at the Gaiety Theatre, Chatham to sing her hits which include *Down at the Old Bull and Bush.*

June 12th: Ellen Terry, British actress who lives in Smallhythe, near Tenterden celebrates 50 years on the stage.

July 3rd: Kent County Council has warned of the spread of tuberculosis through infected milk.

August 6th: Kent's seaside resorts have never known anything like it as the 90-degree heatwave made this year's Bank Holiday one of the busiest ever.

August 21st: The tramline from Chatham to Rainham has been opened. This is a boon to the people of Rainham who can shop in the bigger town and pay 3d for the fare.

August 26th: The first tram service from Northumberland Heath to Erith has commenced.

Kent Cricket Club are the champions. They have won the county championship in great style, beating Hampshire in the final game at Bournemouth to clinch the title. Among the celebrations planned is a ball at the Royal Crown Hotel, Sevenoaks — the scene of many county dinners.

October 20th: A Swedish freighter loaded with timber has hit the Southern Breakwater in the harbour at Dover. The seaward side of the two main cross girders on the breakwater was damaged and the ship lost much of its cargo. The Hamburg-Amerika company are concerned about the narrow entrance to Dover Harbour. There is a possibility they may revert back to Southampton.

October: The castellated Archdeacon's House at Lympne (built XVth century partly with materials from the nearby Roman remains of Portus Lemanis) has been restored and rechristened.

Bromley library has opened, thanks to a benefaction from the Scottish-born US philanthropist Andrew Carnegie.

November 2nd: London buses are too noisy and many have been taken off the road. The licensing law requiring "no undue noise" has been applied with great strictness by the police.

William Waldorf Astor has completed his restoration of Hever Castle down to the last detail, introducing 20th century plumbing, electricity and central heating and moving both the River Eden and the road in order to create formal gardens and a massive lake. The American millionaire has given his other home at Cliveden to his eldest son Waldorf who last year married Miss Nancy Langhorne, a 27-year-old American with political ambitions.

GREAT HITS OF 1906

*Waiting at the church
How'd you like to spoon
with me.*

August 26th: *A great occasion as the first tram from Northumberland Heath to Erith arrives on time, gaily decorated. The journey to work will be much quicker now.*

Paper mill blaze leaves families homeless

August 12th: Thirty one families in Snodland are homeless following a fire which is without parallel in the annals of the village. The blaze entirely burned out the papermaking mills of Messrs Townend Hook and Co, leaving only the carpenters' and fitters' shops standing at one end of five or six acres of ruins.

In just a few hours this enormous conflagration created damage estimated at almost £200,000, deprived 400 people of their ordinary employment, caused 31 families to leave their cottages, imperilled the parish church, filled the air with fragments of burnt paper resembling a snowstorm and engaged the services of six fire brigades.

The fire owed its origin to repair work which was in progress on Sunday morning. A rope made of cotton caught fire and this was the driving rope of the great double-crank engine which drove the whole machin-

ery of the mill. From the engine room the ropes radiated in all directions and the flames ran along them like fuses setting fire to 1,000 tons of resin, 1,000 tons of printing paper in reels, 400 tons of dry wood pulp and 900 tons of wet wood pulp.

One fortunate circumstance was that the wind was blowing away from the town, otherwise the fire would have travelled up the High Street with results too horrible to contemplate. Even more fortunate is that amid all the ruin no lives were lost or serious personal injury caused.

The mill will now be rebuilt without delay and, by arrangement with the insurance company, as many millmen as circumstances permit will be employed on the rebuilding work. A relief fund has been established and the parish council has undertaken the administration of the money.

W. HEARNE (SCORER) FIELDER K. L. HUTCHINGS HUISH BLYTHE
R. N. R. BLAKER J. R MASON C. H. B. MARSHAM, CAPTAIN E.W DILLON C. J BURNUP
SEYMOUR HUMPHREYS

KENT XI. 1906, WINNERS OF THE COUNTY CHAMPIONSHIP.

Kent cricketers are champions of England

August: Kent has won the county cricket championship for the first time in its illustrious history. Captain C.H.B. Marsham, in his third season at the helm, led his side to 16 victories and only two defeats. With four drawn games Kent won the title in convincing fashion with Yorkshire in second place. It has been a memorable season which the county will never forget.

There have been many highlights. The solid batting of Burnup who topped the national batting averages with 67. The remarkable performances of the amateur Mr K.L.Hutchings, who did not play until Tonbridge Week but then scored 1,454 runs and earned a tribute in Wisden as the "sensation of the season". The centuries scored by the veteran Alec Hearne and the captain Mr Marsham. The return of Lord Harris in the county's first game against the West Indies which Kent won by an innings and 14 runs. The bowling of Colin Blythe which set up several successes. The outstanding performances with the ball by Arthur Fielder who took 172 wickets for Kent alone. The wicket-keeping of Fred Huish who kept brilliantly and made his best score for the country with 93.

However, the most encouraging aspect of the season was the emergence of the brilliant young Tonbridge-born all-rounder Frank Woolley. In his first game for Kent the tall lefthander scored 0 and 64, dropped two catches and took 1-103. He went on to score 779 runs at an average of 31.16 and take 42 wickets at 21.11 apiece. His bowling, deceptive in flight and pace, is likened to that of Blythe. His batting includes a brilliant off drive and an ability to entertain and take opposing attacks apart. He is certainly a star in the making.

Kent's first championship success has been greeted rapturously throughout the county and captain Marsham received more than 500 telegrams offering congratulations. Celebration dinners are being held in almost every town.

The Railway Children in line to become a classic

A new book by the well-known authoress, Edith Nesbit is proving to be very popular in Kent bookshops, particularly in the southern part of the county where she now lives. The book is called *The Railway Children* and features Roberta, Phyllis and Peter who, by their initiative, rescue their father from unjust imprisonment.

Edith has lived in Kent for most of her life. Born in 1858 she moved to Knockholt, near Sevenoaks with her husband and lived close to the South Eastern Railway Company's station (then known as Halstead). She moved to Dymchurch in 1902 and then to St Mary's Bay.

However, it was her years in Knockholt which inspired the book and it is based on her memories of the men cutting the great embankment at Halstead station and then the long tunnel under the North Downs. The miners worked in terrible conditions and, as a founder member of the Fabian Society, Edith Nesbit was most concerned for their well-being.

Her husband has a reputation of being a philanderer; in fact Edith Nesbit shares her home with his mistress,

Alice Hoatson who is the housekeeper and mother of Mr Nesbitt's two children. However, as Edith approaches middle age her writing is making her famous. In 1899 she published *The Story of the Treasure Seekers* in which she first introduced Mr and Mrs Bastable and their three children. She followed this with *Five Children and It* in 1902.

In earlier life Edith Nesbit was an enthusiastic Socialist, a general writer and a poet. As her interest in politics waned she began to write novels for children. *The Railway Children* shows all the signs of acquiring the status of a classic.

Liberals sweep to power with 'lies in Tonbridge and bribes in Maidstone'

February: The Liberals have won a General Election victory of landslide proportions. With the last results now in they have swept to power with 399 seats in the new Parliament against 156 for the Tories. Equally remarkable is the success of the Labour Representation Committee led by James Keir Hardy who have taken 29 seats and trebled its share of the total vote.

In Kent there have been many shocks. The Liberals have taken the Tonbridge and Faversham Divisions for the first time. Chatham has fallen to Labour giving that party its only success in Kent and there is talk again of bribery in Maidstone.

The Liberals who, in reality, have been in power since the Tories surrendered office in December without going to the polls, now have the mandate they wanted from the country to govern and place in office some of their brightest stars including David

Lloyd George, Winston Churchill and Herbert Asquith. Prime Minister Sir Henry Campbell-Bannerman will soon be naming his Cabinet.

The new member for Tonbridge (which includes Tunbridge Wells) is Arthur Paget Hedges a manufacturer of cigarettes. He beat the sitting MP Major Boscawen of Boons Park, near Edenbridge by a majority of 1,283 and astonished the Conservative Party who immediately accused the Liberals of stooping to the most woeful methods to obtain success.

They are supported by the *Courier* newspaper who wrote: "The constituency was saturated with a flood of political falsehoods regarding the wages that Major Boscawen pays to his employees at Boons Park. Many of these lies were exposed but only those who have engaged in political strife can

appreciate the difficulty of overtaking a falsehood. A Radical has been returned in an unparelleled political accident."

In Maidstone the Conservative Party — still seething over the fiasco in 1900 when the successful Liberal candidate was disfranchised on bribery charges — are even more convinced that their 1906 opponents are guilty of corruption once more. The Tories won the seat with a small majority of 132 but still plan to lodge a petition against the tactics of Sir Francis Evans and his Liberal team.

Chatham returned a Labour MP only because the Liberal candidate stood down in favour of the newly-found socialist party for fear of splitting the working-class vote. Led by

continued next column

THE FIRE AT HEADLEYS &

continued

the successful candidate John Jenkins they claimed that the Tories, if elected, planned to impose tariffs on foreign goods in order to boost trade with the Empire. And that would make food very dear. Jenkins had a thumping majority in Chatham of 2,672.

One of the closest contests was in Sevenoaks where the Liberal candidate forced a recount. The Tory member retained the seat by just 364 votes.

Another close encounter was at Hythe where Sir Edward Sassoon held on to the seat by 899 against a Liberal who had been convinced he would take it. In Faversham, Thomas Napier, a barrister wrested control for the Liberals after 21 years of Conservative domination.

There were few surprises in the other constituencies. Kent, unlike the rest of the country, remains a Conservative-Unionist stronghold.

11,000 sixpenny novels lost in Ashford fire

September 14th: In the early hours of this morning a disastrous fire entirely destroyed the printing works of Messrs Headley Bros, Ashford. The blaze was first seen in the early hours and in less than half an hour a vast mass of flames made it impossible to save the building. The glass roof fell in, the machinery caught fire and soon this famous printing works was reduced to smouldering ruins. The only salvage effected was the recovery of the safes which remained intact.

The damage, estimated at more than £20,000, is covered by insurance from the Norwich Union but more than 100 employees are now out of work.

Headley Brothers, a renowned firm of printers, lost a consignment of 11,000 sixpenny novels and other publications and hundreds of cases of type which were reduced to large lumps of lead. Part of the works will move to the back of the old Wesleyan chapel in Middle Street and the head office staff will be transferred to the stationer's shop in the High Street.

Marie Lloyd, on the right of the picture, one of the greatest of our music hall stars, with her three sisters.

No dilly-dallying as Marie Lloyd is divorced

September: Percy Courtenay's application to be set legally free from all marital responsibilities from his wife Marie (nee Wood) has been heard and approved by the Divorce Court. Few people, however, are aware of the sensational nature of the hearing, for Mrs Courtenay is better known throughout England as one of the greatest music hall stars of all time. Her stage name is Marie Lloyd. Marie, born in 1870, has been living with her husband at 196 Lewisham High Road since they were married in 1887 when she was just a girl of 17. But if the marriage has not been a great success the same cannot be said of Marie's music hall career. Her speciality is warm-hearted songs about everyday life, made saucy with the help of her famous wink.

Well known in Kent she has appeared in music halls throughout the county where her naughty songs such as *She'd never had her ticket punched before, A little bit of what you fancy does you good* and *Don't dilly-dally on the way* has delighted thousands of people lucky enough to have seen her perform.

Nature is confused. Following a chill spring and a moderate summer until August, the temperatures rose to the nineties in September and, in October, out again came the blossom. This chestnut tree a "freak of nature" is at Birling near Maidstone and the date on the postcard is October 18th.

The funeral procession in Orpington of the men who died in the Vanguard Omnibus tragedy at Handcross Hill.

10 firemen killed in omnibus tragedy

July 13th: The St Mary Cray and Orpington Volunteer Fire Brigade has lost 10 members of its valuable crew in the worst motoring accident ever known. It occurred yesterday on the London to Brighton road at Handcross Hill when the driver of a Vanguard Omnibus, taking the men on their annual outing to Brighton, lost control when the brakes failed. Tragically an overhanging branch of a tree hit the bus, completely ripped away the upper deck and pulled the vehicle into the bank.

The inhabitants of the villages of Orpington and St Mary Cray are devastated by the news. Among those who died is Mr Hutchings, captain of the brigade and the local undertaker.

London Motor Omnibus Company Ltd has been operating a regular service between London and Brighton using Milnes-Daimler double-deckers from its London bus fleet. There have been other mishaps but nothing as serious as this. Apparently the brakes failed at the top of Handcross Hill and then the gearbox disintegrated. With insufficient braking force the driver attempted to slow the vehicle by running the wheels along the verge. To some extent it worked but when the overhanging branch struck the wooden framework the upper deck just came away.

Questions are being asked about the future of the long-distance bus service in the light of this tragedy.

March: During a road-widening project on Dover Hill, Folkestone, 36 Anglo-Saxon graves, complete with skeletons, have been discovered. The borough engineer Mr A.E.Nichols has halted the road scheme in order for an accurate plan to be made of the site and the skeletons photographed. Newspapers are full of stories about "warriors falling in battle" but archaeologists believe it to be a regular Saxon cemetery. Picture shows Folkestonians examining one of the graves.

March 9th: A second hand clothes shop in Rochester High Street has been completely destroyed by fire which also badly gutted the premises next door. The blaze was started when the proprietor, Mr Joseph Martin, accidentally upset a paraffin lamp in his shop. This ignited clothes and spread so quickly that Mr Martin and his housekeeper had only just enough time to rush from the building. Rochester Volunteer Fire Brigade arrived quickly but the fire had gained such a hold that they turned their attention to saving the adjoining block of shops.

'I've seen thousands of boys...hunched up, miserable specimens smoking endless cigarettes' — Robert Baden-Powell explaining why he formed the Boy Scouts.

January 5th: Lloyds paper mill at Sittingbourne has been badly damaged by fire. The local brigade were quickly on the scene but the factory has been gutted and machinery and paper destroyed, despite ample water supply. Edward Lloyd, who prints the *Daily Chronicle*, moved his business here from Bow in 1880.

In a petition held in the Sessions House, Maidstone, judgement has been given in favour of Lord Castlereagh, the Conservative candidate, on the grounds of widespread bribery by the Liberal party in the 1906 general election.

January 21st: Chatham and Ashford Grammar Schools for Girls have opened on the same day.

February 14th: At dusk today mounted police broke up a peaceful protest by suffragettes who were demanding the vote. The horses rode into the procession at Westminster and many women were hurt and their clothes torn. 72 women and two men will appear in court charged with disturbing the peace. Among the defendants will be Christabel Pankhurst.

March 22nd: 72 Suffragettes have been jailed for refusing to pay fines for demonstrating outside parliament.

April 8th: The National Telephone Company has begun to erect telephone poles in many parts of Kent.

April 25th: The bill to facilitate the construction of a railway tunnel under the Channel has been withdrawn by parliament. The War Office declared its opposition to the bill some three months ago.

April: The well-known engineering firm of J and E Hall of Dartford has completed its first omnibus, pictured here on a test run on the Hawley Road. The company has every confidence that the bus will ply the route between Dartford and Farningham for many years to come. The bodywork of this magnificent vehicle is a char-a-banc on an early Hallford lorry chassis, built by George Stubbs of Wilmington. The son of the owner of this firm, Charles Carpenter is seated next to Hall's test driver, Walter Dunmall.

Maidstone brewers Style and Winch have been listed in the *Financial Times* as the second most profitable brewery in the country. The company, which has now acquired more than 350 tied houses, began in 1899 when A.F. Style of Maidstone and E. Winch and Sons of Chatham, amalgamated.

A bird reserve has opened at Dungeness. It is the first conservation site of this kind in Kent.

July 29th: Robert Baden-Powell has formed the Boy Scout movement after taking a group of Londoners to an experimental camp on Brownsea Island.

August 2nd: The British Medical Association at their annual meeting has attacked the evils of smoking, particularly among children. A GP claims that the nation is deteriorating because of smoking and he says that it can cause cancer of the tongue and lip.

September 17th: Louis Bleriot has flown 184 metres in his aeroplane before crash landing.

Goudhurst iron works has closed, bringing to an end the village's connection with the great iron-smelting industry which once brought prosperity to the area.

October 11th: *The Lusitania*, a Cunard ship, has won the Blue Riband trophy for crossing the Atlantic in four days, 52 minutes. She is now regarded as England's "Queen of the Seas".

December: The Nobel prize for literature has gone to an English writer for the first time. Rudyard Kipling's classic *Jungle Books* and his *Just So stories* are delighting both young and old.

October 24th: Lloyd George has approved plans for a Channel ferry from Dover to Calais.

November 25th: A whirlwind which lasted little more than 10 minutes inflicted terrible damage on Orchard Farm, Sholden, Deal. Machinery has been mangled, roofs blown off and a haystack deposited on top of a Russian ship at anchor in the Downs.

New church: St Lukes, Well Hall, Eltham.

January 22nd: It has become known as the greatest show-stopper ever to hit the London stage. Striking artistes have caused 25 music halls to close. Among those who reckon they are getting a raw deal from hall managers is the popular singer, Harry Relf of Cudham.

Harry, better known as "Little Titch", is one of the organisers of the strike. From his picket post this week he claimed that his colleagues could put on 20 shows a week and get paid for only 12. In retaliation the managers say that the British artistes are the highest-paid in the world.

Certainly Harry Relf is well paid. He is the founder of the Variety Artistes Federation but better known for painting his face black and performing brilliantly in music halls all over the country. Harry was born at Cudham in 1867 where his father kept the Blacksmith's Arms. He has six fingers on each hand and stands at four feet five inches high.

Although there is little sign of a solution it is hoped that the pay dispute will be settled after mediation and the music halls will reopen.

1907

Summer: Increasing demand from urban centres and jam factories are encouraging farmers with sufficient capital and fore-sight to expand into fruit growing. There are now more than 22,000 acres in Kent specialising in fruit which is packed into baskets and despatched to its desti-nation via the South Eastern Railway. One problem facing farmers is that the baskets are not all being returned and many have remained abandoned in railway sidings. Picture shows the fruit pickers at Paxton Farm, Bewley, Ightham. The fruit growers are Albert, Frederick and Mrs Phoebe Crowson.

Sir Edward Watkins may be disappointed by the suspension of the Channel Tunnel Works but there is another pioneer in the area who is delighted by the progress his company has been making underground. Arthur Burr, head of the Kent Coal Concessions Ltd, has now sunk several shafts and is highly confident that some collieries may soon be operational. Some 20 years ago geologists made it clear that coal existed in Kent and when the tunnel workings at Dover were first postponed an opportunity existed to test the theory. It was in 1890 that borings, at the base of Shakespeare Cliff, revealed several seams of coal and the race was on to look for more. Tragedy struck in 1897 when water rushed in and six miners were drowned but, undaunted, men and machines continued with the exploration as this photograph of the activity at Dover clearly shows. Kent may never have a tunnel under the sea but one day there may be coal fields, providing employment for hundreds of local people.

French invasion fears kill Channel Tunnel Bill

April 25th: The Channel Tunnel Rail Bill has been withdrawn after objections by the War Office who say the tunnel will be a threat to the nation's defences.

Twenty years ago the tunnel nearly became a reality when the British and French governments agreed to start exploratory shafts under the Straits of Dover between Shakespeare Cliff and a point west of Sandgate. For the English side there were two rival designs — one by William Low, the British mining engineer who had assisted Brunel on his Great Western railway and the other by Sir John Hawkshaw, a successful tunnel and canal engineer.

Sir Edward Watkin, Chairman of the South Eastern Railway Company and MP for Hythe adopted Low's scheme for two parallel tunnels with trains drawn by compressed air engines. Shafts were sunk, headings were driven obliquely under the sea and plans were drawn up for underground stations at each end of the tunnel which would measure 23 miles. The engineers and their families even had lunch under the sea in an atmosphere kept fresh by the boring machine.

Opposition to the proposal, however, was gaining momentum. The main objection was fear of invasion from France. Britain would no longer be wholly protected by the sea and the world's greatest navy. *The Times* even suggested that a few thousand men could land on the Kent coast and hold the English end of the tunnel for a few hours while the main invasion force came through.

Edward Watkin offered to construct two forts to cover the English end with a battery and said the portal on the English side could be demolished immediately by explosives. Despite a petition presented to Parliament by Alfred Lord Tennyson, Watkins kept his engineers working, hoping the War Office would not object to the scheme.

With War Office objections, the withdrawal of the bill and the continuing hostile reaction to the scheme by the public, the sponsors accept that there is little chance of a tunnel under the sea being constructed in the foreseeable future.

'Travelling on Mr Brennan's monorail will be more like riding on a moving hotel or ship on shore than in the usual form of railway carriage'— Charles Hands of the Daily Mail.

January 7th: Kent cricketer Arthur Fielder is the hero of England. Amid rising tension at Melbourne the fast bowler, batting number 11 for his country, helped Sydney Barnes score the 39 runs needed to beat Australia in the closest Test Match yet played overseas.

February 16th: Lord Northcliffe takes control of *The Times*

April 1st: In one of the final steps in the reform and modernisation of the British Army, the Yeomanry, the volunteer cavalry corps and the Volunteers have merged. The new force will be known as the Territorial Army. It will be split into 14 infantry divisions and the same number of cavalry. Training will be linked to that of the regular army commanded by the General Staff.

April 12th: Sir Henry Campbell-Bannerman has resigned as Prime Minister due to ill health and his place has been taken by Herbert Henry Asquith. Other appointments include David Lloyd George as Chancellor and Winston Churchill as President of the Board of Trade.

April 18th: Trams have started to run over Rochester Bridge to Strood and Frindsbury. For the people of the Medway towns, Cobham and Cobham Woods are now within reach for a day out.

Easter Monday: England's greatest cricketer, Dr W.G. Grace, who now lives in Kent, has played his final game. He took the field for the Gentlemen of England against Surrey and scored 14 and 25 despite snow on the pitch. In all first-class games he has amassed 54,211 runs and taken 2,808 wickets.

May 7th: Mr Asquith has announced the Government's intention to introduce an old age pension of 5/- a week for everyone over 70 or 7/6d for married couples. Excluded from this are those who have failed to work, prisoners, the insane and paupers.

Spring: More than 100 men of the West Kent Imperial Yeomanry assembled on bicycles to take part

The monorail car invented by Louis Brennan of Gillingham. His factory is in Piers Road and he is anxious to persuade the British Government that the idea has exciting commercial possibilities.

in an exercise which entailed attacking the Hildenborough Village Hall held by the Infantry of Volunteer Battalion of the West Kent Regiment.

June 11th: The Rotherhithe tunnel has opened under the River Thames.

July: After two years of building and planning, the London Olympic Games has finally got under way at the new White City stadium. The spectators will be treated to 21 different sports.

Girls in white representing 44 other towns all over the world, all called Dover, have appeared in a spectacular pageant in what is now known as "the Gateway of England".

July 15th: Fireman Temple of Broadstairs was killed today on his way to a blaze at the Old Fish Market, Broadstairs. The brigade, called by maroon, dragged out the pair-horse manual engine and proceeded to draw it by hand to the fire. On the hill to the railway station the machine ran out of control, threw Temple off and both wheels passed over him.

Action brought in the High Court by the Oyster Fishery Company accusing Faversham Town Council of discharging crude sewage into the creek and polluting oyster beds has been proved. The Corporation must pay damages and costs of £4,250 and establish a sewage disposal works.

August 13th: The first submarine built at Chatham, the C17, is launched.

Autumn: Sylvester's Hippodrome Theatre, Maidstone is destroyed by fire.

September 21st: The funeral took place today of General Charles Luard of Frankfield House, Seal Chart, near Sevenoaks, who committed suicide by throwing himself under the wheels of an engine as it

passed Teston where he was staying with a friend. General Luard was the central figure in one of the most gruesome murders ever known. In August, his wife Caroline, 58, was shot dead in the garden summerhouse where she was resting. Several rings were missing from her fingers but the case has completely baffled Scotland Yard detectives and, with the General's untimely death, it may now never be solved.

October 24th: Emmeline Pankhurst, the Suffragette leader and her daughter Christabel have been imprisoned for "causing a breach of the peace by inciting the public to rush the House of Commons". David Lloyd George and Henry Gladstone, two cabinet ministers spoke in their defence.

Everyone is talking about a new book written by the secretary of the Bank of England, Kenneth Grahame. This delightful fantasy is called *The Wind in the Willows* and many predict that it could become a classic.

Lord George Sanger's amphitheatre at Ramsgate has now been remodelled as the Palace Theatre. The development includes six shops and a pub, Sanger's Hotel. Eight statues bearing lanterns line the pavement outside the theatre and shops.

County Medical Officer, Dr William Howarth has estimated that there are 74,748 hop-pickers scattered throughout the county, a figure which excludes about 5,600 gipsies and home pickers. In the Tonbridge area alone there are 12,000 local residents picking.

New churches built this year include St Michael and All Angels, Abbey Wood, St Michael and All Angels, Beckenham, Good Shepherd, Borough Green, and St Hilda's Crofton Park, Lewisham.

Letter writer in Gillingham: "The cry of the chimney sweep, the ting-a-ling of the coal bell, the tintinnabulation of the muffin man, the familiar cry of the woman who sells eels and the fine round nightly call of "oysters" positively charms us. My milkman warbles his "milk-ho" every morning in the sweetest of falsettos. The dolorous singing of the vagrant is more trying — all appear to be allowed absolute freedom."

Louis Brennan with his first model. The air-tight containers housing the gyroscopes were made by a blacksmith at Gillingham gas works, the air being withdrawn by using a bicycle pump. Mr Brennan experiments with various designs and models before converting his idea to a full-sized vehicle.

Brennan's monorail — a 'wonder of the age'

October 26th: Despite a recommendation from the Army Council that they did not want to press ahead with any more trials, Gillingham's well-known inventor Louis Brennan is continuing to experiment with his gyroscopically-stabilised monorail car which many informed people believe could revolutionise the transport system all over the world.

The engineer, already famous for his torpedo, is under no doubt that a monorail system of transport could be the answer to modern traffic problems. The inspiration came from a visit to Australia where he saw an obvious need for a rapid transport system which required a simple track laid across rough country without becoming a vast engineering project. To his mind a single rail would provide the answer but how to balance a train on it, like a tight-rope walker, was the problem.

From his home at Woodlands, Woodland Lane, Gillingham, Mr Brennan built a model and experimented with gyroscopic mechanism, recognising that this could be the potential for solving his problem of keeping rolling stock upright on a single rail. The model experiments

were successful and the inventor gave rides to local schoolboys who were fascinated by the gyroscopes and road motors which were driven electrically by accumulators carried in the model itself.

Last year Brennan gave a press demonstration at Woodlands and a reporter from the *Daily Mail* offered to ride the model which ran on a track above the heads of the audience. The following day newspapers gave technical details of the monorail but most articles concentrated on the exciting commercial possibilities of this new means of travel.

Today Mr Brennan has a full-scale monorail car and a factory at Piers Road, Gillingham and demonstrations are given regularly. Although they have vast sums invested in a dual-rail system, the British Government is showing more interest in the idea and so are the Australian, Indian and Japanese Governments. The latter has described the gyroscopic monorail as one of the "wonders of the age".

Louis Brennan's next big demonstration will be at the Japan-British Exhibition at the White City next year.

MEDWAY WITH P.S. "CITY OF ROCHESTER".

Summer: A great amenity for local inhabitants is the introduction of another City of Rochester pleasure steamer to replace the one which has now been broken up. The steamer will continue to ply between Rochester, Chatham, Southend and Sheerness taking thousands of people on pleasure trips. Here are some happy trippers on their way to Southend.

Canterbury mayor and the mystery of the Irish Crown Jewels

January: Canterbury's charismatic mayor, Francis Bennett-Goldney, linked for some time with the mysterious disappearnce of the Crown Jewels of Ireland, has been asked to resign from his position as Athlone Pursuivant of Arms in Ireland. Although the jewels disappeared while they were in Mr Bennett-Goldney's custody he vehemently denies he is reponsible and is devastated by the King's desire that he should sacrifice his heraldic career.

The Canterbury mayor has already given evidence to the inquiry set up to investigate the loss of the jewels and he has written a long letter to *The Times*

This week, however, an interesting sideline to the story has come to light in the shape of a blue Garter that has been seen on display at the Beaney Museum Institute in Canterbury.

A similar blue Garter belonging to the Duke of Marlborough disappeared from Dublin Castle at the time the jewels were taken. As Mr Bennett-Goldney is also director of the Beaney Institute it is possible that he knew something about the Garter in the Museum but that, too, has been suddenly withdrawn from the case.

By whom, when or how is not known.

Massive demonstration by Kentish hoppers

May 16th: Thousands of hop-growers, labourers and pickers from farms in 33 districts of Kent took advantage of the special trains laid on by the South Eastern and Chatham Railway Company today to attend the great hop demonstration in Trafalgar Square, London. The event was an object lesson in organisation and a striking commentary upon the depressed condition of an industry upon which Kent largely depends for its prosperity in town and country alike.

More than 50,000 people took part in the procession and it was long enough to take an hour and a quarter to pass a given spot. Hundreds of banners were exhibited, all suggesting or demanding a duty on imported hops and denouncing the conditions under which England admits foreign hops to compete with home growth.

Rolvenden had a banner with the motto: "We request the Government put a duty of 40s on foreign hops. British workmen want work." A party of blacksmiths from the Isle of Oxney carried a verse: "Under the Kentish chestnut tree, No Kentish smithy stands; The smith a brawny man was he, But now he wrings his hands."

Tenterden's banner attracted much attention. "Hops grubbed, labour displaced, oasthouses empty, workhouses full". A London flag bore the words: "London join hands with Kent; one month's holiday pays the rent". Paddock Wood carried a mourning card which said: "In loving memory of the hop gardens of old England". Another flag read: "We want employment, not charity."

The Wingham contingent reminded everyone that "charity begins at home". Minster and Monckton carried a banner: "Driven from the land, remedy 40s", and Maidstone said: "40s or the workhouse."

The procession was followed by a rally in Trafalgar Square and many stirring speeches. Mr W.F. Winch of the Maidstone brewers Style and Winch moved the resolution that they were there to try and save an industry which the foreigner had striven to kill. "The home demand for English hops", he said, " is far greater than the supply. There is no hop grown in the world that could be compared with the English hop."

Wigmore is the new site for an English Garden City

April 28th: The directors of British Gardens Cities Ltd who propose to establish a series of garden cities combining philanthropy with business, have secured a site known as Wigmore, situated about a mile and a half from Rainham station. Having an area of some 365 acres Wigmore commands a fine view of a long stretch of the Medway and also of the Thames beyond Sheerness. It will be difficult, in Kent, to find a more charming spot for a garden city. With the extension of the tramway from Chatham to Rainham which is shortly to be carried out, the electric tramways will run within ten minutes' walk of Wigmore.

Ramsgate Sands with the bathing machines which are drawn up and down by horses as the tide comes in and out.

Bank Holiday heatwave draws the crowds to Thanet

August: A 90-degree heatwave and continuous sunshine throughout has made this Bank Holiday one of the busiest ever. The numbers of visitors to Thanet on Saturday and Monday must have constituted a holiday record for the island. Thousands arrived by train and tram and this did not include those who walked, cycled or drove by horse and carriage, only to find that letting houses and hotels were full, forcing many to sleep on the beach.

Ramsgate has been particularly popular. The Promenade Pier (admission 2d, children 1d), the Marina Hall and the Royal Victoria Pavilion were thronging with visitors who thoroughly enjoyed the music shows, the dances and the aquatic displays. The entertainment troupes on the Sands also drew vast crowds.

It appears that most of Ramsgate's visitors are from London. One regular holidaymaker said her family travels by railway and "there is always great excitement when the train pulls in at Whitstable and we get the first glimpse of the sea. We like the pure air and the lodgings are fine. We bring the food for the holiday and the landlady cooks it and serves our meals."

Another said: "We come down from Tower Bridge all the way to Margate Pier on the *Royal Sovereign*. We sent our luggage in advance by putting a card in the window of our house in London saying 'Pickford's Wanted'. A van man saw the card and picked up the trunk. It was as easy as that."

The estate workers at Lullingstone Park, the home of Oliver Hart-Dyke, whose family have owned Lullingstone Castle and the Park since

...out 1500, enjoy a picnic while carrying out the annual deer cull. The venison will provide them with a healthy addition to their diet.

Knole, the magnificent stately home in Sevenoaks, which has 365 rooms — one for every day of the year.

The scandal of the Sackville peerage

November: Knole, the stately home of the Sackville family which stands in its great park at Sevenoaks is to be locked and bolted while its ownership is determined in the law courts. The petition is likely to become the scandal of the century.

Following the death of the 2nd Baron Lord Sackville it was expected that the title and inheritance would pass to Lionel

Lord Sackville's daughter Victoria who acted as hostess

Sackville-West who is both his nephew and son-in-law. But to the surprise of the staff at Knole and the people of Sevenoaks, Henri E.J.B. Sackville-West, the 2nd Baron's youngest son by his mistress Pepita claims that he is the rightful heir and has filed a suit of legitimacy.

Henri claims his father was married to Pepita at the time of his birth and will prove so in the High Court of Justice. He says the title and the great Knole estate is legally his.

The white bearded old gentleman who died in his eighties at Knole earlier this year was a legendary figure in the town but remembered by many as a well travelled, successful English diplomat in his younger days. In 1852, as the Hon Sackville-West, and on holiday in Paris, he met the beautiful Spanish dancer Pepita and fell deeply and instantly in love. Pepita was 22, married but separated. He was 25.

Although they were, by law, unable to marry, the British diplomat and the great dancer managed to forge a long liaison and seven children were born to them including Victoria in 1862 and Henri in 1869. Tragically Pepita died shortly after giving birth to her seventh child.

In 1881 Sackville-West was appointed head of the British Legation in Washington and, astonishingly, it was agreed that his daughter Victoria should act as his hostess. In true Cinderella fashion this insecure, illegitimate but very attractive girl became the most courted and most admired hostess in Washington. Later as mistress of the family house at Knole she fell in love with, and married her cousin, Lionel Sackville-West.

The death of her father is a tragedy for Victoria but even more devastating is the news that her younger brother Henri is claiming the title and inheritance. She must now go to court and listen to her most intimate secrets recounted by lawyers engaged to help her fight for her husband and Knole. She must reiterate her own illegitamacy, the subject from which she has always shrunk and she will be in the glare of world-wide publicity.

It is now legally necessary for Victoria to shut up the great house and lock the park gates until the ownership is finally determined. There is little doubt that it will be the scandal of the day.

'At sea let the British their neighbours defy —The French shall have frigates to traverse the sky.'
Philip Freneau: *The Progress of Balloons*, 1784

January 1st: Hundreds of happy pensioners throughout Kent invaded post offices today to draw their first weekly pension of five shillings. Many old people expressed delight that the pensions were paid by the state and were not like poor relief.

February 17th: A Royal Commission on Britain's poor laws has recommended that no more children should stay in workhouses; help will be given to the unemployed of "good character", boards of guardians will be scrapped and powers will pass to the county boroughs. The commission is united in its condemnation of the present system.

Northfleet United football club has won the Kent Senior Cup, the Kent League and the Thames and Medway Combination in what has been the most successful year in the club's history.

April 16th: King Edward has authorised Tunbridge Wells to style itself as a Royal Spa. It is a title held only by Leamington, a town which secured this status from Queen Victoria in 1838.

Concern about animals on their way to and from market has led to the introduction of a drinking fountain at Pembury supplied by the Drinking Fountain and Cattle Trough Association. Others already exist at Canterbury, Tunbridge Wells, Birchington and Sevenoaks.

April 29th: The most radical budget in the nation's history has been introduced by David Lloyd George, Chancellor of the Exchequer. Its purpose is to finance re-armament and the new old age pensions through higher taxation. One new, unpopular innovation is the introduction of death duties.

May 3rd: The Aeronautical Association in London has presented the Wright Brothers with a gold medal for achievement.

June 13th: Lieutenant Edward Shackleton arrived in Dover today from his Antarctic expedition. After a dramatic journey through storms and blizzards, Shackleton and his explorers came to a halt less than 110

1909

March 6th: *East Kent villages have been totally cut off following the third great blizzard of the winter. On this occasion it snowed without interruption for 36 hours and many motorists, unaware of the incompatibility of car and snow, found themselves stranded, particularly on Sandgate Hill. Picture shows a one-horse snow-plough at work in the Folkestone area.*

miles from the elusive South Pole. It is believed that Shackleton will receive a knighthood.

July: A 400-acre site at Eastchurch on the Isle of Sheppey has been purchased by the Royal Aero Club.

July 25th: Frenchman Louis Bleriot has landed in the grounds of Dover Castle after his epic flight across the Channel. He has won the *Daily Mail* prize of £1,000 for the first aviator to achieve this feat.

July: Farnborough Fire Brigade has resigned en bloc. The reason for the dispute concerns the responsibility for the lighting and care of the fire station lamp.

September 4th: The first Boy Scout parade has taken place at Crystal Palace. Hicks Own scout troop has been formed in Sevenoaks by a schoolteacher of that name.

September 7th: Lord Northcliffe, owner of *The Times*, has claimed that Germany is rapidly preparing for war with Britain.

October 15th: The Prince of Wales has opened the newly completed harbour at Dover.

October 26th: Rivers in East Kent have burst their banks after days of torrential rain. Many town centres are flooded.

November: Lord Brabazon has completed the first circular mile in an all-British plane on the Isle of Sheppey.

November 23rd: The Salvation Army is feeding as many as 640 vagrants every night. The unemployed down-and-outs congregate on the Embankment, knowing it offers their one chance of food and shelter.

November 30th: The House of Lords has thrown out the Chancellor's "People's Budget" after a controversy lasting seven months. There will now be a General Election in the New Year.

December 3rd: The King has dissolved Parliament. Taxes on beer, spirits, tobacco and cars have been lifted because the Budget has not been passed.

December 31st: Guglielmo Marconi of Italy has won a Nobel Prize for his contribution towards wireless experiment.

Harry Hanoel Marks, MP for Thanet since 1904 has retired from his post as proprietor of the *Financial News,* London's first daily financial paper which he had started in 1883. Mr Marks who will not stand at the next election lives at the magnificent Callis Court in Broadstairs.

Norwood Street Drill Hall Ashford has become an electric palace following parliamentary legislation of the cinematography act.

New church; St Luke's Gillingham.

GREAT HITS OF 1909

I wonder who's kissing her now?

Moonstruck

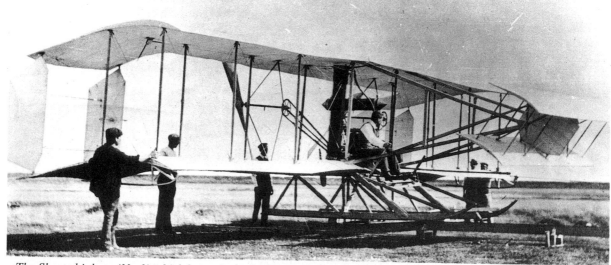

The Shorts biplane (No 1) which has a front elevator and wing-tip rudders and is fitted with an automobile engine as no British aero engine is yet available. Sadly, the engine is too heavy and the biplane has not been able to leave the ground. Another flight will be attempted in November.

Short Brothers open aerodrome on Sheppey

July: Three brothers, who set up a partnership as the world's first aircraft manufacturers in 1908, have now opened their new aerodrome on unobstructed marshland near Leysdown on the Isle of Sheppey. Horace, Eustace and Oswald Short, who are working closely with Orville and Wilbur Wright, Frank McClean, Charles Rolls and other air pioneers, have called their aerodrome Shellbeach. They are constructing Flyers to the Wright Brothers' design at their factory in Battersea but experiments are taking place at Shellbeach.

There have already been some attempts at powered flights. A 30hp Nordenfelt car engine was fixed to one Flyer and launched from a trolley on a slightly downhill rail. Unfortunately, the pilot Frank McClean failed to become airborne. Charles Rolls has achieved a few short hops but sustained some damage to his machine. He intends to make his next serious attempt in early November.

The three Short brothers have inherited their engineering ability from their father who served his apprenticeship with Robert Stevenson. The two younger boys Eustace and Oswald taught themselves to fly a second-hand coal-gas Spencer balloon and went on to carry passengers on joy rides from Battersea gasworks. Elder brother Horace, an engineering genius, collaborated by designing the pressurised aluminum spherical gondola for a proposed hydrogen balloon ascent into the stratosphere. Sadly, no sponsors could be found.

There were more ascents from Battersea in balloons built by the Short brothers but their greatest success to date was the construction of a 78,500 cubic feet Britannia balloon for Charles Rolls who then achieved a 26-hour flight from Paris to Norfolk in 1905.

The Wright brothers, who made their historic flight in their "Flyer" back in December 1903, heard of the achievements of the Short brothers and gave them British rights for the licence production of six new Flyers. Horace made a sketch of the Wrights' Flyer from which working drawings were then made.

Horace Short is working on an aircraft in which J.T.C Moore-Brabazon will attempt a circular mile later in the year. The *Daily Mail* has offered a £1,000 prize for the first entirely British designed-and-built aircraft to achieve this feat.

October : J.T.C.Moore-Brabazon flew nearly 500 yards in his own Voisin, which he called "Bird of Passage" from the Royal Aero Club at Leysdown — the first by a British pilot in Britain. The aircraft above is Shorts' triple-twin with two rotary engines.

March 5th: Two men were killed at Tonbridge today when a boat train from Charing Cross to Dover collided with the 8.30 am Charing Cross train arriving from Redhill, on the main-line curve just outside the station. Eye witesses said the driver of the Redhill train missed the warning signal, crossed in front of the boat train and its tender was hit by the engine. Henry Howard, fireman, and R.L.Rowley, loco inspector, who were both on the Redhill train, were killed. A major disaster was averted by a ticket inspector, Mr Agnew waving a warning to an approaching express from Margate. The train came to a halt just 150 yards from the wreckage.The incident occurred 40 minutes before the Royal Train was due to pass through Tonbridge.

Sevenoaks family may return Cromwell's head

March: The embalmed head of Oliver Cromwell which has been in the possession of the Wilkinson family of Seal Chart, near Sevenoaks for many years, is now likely to be restored to its proper resting place in Westminster Abbey. Mr Horace Wilkinson who died last December has made this clear under his recently-published will.

History has it that the head, after being exposed on the top of Westminster Hall for several years, was blown down one windy night and secreted by a sentry who kept it until he died. Ultimately, at about the time of the French Revolution, it passed into the hands of Mr Wilkinson, a medical man of the day — and remained in his family.

The circumstantial evidence as to identity is strong and curious. Flaxman, the great sculptor, who went as a sceptic to view the skull, came away convinced because of the way it responded to certain crucial tests. If it be not Cromwell's head, then it is the only head in history known to have been embalmed and afterwards beheaded!

The author Frederick Harrison believes the Home Secretary should ask a small commission to investigate the possibility of returning the head to Westminster Abbey. "It is really cruel to think that the grandest head that ever sat on English shoulders is lying loose in the house of a private owner. The head, be it remembered, is that which Parliament so foully disinterred, cut off and set up in mockery at the gateway of Parliament."

April 16th: Tunbridge Wells, the bustling, beautifully sited spa town on the borders of Kent and Sussex, has proudly acquired a prefix to its name. It is now Royal Tunbridge Wells. The final decision was made by the King this week who wrote: "I am graciously pleased to accede to the application of the burgesses of Tunbridge Wells by resolution of the Town Council that the borough be authorised to style itself a Royal Spa". Among other towns in England, only Leamington Spa has such a proud prefix which was secured from Queen Victoria in 1838.
No great celebration has been planned in honour of the occasion. Life will continue in this fashionable town at the same elegant pace — a pace clearly shown in this modern photograph of the Pantiles, the town's famous terraced walkway with shops behind a colonnade and a row of lime trees.
Kings and Queens of England, including Queen Henrietta Maria, Queen Anne, King Charles II and Queen Victoria have paraded at the Pantiles, admired the terraces and villas and taken the spa waters. Royal Tunbridge Wells deserves its new-found status.

Electric palaces in Kent for moving picture shows

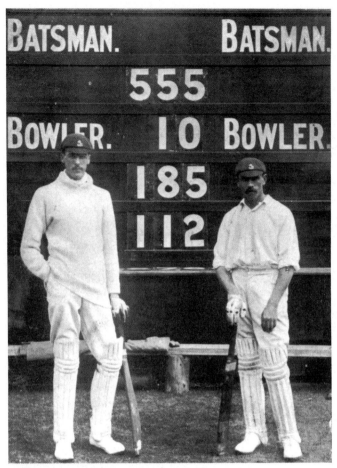

July: Kent cricketers, Frank Woolley and Arthur Fielder have created a record that may never be beaten. In the match against Worcestershire at Stourbridge, Fielder, batting number 11, scored an unbeaten 112 and helped his young colleague to add 235 runs in 150 minutes for the last wicket.
Woolley who scored 185 also made his first appearance for England during the summer earning an accolade from Wisden as a "colt to be watched".

October: Thirsty for entertainment, the public in several Kent towns is welcoming the decision by local businessmen to establish permanent picture palaces. Halls, theatres, redundant churches right across the county are being converted. In Dartford, the Conservative Club in Spital Street has already shown Poole's Myorama, Ramsgate's Excelsior Picturedrome has been open for several months and in November Ashford plans twice-weekly film shows in the Norwood Street Drill Hall.

A far more ambitious project is nearing completion in Dover where, it is hoped, a 500-seat picture house will open in the former Congregational Chapel in Queen Street in time for a Christmas showing. Electric Pictures (Dover) will retain the side galleries plus the main gallery facing the pulpit. There will be a foyer with a separate paybox for a "circle" upstairs. Entry will be by token and each patron will be given a programme.

There is great excitement over the availability of moving picture shows. The first 'cinematograph' flickered into life in Folkestone, Dover and Ramsgate some years ago but the modern "flickers" — the consequence of almost simultaneous inventions by Thomas Edison in America and the brothers Louis and Auguste Lumiere in France — are far more sophisticated.

Next year picture palaces are planned to open all over Kent including the Oxford Animated Picture Hall at Whitstable, the Marina Picture Hall in Deal, the public hall in Gravesend and the Empire Electric Theatre in Maidstone.

Floppy hats and brooksticks for Bill Hicks' Scouts

April 10th: Two years after Sir Robert Baden-Powell's experimental camp on Brownsea Island and the great success of the journal *Scouting for Boys*, scout patrols and troops have been springing up in profusion all over the country. One of the first to be formed in Kent is at Sevenoaks and this week the scoutmaster William Goss Hicks took his boys to camp at Fawke Common on the edge of Knole Park where he taught outdoor skills such as woodcraft, fire-making and tracking.

Bill Hicks and his pupils obviously enjoy each other's company because it is not only at weekends they are together. Bill is a master at Lady Boswell's School, Sevenoaks and the boys seem to be delighted with this outdoor extension of hours.

Bill Hicks was himself a pupil, then pupil-teacher at Lady Boswell's and his father was, for many years butler to the Sackville family at Knole. Today he lives behind the Manor House in the Upper High Street.

Until a more official uniform is available, the boys will wear knee breeches and socks and heavy boots. They must carry a brookstick and a floppy hat and remember they are pioneers — the 1st Sevenoaks Scout Troop, the forerunner to many which may be formed in the district.

Bleriot flies into history

July 25th: Aviation's latest hero, Frenchman Louis Bleriot landed in the grounds of Dover Castle today just 43 minutes after taking off from Sangatte, near Calais. He has become the first man to fly across the Channel and wins the £1,000 prize offered by the *Daily Mail.*

It is a wonderful amd historic feat. Bleriot had to wait at Calais for several days until the weather conditions improved but this morning, despite a brisk wind, he took off at 5am. His monoplane, which was driven by a three cylinder engine attached to a two-bladed propeller soared into the sky over the sea and headed for the English coast.

The French Government laid on a destroyer in mid-Channel with instructions to rescue Bleriot should his machine crash in the sea but he quickly left the ship behind, disappeared immediately into a cloud, almost came down off Deal and then felt a severe buffeting from the wind as he approached the White Cliffs. Here, a colleague was waving a French tricolour flag. Bleriot spotted it and was guided down to a suitable landing spot. His 43-minute flight covered 31 miles at an average speed of 41 mph.

The flight across the English Channel has been the goal this year for all the top aviators but Bleriot, who carried neither compass or watch, beat them all.

These are the words of M Bleriot, in his own description of the historic flight
"At 4.30 we could see all around. Daylight had come. 4.35. All is ready. Le Blanc gives the signal, and in an instant I am in the air, my engine making 12,000 revolutions — almost its highest speed — in order that I may get quickly over the telegraph wires along the edge of the cliff. As soon as I am over the cliff I reduce my speed, There is now no need to force my engine.

"I begin my flight, steady and sure, towards the coast of England. I have no apprehensions, no sensations, *pas du tout*. The *Escopette* has seen me. She is driving ahead at full speed. She makes perhaps 40 kilometres (about 26 mph). What matters? I am making at least 68 kilometres (42 miles). Rapidly I overtake her, travelling at a height of 80 metres (about 250 feet). The moment is supreme, yet I surprise myself by feeling no exaltation. Below me is the sea, the surface disturbed by the wind, which is now freshening. The motion of the waves beneath me is not pleasant.

"I drive on, 10 minutes have gone. I have passed the destroyer and I turn my head to see whether I am proceeding in the right direction. I am amazed. There is nothing to be seen, neither the torpedo-destroyer, nor France, nor England. I am alone. I can see nothing at all. For 10 minutes I am lost. It is a strange position to be alone, unguided without a compass in the air over the middle of the Channel.

"I touch nothing. My hands and feet rest lightly on the levers. I let the aeroplane take its own course. I care not whither it goes. For 10 minutes I continue, neither rising, nor falling nor turning. And then 20 minutes after I have left the French coast, I see the white cliffs of Dover, the Castle, and away to the west the spot where I had intended to land.

"What can I do? It is evident that the wind has taken me off my course. I am almost at St Margaret's Bay and going in the direction of the Goodwin Sands.

"Now it is time to attend to the steering. I press the lever with my foot and turn easily towards the coast, reversing the direction in which I am travelling. Now indeed I am in difficulties; for the wind here by the cliffs is much stronger and my speed is reduced as I fight against it. Yet my beautiful aeroplane responds. Still steadily I fly westwards, hoping to cross the harbour and reach the Shakespeare Cliff. Again the wind blows. I see an opening on the cliff. Although I am confident that I can continue for an hour and a half, that I might indeed return to Calais, I cannot resist the opportunity to make a landing on this green spot.

"Once more I turn the aeroplane, and describing a half circle, I enter the opening and find myself again over dry land. Avoiding the red buildings on my right, I attempt a landing; but the wind catches me and whirls me round two or three times. At once I stop my motor, and instantly my machine falls straight upon the land from a height of 20 metres. In two or three seconds I am safe upon the shore." — Louis Bleriot.

1. BLERIOTS ARRIVAL AT DOVER 25/7/09.

25.7.09
Photo Wharwell
Dover

July 25th: *Aviation history is made as Frenchman, Louis Bleriot lands at Dover to be greeted by a large number of admirers who quickly gather round his monoplane.*

A horse and cart in the floods between Black Bull Road and Bradstone Avenue, Folkestone

The wild waters of east Kent

October 26th: In three extraordinary days, 5.99 inches of rain has fallen on east Kent turning streams and even harmless little brooks into wild, destructive, fast-flowing rivers. Among those to show their ancient powers is the Pent at Folkestone. So dramatically did the water level rise this morning that residents have had to abandon their homes and even link arms toavoid being swept away in the raging floods.

In Canterbury there has been great excitement. The whole of the district between the town and Fordwich has the appearance of an inroad of the sea and the Stour valley one expanse of water. In St Peter's Lane the flood water has been surging in the front doors of many homes sending residents upstairs and rowing boats have been used in the town centre..

Canterbury under water in October.

'No man can be ignorant that he must die, nor be sure that he may not this very day' —
Cicero: *De Senectute*, c.78 BC

January 21st: Miners in Northumberland and Durham, angry about proposed eight-hour shifts and round-the-clock working, have gone on strike and, in many collieries, there is rioting.

January 31st: The wife of an American, Dr Hawley Harvey Crippen has vanished from their home in Camden Town.

February 1st: 80 labour exchanges open in England and are immediately inundated with job hunters.

February 2nd: The National Horse Supply Association says Britain will be seriously short of horses should war break out. Germany and Austria spend £200,000 annually on horse breeding, Britain less than £5,000.

February 14th: The last general election result is in and there has been a deadheat between the major parties. The score card reads: Tories 273 seats, Liberals 273, Nationalists 82 and Labour 42. Mr Asquith and his Liberal Government stay in power, certain of support from Labour.

February 16th: A suit of legitimacy filed by Henri E.J.B. Sackville-West has been dismissed in the High Court of Justice. Today Lord and Lady Sackville will make their triumphant return to Sevenoaks and to Knole.

March 8th: The Royal Commission on Divorce has stated that separation orders are now running at 2,000 a year. There are a large number of couples living immorally and there is an illegitimate birth rate of about 36,900 a year.

March 10th: A film made in Hollywood, a suburb of Los Angeles, goes on release today. It is called *In Old California*. Hollywood may prove to be a popular site for film companies moving into Los Angeles.

May 6th: King Edward VII has died of pneumonia after a short illness. Prince George, Prince of Wales is due to take his oath as King.

July 16th: A red letter day for Whitstable. The conversion of the parish hall to a picture palace is completed in time for the public to see the film of the funeral of Edward VII.
The Oxford Animated Picture Hall, as it is now known, has many special features including free matinees for children and a special curtain that can be drawn around adults — to reduce draughts, not for privacy. Other picture houses which have opened recently include the Marina Picture Hall at Deal, the electric cinema in Station Hall, Maidstone and the Cinema de Luxe in a converted shop in Chatham.

In his aviation works on the corner of Hilda Vale Road and Sevenoaks Road, Farnborough, Mr C.H. Anderson has constructed a Candeler-Stella monoplane, which he calls The Monotail. It has aerofoil wings of 26 ft by 6ft, a tail of 12 feet and in appearance is similar to the type that Bleriot used in his historic flight.

May 26th: A French submarine, *Pluvoise* has collided with a steam ship in the English Channel. 27 have been killed.

May 31st: Sir Robert Baden-Powell and his sister Agnes are now forming a youth movement for girls. It will run along the lines of the Boy Scout movement and teach living to be obedient, clean living and resourceful. It will be called the Girl Guides.

An Anglo Saxon cemetery has been excavated in the grounds of Valletta House, Broadstairs. The skeletons of four men and three women were found all furnished with grave goods including iron buckles and knives, spearheads and pottery bottles. Scraps of Iron Age pottery were also found suggesting an early Iron Age settlement had existed.

Lord Cornwallis has been appointed chairman of the Kent County Council for the third time.

July 12th: The Hon Charles Stewart Rolls, the famous British aviator, died when his aircraft crashed today during a flying competition at Bournemouth.

July 31st: Dr Hawley Harvey Crippen, wanted for murder, was arrested today aboard ship. He is the first criminal suspect to be caught by radio. If he is found guilty he will almost certainly be hanged.

August 13th: Florence Nightingale, the founder of nursing, has died aged 91. A memorial service will be held at St Paul's Cathedral.

August 27th: The American inventor Thomas Edison has pioneered "talking pictures". His process involves the use of a device which is part camera and part phonograph, enabling picture and sound to be recorded simultaneously.

November 18th: The Prime Minister, Herbert Asquith announced today that the King will dissolve Parliament and there will be another general election. The constitutional crisis has arisen over the House of Lords' veto of the 1909 budget. Women, of course, will not be allowed to vote.

November 19th: Suffragettes have again stormed the House of Commons and 119 women have been arrested. Winston Churchill orders charges against them to be dropped.

December 17th: A 14-year-old boy has been burnt to death in a fire at Messrs Dennis Paine and Company's draper's shop in High Street, Maidstone. The shop is completely destroyed.

December 20th: The general election has produced another remarkable tie — 272 seats each for Liberals and Tories. Mr Asquith continues as Prime Minister with the backing of 42 Labour MPs and 84 Irish Nationalists.

December 22nd: In one of Britain's worst mining disasters, 350 are feared dead following an explosion underground at Hulton Colliery, Lancashire. It is believed that 1,000 childern are orphaned and one mother has lost her husband and four sons.

GREAT HITS OF 1910.

Ah! Sweet mystery of life.

Chinatown, my Chinatown.

The skeletons of two male persons in chains have been found about 70 feet to the west of the Gravesend viaduct which was built in 1886 by the London Chatham and Dover Rail. About 100 years ago a gibbet stood in this area and many Gravesend malefactors were hung. The two recent chained skeletons were discovered at the west end of Rope Walk. It is proposed to give the iron manacles to the local museum.

HON. C.S.ROLLS'S

CONQUEST OF THE CHANNEL, 2ND June, 1910.

RETURN JOURNEY DONE WITHOUT LANDING.

Start from Dover	6.30 p.m.
Over Sangatte, France	7.15 p.m.
Return to Dover	8.0 p.m.

June 2nd: More aviation history was made today when the Hon Charles Stewart Rolls flew over the English Channel — and back again. His aircraft was a Short-built Wright biplane. He left the grounds of a school in Dover and landed briefly in Sangatte where he gave greetings to the Aero Club de France from the Aero Club of England. The return flight, 80 miles in total, took 90 minutes and Rolls circled Dover Castle before landing in a field.

Pioneer aviator and motorist dies in crash

July 12th: Pioneer aviator, the Hon Charles Stewart Rolls, was killed today when his French-built Wright biplane crashed during a flying competition at Bournemouth. Mr Rolls, the son of Lord and Lady Llangattock, was well known on the Isle of Sheppey where many of his early flying experiments were carried out.

His death at the age of 33 is a great tragedy, for Mr Rolls was one of the country's most distinguished aviators. Only a month ago, in June, he became the first person to fly both ways across the Channel without stopping. He was also a renowned pioneer motorist winning the 1,000 miles trial in 1900 and was a partner in the Rolls Royce manufacturing company which bears his name.

Mr Rolls flew regularly from Leysdown where the Royal Aero Club had established its headquarters in a house nearby known as Muswell Manor. He was the second pilot in history to receive an RAC certificate — the first going to Moore Brabazon — and he helped Frank McClean open a new aerodrome on the Isle of Sheppey at Eastchurch.

Eye witnesses who watched Mr Rolls' fatal plunge into the ground said the rudders appeared to break as he tilted the aircraft. "There was a crack, a wooden strut fell, the tail bent upward, and the whole machine came forward with a heart-rending crash."

The death of Charles Rolls is a particular blow for the Short brothers who have just moved their factory to the new location at Eastchurch and are now producing experimental pusher biplanes of the French Farman type. Other pioneer aviators, Lieutenants Samson, Longmore, Gregory and Gerrard have arrived at the site and a Mr C.R.Fairey has joined the company as works manager.

Controversial mayor takes Canterbury seat

December 20th: The general election — the second this year — has produced a remarkable tie. The Liberals and Tories have won 272 seats each and the great constitutional crisis over the Budget, which the House of Lords refused to accept, seems set to continue.

Just as remarkable is the result in Canterbury. The controversial (some say devious) mayor Francis Bennett-Goldney, who has been accused of falsifying city documents, among other alleged crimes, has taken the city as an Independent Unionist from the sitting Conservative member and then been immediately expelled from the local Conservative club.

Mr Bennett-Goldney will take his seat in the House of Commons as the Peers versus People battle is fought with increased venom. Mr Asquith continues as Prime Minister with the reluctant backing of 42 Labour MPs and 84 Irish Nationalists. The election earlier this year also produced a tie between the major parties.

Crippen is led down the gangway from SS Montrose accused of the murder of his wife.

North Forelands radio captures Dr Crippen at sea

July 31st: A message from the captain of the *SS Montrose* to the North Foreland Radio Station has led to the arrest of Dr Hawley Harvey Crippen, wanted for the murder of his wife. Dr Crippen is the first criminal suspect to be caught by radio and the staff of North Forelands are delighted by the success of the operation.

The station, established by the Post Office for communication with ships at sea, received the message from captain Henry Kendall who said he was suspicious of a passenger and his young colleague, travelling under the names of Mr Robinson and son. Having seen the two men "holding hands" he wondered if they could possibly be Crippen and his 27-year-old mistress Ethel Le Neve who had disappeared on July 9th.

Chief Inspector Walter Dew of Scotland Yard who has been investigating the murder ever since the mutilated and dismembered body of Mrs Crippen was found beneath the cellar floor in a house in Camden Town, caught a faster boat, overtook the *SS Montrose* off Canada, boarded the ship, forced a confession from the couple and then arrested "Mr Robinson and Son".

Right: Ethel Le Neve disguised as a boy

February 16th: Crowds surge around the gates of Knole Park as Lionel, Victoria and Vita return home in triumph. On their way they passed under a the triumphal arch erected over London Road, Sevenoaks.

Lord and Lady Sackville return to Knole in triumph

February 16th: Lionel and Victoria Sackville-West have won their battle in the High Court. The title, the inheritance and the great house of Knole is theirs. Henri, Victoria's brother, has lost his legitimacy claim.

The outcome of this strange case, which lasted six days and was covered by every daily newspaper in Britain and America, has been received with great delight by the people of Sevenoaks.

Today the couple made their triumphant return to Knole accompanied by their 17-year-old daughter Vita. From London they travelled by car to the foot of Tub's Hill where a pair-horse victoria awaited them. In this, the delighted couple travelled to the top of the hill to a triumphal arch erected over London Road at the end of Lime Tree Walk. At the arch the horses were taken out of the shafts, men of the fire brigade and many helpers drew the traces and, escorted by cheering inhabitants, took the carriage through the town, past the church, down the drive, through the lodge gates and up the hill.

Lord and Lady Sackville had come home to Knole.

Kent mourns the death of Edward VII

May 20th: Kent today mourned the death of the great peacemaker. King Edward VII was buried in the family vault in St George's Chapel, Windsor Castle. He died from pneumonia on May 6th after returning from what was intended to be partly a convalescent holiday in Biarritz. He continued to work despite breathing difficulties and then became very ill.

The sovereign was personally well known by many people in Kent. He had been a frequent visitor to Eastwell House, Ashford and had attended garden parties at Knole, Hever and Cobham. He regularly travelled from Dover to the Continent and just a few months ago he left from Port Victoria, Isle of Grain, with the Queen in the royal yacht in order to visit the Czar. He met the sailors at Sheerness, inspected the Royal Engineers at Maidstone, unveiled a memorial arch at Chatham and opened the naval hospital at New Brompton.

The funeral procession in London was watched by crowds of up to 500,000. The King's coffin was placed on a gun carriage and pulled by members of the Blue-jackets from Westminster Hall to Paddington and on to Windsor.

Among the kings and queens, dukes and duchesses, princes and princesses from across Europe was Edward VII's nephew, the German Emperor, Kaiser Wilhelm II who escorted Queen Mary, wife of the new King, George V. In respect, Chatham dockyard closed for the day without loss of pay for the workers.

May 23rd: Today the Kaiser travelled by special train to Port Victoria for his journey back to Germany. He was greeted by a royal salute of 100 men.

Hundreds turn out in Dartford to see the memorial procession.

Ethel Smythe, born and raised in Sidcup and one of our most celebrated composers, has put aside her latest operatic composition to concentrate on an anthem in support of the suffragette movement. *March of the Women* will be "at once a hymn and a call to battle". Miss Smythe was born in 1858 at the height of the Victorian era and has had to battle constantly against male prejudice to pursue her vocation. Her first opera was *Fantasia,* followed by *Der Wald* which was a tremendous success at Covent Garden in 1902. Many consider *The Wreckers* to be her best work to date. That was performed at the Queen's Hall two years ago and conducted by Sir Thomas Beecham.

1910

Pride of Prussia dies on the rocks in St Margaret's Bay

November 7th: The five-masted German sailing ship, *Preussen,* known throughout the world as the Pride of Prussia, lies wrecked on the rocks of St Margaret's Bay, near Dover. The sailors have been rescued but only after tremendous bravery by Dover lifeboatmen and the crew of 12 tugs who came to the rescue. The ship was on her way back from South America, with a cargo which included 100 grand pianos, when she was rammed by the Newhaven-to-Dieppe steamer, *Brighton,* which had attempted to cross her bows. Tugs tried to tow the *Preussen,* the largest ship of her kind in the world, through the eastern end of Dover harbour but she drifted away, smashed on the rocks and lay there all night with a broken back. Hundreds of spectators, drawn by the terrifying noise of the great iron ship being battered by mountainous seas, saw lifeboats, tugs, coastguards with rocket firing apparatus and even a party of volunteers attempt to reach the stricken German sailors. It has been a night of high drama.

New airfield for Vickers at Joyce Green, Dartford.

August: The Crayford-based firm of Vickers and Son and Maxim, now simply known as Vickers Limited, is planning to buy land at Dartford Salt Marshes with a view to constructing a rudimentary airfield for the testing of prototype aeroplanes. The site comprises a number of small fields separated by drainage ditches, bounded on the west by the River Darent and on the east by Joyce Green Lane which leads to the embankment of the River Thames.

Vickers hope to test their single-winged monoplane on the airfield which is currently being built under licence at Vickers' Erith Works to a design by the French aviation pioneer Robert Esnault-Pelterie. The single wing is a radical idea that is proving unpopular with would-be buyers. The Admiralty have declined to place an order which is a blow to Vickers but they are not going to be put off and have high hopes of taking the Number One Monoplane, as it is called, on its maiden flight next year. The pilot will be Captain Herbert F. Wood.

Sir Hiram Maxim, whose "flying machine" flew 100 feet at the end of the last century, also continues to show an enthusiastic interest in the future of aviation. He has now moved from Baldwyns Park to Rycrofts, a house at Dulwich Common where he has designed his latest machine. Sadly, for Sir Hiram, the engine was wrecked during trials at Joyce Green.

November 6th: Flying experiments are also continuing at Eastchurch. Here Aero Club owner Frank McClean takes W.J.S.Lockyer for a ride on Shorts Number 3.

Moissant and Fileux, under the wreckage at Heaverham, near Kemsing, carrying out vital repairs watched by a large crowd.

Paris to London by air — in three weeks!

September 9th: A Frenchman and his mechanic have become the first airmen to fly between Paris and London. Their journey, dogged by ill-luck throughout, has taken just over three weeks but they have each won a silver cup from the *Daily Mail*.

The airman, Jon Moissant and his passenger Fileux bought a two-seater Bleriot monoplane in Paris and after a few practice flights decided they could emulate the great French pioneer by flying the Channel. They set off from Paris in early August and, after an overnight stop, eventually landed on the sand near Calais and refuelled.

Moissant and Fileux successfully crossed the water but made a heavy landing at Telegraph Farm, Tilmanstone. The vicar gave them a picnic lunch during which a large crowd of spectators gathered. People from as far away as Dover and Deal had walked out to see the intrepid flyers take off again. This time they came down with a bump in a turnip field at Sittingbourne.

They managed to become airborne again and headed for Crystal Palace where a huge money prize awaited them if they could get there within a certain time. Alas, ill-luck struck again. Moissant and Fileux came down in a brickworks at Upchurch after magneto failure and, in a heavy landing, damaged a propeller. The Short brothers who had just opened their factory at Eastchurch came to the rescue and ordered a new one. Some days later it was delivered.

The intrepid flyers took off again but the strength of the wind, the flimsy condition of their machine and sheer bad luck did not mix easily and they made forced landings at Rainham, Chatham and Wrotham where they managed to buy petrol from a local garage. By now the *Daily Mirror* was reporting their adventures daily.

Their worst landing was at Heaverham, Kemsing where they ran into the side of a hill near the Beachy Lees Estate. The plane and the propeller were smashed again but Fileux said he could cope. He bought whipping and glue and repaired the airframe. Another propeller was obtained by the *Mirror* from Bleriot himself in Paris. It was delivered to Moissant and Fileux who stayed at St Clere for a few days while Mr Akehurst, of the Rose and Crown, provided a carriage and pair for their use.

In setting off again they hit a tree and crashed once more. It was now September 6th and there was little chance they would win the prize money but they managed to become airborne yet again. Great gusts of wind brought them down in the valley near Otford and the flyers waited for the wind to subside before taking off again, for Crystal Palace.

Sadly Moissant and Fileux could not find the special landing ground so they came down on a cricket pitch at Beckenham, obtained directions, took the monoplane to Crystal Palace and missed the deadline by just a few hours. Thousands of people were there to greet them.

Jezreel's tower is faced with yellow brick and can seat more people than St Paul's Cathedral.

Great tower remains as Jezreelites go bust

October 6th: The Jezreelites of Gillingham and "Prince Michael", their self-styled leader are in the news once more. This week the few eccentric members that remain of the New and Latter House of Israel have been ejected from their house in 555 Canterbury Street for arrears of rent — so continuing a saga which has fascinated the people of Gillingham for more than 30 years.

"Prince Michael's" real name is Michael Keyfor Mills. He sports a long white beard and moustache, long luxuriant hair over his shoulders and dresses in bright blue suits. He has great charm and is a fluent and persuasive speaker. Like his predecessor, James Rowland White, who founded the sect, he declares himself to be the Messenger of the Lord.

His followers — the Jezreelites — are regarded locally as harmless. They number about 150 but before the turn of the century more than 1,500 lived in the locality, in communes, and worked in the Jezreelite shops in Gillingham which were owned by the sect. They had a reputation for fair dealing and prospered to the point where they were able to go ahead with the building of a great tower — still partially standing at the top of Chatham Hill.

The tower, 144 feet long, broad and high was designed to house 12 printing presses, contain an assembly hall able to seat 5,000 with galleries, offices, reading rooms, staircases and lit by both gas and electricity. As the building work neared completion it dawned on the locals that it was going to be the biggest church in England, capable of holding more people than St Paul's Cathedral.

The buildings and the ambitious plans drained the work of the community coffers. Jezreelites lost their money and their faith and many went back to America. The numbers dwindled rapidly, work on the tower was suspended and the builders repossessed it.

Today, in 1910, the great unfinished tower stands as a notable landmark beside the A2 at Gillingham. Some Jezreelites have been living there and there was great controversy a few weeks ago when builders arrived to knock off some top bricks in order to put a roof on the building. The occupants refused to move and there was a scuffle.

What will become of the great building, no-one knows. There are rumours that it may be converted into a factory, or even a school. But the Jezreelites claim that it still belongs to them.

'With open mouth he drank the sun as though it had been wine' — Oscar Wilde, Ballad of Reading Gaol

1911

January 3rd: A house in Sidney Street off the Mile End Road in the East End of London was devastated by fire today. Three anarchists were trapped inside after a gun battle with more than 1,000 troops and armed police. The men had already killed three policemen.

February 1st: The first Dreadnought, *HMS Thunderer* has been launched in the Thames.

February 21st: James Ramsay MacDonald, the new Labour Party chairman in succession to Keir Hardy, has made his maiden speech at Westminster supporting a bill to curb the powers of the House of Lords.

March 22nd: With an initial capital of £4,000 a new company known as Maidstone and District Motor Services has been formed to operate omnibus services in mid Kent. The fleet consists of five Hallfords dating from 1908, with a 24-seat char-a-banc body and operates on a route from Maidstone to Gravesend. Two single deck Hallfords have been ordered to supplement the fleet.

May 12th: The King and Queen have opened the Festival of Empire at Crystal Palace in south London.

Edward Sharp, confectioner manufacturer of Maidstone who recently introduced a "kremy toffee" has found it so successful that the company will need a new factory covering half an acre and a workforce of nearly 300. Business has expanded so briskly that the *Kent Messenger* has carried an advertisement for 100 young female workers and Sharp has offered to pay railway fares from surrounding villages.

June 1st: The Canterbury Electric opens at St Peter's Street. It is hoped that a second cinema called Palais de Luxe will open at St George's Street later in the year.

June 10th: After demolishing a lamp post, pillar box and brick wall a runaway steam roller came to rest outside Houghtons the photographers at the corner of

April 2nd: *Herbert Kitchener, British Commander-in-Chief in the Boer War, arrived at Dover today having been summoned back from a long holiday in Africa with the instructions to command the troops at the forthcoming Coronation of King George V. Anxious to live in Kent, Kitchener is negotiating for the purchase of Broome Park near Canterbury from the Oxenden family for £14,000. The impressive 500-acre estate includes stable and outbuildings which are in need of repair. Kitchener plans to engage architects to design new terraces in the garden and raise the height of floors in the house.*

Belmont Road and High Street Broadstairs. No-one was hurt.

June 23rd: Tens of thousands of people lined the streets on the way to Westminster Abbey to catch a glimpse of King George V and Queen Mary on their way to the coronation ceremony. People in every Kent town and village celebrated this great occasion in festive style.

June 17th: Over 50,000 supporters of the enfranchisement of women formed a five-mile long procession as they marched through the streets of London. Among them were 700 women who had been imprisoned for the

cause, each displaying a silver arrow as a mark of their suffering.

June 30th: Farringtons Girls' School, Chislehurst has opened.

July 11th: The maiden flight of Vickers' No 1 Monoplane took place today under the skilled control of Captain Herbert Wood. He has now been appointed manager of Vickers Aviation.

August 7th: The Red Lantern Cinema has opened in Herne Bay High Street. For several weeks films have been showing at the Town Hall in the High Street.

August 8th: The country is grinding to a standstill as a nationwide strike by railwaymen, carters, stevedores and other trasnport workers begins to bite. In Liverpool two men have been shot dead as rioters came up against 50,000 armed troops.

August 9th: The temperature at Canterbury today reached 98F, the hottest reading ever registered in Britain. The record-breaking heatwave has sent Britain's death rate soaring and London has been named as the second most unhealthy city in the world.

September 6th: Thomas Burgess, a Yorkshireman, swam from Dover to Cap Griz Nez to become only the second man to swim the English Channel. It took him 22 hours and 30 minutes — an hour longer than Matthew Webb who set the record 36 years earlier. It was Burgess's 13th attempt to swim the Channel.

September 20th: Bromley Grammar School for Boys, originally known as the County School, has been opened by the mayor.

October 23rd: Winston Churchill has switched from the position of Home Secretary to become First Lord of the Admiralty.

November 13th: Andrew Bonar Law has succeeded Arthur James Balfour as leader of the Tory party.

December 18th: The Picture Palace, the first cinema in Ashford has been opened in Tufton Street. Ashford is one of the few towns in Kent with a cinema but without electricity.

More cinemas have opened in Kent including Shanly's electric theatre at Snargate Street, Dover and the Apollonian also at Snargate Street. In Sandwich the Empire Electric Theatre is up and running and films are being shown in the Queen's Hall, Deal.

GREAT HITS OF 1911

Alexander's Ragtime Band

Coronation celebrations are quite electric

June 23rd: George V was today crowned King of the United Kingdom of Great Britain and Ireland and of the British Dominions beyond the seas, Defender of the Faith and Emperor of India. The ceremony at Westminster Abbey lasted seven hours and, outside, crowds stood in their tens of thousands.

There is no need to go to London to celebrate. Towns throughout the county observed the occasion in great style with concerts and fireworks and sports for children, delighted to have the day off.

Rainham, well-known for its ability to unite the town on such occasions, began the day at 8 am with a 21-gun salute from the church tower. The vicar also sounded the Royal Salute on a bugle. Soon after noon all schoolchildren of seven years and upward assembled in Station Road and, together with the Friendly Society and the Fire Brigade, marched to the parish church for Divine Service. A sports afternoon followed in the meadow behind the National Schools and, in the evening, a torchlight procession led the way to Bredhurst Lane where a huge bonfire was lit.

The coronation celebrations in many towns provided one historic opportunity — to illuminate churches and public buildings by electricity for the first time. In Bromley this concession to a comparatively modern invention was resisted by considerable numbers but the organisers got their way and the parish church was a spectacle to behold.

Sevenoaks, not quite so advanced, also lit up the town centre by using large coloured cut-glass designs illuminated from the back by gas jets. It was an effective display but, one suspects, it will never be used again as the "age of electricity" is certain to catch up with this West Kent town.

Hero returns to the town he loved

January 3rd: James Wolfe, who was born in the vicarage during a thunderstorm, grew up in the town, received a commission when he was just 14 and went on to become the greatest general of his generation, has come home to the town he loved so much. Thousands of cheering inhabitants crammed into Westerham yesterday to see the statue of General James Wolfe unveiled on the green. Sword aloft, he looks towards the West and the scene of his last triumphant battle.

It was in the summer of 1759 that this local boy, then 32, took his warriors up the cliff to the Plains of Abraham outside Quebec to surprise the French and bring under our flag a piece of America, greater than the United States. In winning Canada for the grateful King, James Wolfe laid down his life.

In Quebec there is a Wolfe

Memorial and the soil that contains the flowers comes from the vicarage gardens in Westerham. There were Canadians at the unveiling ceremony and they were reminded that young James went to the local church of St Mary's and was baptised at the font. He trampled every yard of the town,

January 2nd: Scenes at Westerham during the unveiling of the Wolfe statue on the green.

usually with his great friend John Warde of Squerryes, in which splendid house James received his commission.

Ramsgate Harbour in 1911 — one of only three ports where the sailing trawler can be seen in numbers. Their tonnage is about 25-40 tons and length from 50 feet to 63 feet. The best weather for fishing is a stiff breeze.

Ramsgate trawlers lost in terrible gale

October 11th: More than a week has passed since three vessels of the Ramsgate fishing fleet failed to return to harbour after one of the most violent storms ever known. A town in mourning has finally accepted that the 10 brave smacksmen who crewed the trawlers *Progress, Idessa* and *Criterion* have become victims of the cruel sea.

The gale occurred during the night of Saturday September 30th and Sunday October 1st when the whole of the fleet was in the Channel. All night the wind blew with hurricane force, the seas heaved and mountainous waves kept an anxious community awake. The next morning, one by one, the battered smacks limped back into the harbour, many having undergone unnerving adventures which the crews never expected to survive. With the favourable winds which followed the gale the three missing boats were expected to follow.

Anxiety concerning the safety of the vessels grew daily. The familes waited in tortured suspense and to the repeated enquiries the reply was the same — 'no news yet'. The gloom is now complete and the fishing industry has accepted the inevitable.

Among those who have died is Richard Chandler, skipper of the *Progress* whose nephew and son were on board. His other son died at sea a year ago and he was mourning also the death of his wife. At home, 10 Percy Road, there is now only a daughter and her younger brother.

It is believed that the *Progress* was fishing off the Dutch coast and the *Idessa* and *Criterion* abreast of Lowestoft when the storm brewed up.

One trawler which managed to survive the tempest is appropriately named *The Gratitude*. She was in a deplorable condition with her sails torn away, a small boat lost and everything on deck swept clean away. There were four men on board including the cook and, in the wildest weather they had ever seen, they did everything they could to keep the vessel before the wind.

Provision will be made for the widows and children by the Royal Provident Fund for Sea Fishermen and the local Fisherman's Accident Fund. Under the former, a widow will receive the sum of 5s a week for four years and 1s a week in respect of each child under 14. The accident fund will make a funeral grant of £10 for each family.

Traffic on the Medway — the golden age may be over

The Tonbridge Navigation Company, which has controlled the movement of river traffic since the Medway became navigable in 1740, has been wound up. Faced with numerous setbacks, such as the decision to switch the lucrative hop and coal traffic to road and rail, the increase in zymotic diseases caused by river pollution and the damaging Chancery lawsuit with the rival Penshurst Canal Company, the TNC has decided that there can be no return to the golden age of commercial traffic. The Medway is in terminal decline.

The Upper Medway Conservancy Board will now assume public control. They propose to close the river to traffic for about four years while ten new locks are built and the flood control system improved. Then they will make strenuous efforts to revive commercial activity.

Older people still recall the boom years on the river. Stone for building and coal for the gasworks came inward while timber and iron from the Weald went downstream. In fact the Rose and Crown in the High Street and the Bull in Bordyke were refaced by imported stone but as trade grew so did river craft and the old medieval bridge across the High Street had to be rebuilt.

The decline in river traffic began when the railway arrived in 1842 and the navigation company made the error of trying to compete instead of co-operating.

Picture theatres are here to stay

April 22nd: More electric theatres are opening in Kent this year, including the National Electric at 205 High Street, Chatham which has seating for 639 people and showed its first film last week (April 15th). The *Chatham Rochester and Gillingham News* wrote: "Ever since cinematograph pictures have been placed before the public they have proved remarkably popular and theatres for this form of entertainment have sprung up with startling rapidity all over the country but particularly in this district where the demand is well-nigh insatiable. That they have evidently come to stay is fully borne out by the fact that during the past 12 months no less than eight picture theatres have been established in Chatham, Rochester, Strood and Gillingham and, what is more, audiences are steadily on the increase."

Frances Hodgson Burnett who was born in 1849 and lived in Rolvenden. A portrait taken in 1888

Frances' *Secret Garden* created in Rolvenden

A new book published by the American author, Frances Hodgson Burnett has delighted the inhabitants of Rolvenden, near Tenterden — for the plot in the novel was conceived during the years she lived in the village. It is called *The Secret Garden* and tells the story of a spoilt child transformed by her discovery of a long closed-up garden which she begins secretly to cultivate. The book is a classic and well up to the standard of her previous novel, *Little Lord Fauntleroy.*

Frances Hodgson Burnett lived at Great Maytham Hall, Rolvenden between 1898 and 1907. It was then just a small house and only converted into a mansion in 1909. Burnett, herself an enthusiastic gardener, was greatly attracted to the beautiful old walled garden at Great Maytham Hall and wrote to her son in America: "It was entered by a low, arched gateway in the wall, closed by a wooden door. The ground underneath the twisted, leaning old apple trees was cleared of all its weeds and thorns and sown with grass and then, at every available place, roses were planted to climb up the ancient trunks and over the walls."

This was *The Secret Garden*, planned at Rolvenden and written at Plandome. Long Island, New York.

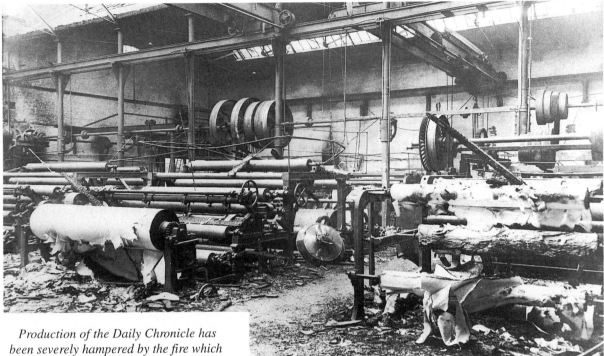

Production of the Daily Chronicle has been severely hampered by the fire which destroyed Lloyds Paper Mill at Sittingbourne. Machinery, manufactured rolls of newsprint and other equipment have been devastated and the owner Edward Lloyd might be regretting his move from Bow several years ago — for this is the third big blaze at the mill. The Sittingbourne Fire Brigade, led by the enthusiastic Hedley Peters, was quickly on the scene and made some progress in controlling the fire, although the extent of damage can be seen in the photograph. For his efforts, however, Captain Peters has been presented with a silver cigarette case by the grateful management of Lloyds.

Daily Chronicle Paper Mills.   Sittingbourne.

August 9th, 1911 — the hottest day ever known

The great heatwave shows no sign of letting up. Day after day the sun continues to bear down from a cloudless sky onto a parched earth. Through May, June, July and now August, Kent has been wilting in the torrid conditions of the hottest summer ever known. Food is being thrown away. People are walking only on the shady side of the street. Cattle are dying for lack of water. Massive fires are breaking out all over the county, and yesterday, in Canterbury, the temperature reached an unprecedented 98F.

It is hard to believe that snow in April led to terrible losses of lambs, fruit and potatoes right across the county and deep drifts impeded all forms of transport. It is almost inconceivable that the Staplehurst mail cart took nearly six hours to travel to Maidstone and huge icicles festooned buildings in Rochester.

Now the fields are parched, the cattle are being fed hay, the crops are burning, fruit is shrivelling and people, in their thousands, are rushing to the coast. Thanet is having another record season and it is estimated that there were more than 4,000 on the beach at Margate during the Bank Holiday weekend. Even more, it seemed, walked the pier at Ramsgate to take advantage of the slightest breeze.

The fire at Lloyds paper mill is one of many. The gallant firemen are working overtime and there have been many stories of heroic rescues from burning buildings.

An exciting event for the inhabitants of Bexleyheath was the recent opening of the Coronation Clock Tower at the end of the High Street. This new town is growing rapidly. It has already swallowed the village of Bexley and an unbroken line of buildings is now encroaching on the Erith marshes .

Come to Margate and practically live for ever!

August 7th: The mayor of Margate, Alderman W.B. Reeve, in accordance with the wish of the Town Council has formally opened the new Margate Pavilion and Winter Gardens which has been constructed on the site of Fort Green. He therefore consummates what has for years been recognised as a necessity in the welfare of the town, a public hall in which visitors could be entertained when the weather was unfavourable for outdoor concerts.

The Corporation have wasted no time in building this magnificent amenity. The plans were approved last year, the first sod cut in December and the foundation stone laid on March 15th. The chalk was excavated from the green without any mechanical aid other than picks and shovels and only local labour was used in the entire operation. Sadly a workman was killed in a fall but the pace did not slacken, for the entire pavilion was erected by July.

The opening on Thursday was a grand affair. All the members of the Corporation were assembled by midday. Then, headed by mounted police, they drove in procession to the main entrance and the formal speeches. A lavish luncheon was held in the Louis XVI ballroom when the mayor in his address spoke about the healthiest resort in England: "While not a matter to be discussed at lunch I am proud to say that the death rate is the lowest for 32 years. So you only have to come to Margate to practically live for ever!"

When work began on the building of the Winter Gardens on the site of Fort Green, the bandstand had to be removed to make way for the complex.

Internally the Pavilion and Winter Gardens have been decorated in a Neo-Grecian style. They consist of a large concert hall, four entrance halls, two side wings and an amphitheatre. Potted palms are in abundance and the buildings can accommodate 2,500 inside and 2,000 in the open-air amphitheatre and upper balconies on the colonnades. The cost of building is in the region of £26,000.

Four naval officers learn how to fly

December: Aviation history was made today when a young naval officer, Lieutenant Charles Samson successfully took off in a Short's biplane from the deck of the great battleship, *HMS Africa* at anchor in Chatham. It is the first flight ever undertaken from the deck of a ship and it represents further progress in man's age-old desire to master the air.

Earlier this year Mr Francis McClean of the Aero Club at Eastchurch generously offered the Admiralty free flying instruction for the officers billeted nearby. The Admiralty asked for volunteers to step forward, re-

Lt Samson RN takes off from the deck of HMS Africa.

ceived more than 200 and chose just four. Each of them had to be unmarried, become members of the Aero Club at their own expense and promise not to fly on Sundays.

Lieutenants Samson, Gerrard, Gregory and Longmore were the four naval pioneers. They were given six months leave of absence on full pay and nervously reported to flying instructor, George Cockburn at Eastchurch on March 1st, uncertain whether they would enjoy the sensation of flying and the dangers it posed to the inexperienced.

Horace Short was at Eastchurch to assure them that instructional flying would only be undertaken in light winds. Each officer was given a pusher biplane and told to crouch behind the pilot and learn how to control the aircraft before launching off on his own. There were two minor mishaps but the men gained their aviators' certificates and proudly invited their brother officers to join them at every opportunity.

By the summer — which brought clear blue skies throughout — the naval officers were taking part in short cross-country flights, disappointed that the six-month agreement with the Admiralty was soon to expire. On August 31st the four men returned to normal duties and then tried, unsuccessfully at first, to persuade the Admiralty to set up its own school of flying.

Maintaining that the navy's reponsibilities were on the high seas and not in the sky the Admiralty eventually

agreed, almost certainly encouraged by the new First Lord, the Liberal MP Winston Churchill.

Now there is a small naval flying school at Eastchurch with two Short biplanes which have been purchased from McClean. Lieutenants Samson and Longmore are in charge of the trials and new officers are being eagerly recruited for flying courses.

The Admiralty is delighted and there is even talk of a Royal Flying Corps being established as a Fleet Air Arm. The future is exciting.

Cooking by electricity at Broomhill

November: The scientist Sir David Lionel Salomons who organised the first motor show — at Tunbridge Wells in 1895 — has achieved another first. Family meals are now being cooked by mains electricity and his home at Broomhill, Southborough has become the first in England to enjoy such an unbelievable luxury.

Sir David is an outstanding engineer and electrician. As early as 1874 there was an arc light in his workshop and by 1882 he had installed 60 lamps of 50 volts from accumulators. Well before the turn of the century a dynamo was providing Broomhill with electricity for one thousand 16 candlepower lights. Now comes electricity for cooking and other domestic work.

July 3rd: Renaux's Farman biplane which was taking part in a European air race organised jointly by the Standard newspaper and the Paris Journal, has been forced to make an emergency landing on Romney Marsh due to a fault in the carburettor. The incident attracted many excited followers who rushed to the site as the machine made a bumpy landing. The Kentish Express described the 11 planes taking off "like a flight of swallows". They flew across the Channel and their course was mapped out by a series of white arrows on the ground. Photograph shows the Renaux near Appledore.

December: Another emergency landing and another crowd of interested spectators. The excitement on this occasion was at Five Oak Green, near Tonbridge.

'The ship was tilting gradually on her nose and the band were still playing. I guess all of them went down' — Henry Bride, wireless operator, who swam for his life as the Titanic sank.

January 1st: The Post Office takes over the National Telephone Company.

January 17th: Captain Robert Scott and his party have reached the South Pole, only to discover that the Norwegians led by Captain Roald Amundsen have beaten them by a month.

February 7th: People in all parts of the English speaking world have today been honouring the centenary of the birth of Charles Dickens. Wreaths have been placed on his grave in Westminster Abbey and there have been numerous tributes in the newspapers. Dickens was born at Portsea in 1812 and he died at Gadshill Place, Rochester on June 9th, 1870.

March 28th: The University Boat Race has had to be re-run as both Cambridge and Oxford sank.

May 26th: A transport strike has brought the country to a standstill.

Lord Wakefield, founder of the country's greatest oil company, has built himself a mansion at Hythe.

June 25th: Prime Minister Asquith has been bitterly attacked in the House of Commons for "force-feeding" suffragettes in prison.

The twice-a-day steamer which leaves Queenborough Port with passengers and freight to Belgium, Holland and Dover will soon be transferred to Folkestone.

A clock tower has been erected in Bexleyheath to commemorate the coronation of George V and Queen Mary.

July 3rd: Captain Smith, captain of *The Titanic,* who died when the ship went down has been found guilty of negligence in a Board of Trade inquiry.

July 22nd: The Olympic Games have opened in Stockholm.

August 1st: An air mail service has begun between London and Paris.

September: George Thomas, proprietor of the internationally-

The pride of Margate, the Winter Gardens, is looking forward to a second wonderful summer season.

famous fruit nursery business at Maidstone has introduced a new dessert apple to the country — the Maidstone Favourite. His principal apple, however, is still the Allington Pippin, a late autumn dessert variety.

September: The giant floating dock, built by Swan Hunter of Wallsend on Tyneside and delivered in June has been officially tested in Saltpan Reach, Gillingham. It is 680 feet long and 144 feet between its towering sides

October 1st: From today the railway station, formerly known as New Brompton is to be called Gillingham.

October 26th: A tunnel under the Thames at Woolwich has been opened.

Tragedy has again struck the Hamilton family of Hythe. Following the death of his three brothers during the Boer War in South Africa, the remaining Hamilton brother, a member of the Worcester Regiment and one of the first members of the Royal

Flying Corps, has been killed in a flying accident.

November 1st: A Vickers machine gun has been introduced into the British army.

November 3rd: Thousands of local people flocked to the Esplanade at Rochester to see a memorial tablet unveiled to the memory of Percy Henry Gordon of Bermondsey by the Countess

of Darnley. Percy Gordon had lost his life rescuing a little girl from drowning in the Medway while visiting Rochester on Good Friday of this year.

November 5th: A "censor of films" has been appointed in Britain in order to ascertain what is or what is not suitable for children.

November 19th: There have been great celebrations as coal was raised from Snowdown colliery for the first time.

December 18th: A discovery has been made near Lewes, Sussex of human ancestor remains known as the Piltdown Man.

The Gaiety Theatre, Chatham has been demolished to make way for the Empire Theatre which has 2,500 seats.

NEW CINEMAS THIS YEAR
Royal Cinema de luxe in Beaver Road Ashford, Cinema Palace in Oaks Road, Tenterden, King Hall Cinema in New Barrack Road, Walmer, Grand Cinema, Herne Bay (spelt out in 292 lights), Palace Cinema, Tubs Hill, Sevenoaks, The Grand, Snodland, the Electric Palace at Borough Green.

GREAT HITS OF 1912

It's a long way to Tipperary

When I lost you (Irving Berlin)

Royal Flying Corps is born

April: A Royal Flying Corps has now been established as a joint army and navy enterprise and the Admiralty facilities at Eastchurch have been expanded. The Naval Flying School whose new commanding officer is Captain Godfrey Paine RNA, now has the use of six large sheds and three portable canvas hangars.

The enthusiastic Charles Samson is now in charge of the naval wing at Eastchurch and his officers include Lieutenants R.Gregory, A.M. Longmore and D. Wildman-Lushington who see themselves as the founders of a Fleet Air Arm.

The flying pioneers want a new name for the airfield at Eastchurch. The one most likely to be adopted is *HMS Pembroke II,* after the Chatham naval barracks which is called *HMS Pembroke.*

British Portland Cement Manufacturers have taken over the giant Wouldham Hall cement works complex. When William Peters of Wouldham Hall first opened his greystone lime works in 1857, it was just a small family business. It began to grow rapidly when his two sons took over in 1866 and by the end of the century it was among the largest cement manufacturers in the world. Today, the new owners (BPCM) inherit a workforce of around 1,000 men and a fleet of 80 barges. Our picture shows some of those barges transporting cement and coal to the works. Bottle kilns can also be seen, the tall chimneys becoming necessary when batchelor kilns were installed.

A Wellcome companion

January 17th: *The Dartford firm of Burroughs Wellcome, known throughout the world for its pioneering work into medical research and the development of pharmaceutical products, is delighted that Roald Amundsen of Norway and Robert Scott of England and their respective parties have both reached the South Pole and are in good health. Both explorers carried a medicine chest prepared by Burroughs Wellcome who are earning considerable fame for supplying the medical requirements to combat the climate and diseases likely to be encountered in various parts of the world. H.M. Stanley of Africa carried a Burroughs Wellcome chest, as did Shackleton and Bleriot.*

Bride found dead in bath

July 27th: An inquest has returned a verdict of death by misadventure on Beatrice Constance Annie Williams (née Mundy) and recently married who was found dead in a small zinc bath at her rented house at 80 High Street, Herne Bay. The jury was told that there were mysterious circumstances about her death but it was assumed that she may have had a fit. She had been found by her husband, Henry Williams, lying on her back under the water. Apparently devastated by the incident Mr Williams inherits her property and a small trust fund left to Bessie, as she was known, by her father.

Many Kent people go down with the Titanic

April 19th: In the worst-ever disaster at sea, more than 1,500 of the 2,340 passengers and crew of the *Titanic* drowned in the icy waters of the North Atlantic early on Monday morning (April 15th). It is believed that a dozen people from Kent are among those lost.

The great ship, proclaimed unsinkable because of its 16 watertight compartments, hit an iceberg and sank within hours. Survivors on the boats watched helplessly as the Titanic, pride of the White Star fleet, slid beneath the waves with all her lights still blazing. One of them said that the great ship tilted gradually on her nose, just like a duck that goes for a dive. Another said he heard the ship's band still playing as she went down.

The last moments of the pride of the White Star fleet

Reports circulated on Monday said that all the passengers had been rescued but later it became known that all the available boats had been filled with women and children (numbering about 708) and these were picked up by the *Carpathia.*

Many stories of bravery are reaching England. Colonel John Astor, cousin to Mr William Waldorf Astor of Hever and well known in the Tonbridge area, declined to join other millionaires in the first boat but instead helped his new bride and many other women and children into the other lifeboats. He remained on board to the end and has almost certainly drowned. It is believed that Mr Norman Craig, MP for Thanet is also among the victims.

Two people from Sittingbourne were on board. They are Miss Kate Buss daughter of Mr and Mrs Buss of Shortlands Road, who was on her way to California to be married, and Mr Richard Rouse, aged 53, a labourer of New Road. The worst is also feared for Bernard Boughton, aged 24, of Hardinge Road, Ashford. He was employed at Ospringe, Faversham before he adopted the vocation of seaman and was on the *Olympic* when it met with a disaster some months ago. Leaving her he was delighted to join the *Titanic* as a steward.

Also among the passengers was Mr Frank Goldsmith of Strood with his wife and nine year old son. They were accompanied by Mr Thomas Theobald of Bower Road, Strood. The men had worked for the engineering works of Aveling and Porter and Messrs Cobb and Son respectively and were on their way to seek new employment in the motor car factories in Detroit, Michigan.

Mr John Simmons from the village of Leigh, near Tonbridge was also on the *Titanic*. Formerly a cricket ball maker with Messrs Duke and Son of Penshurst, Mr Simmons was making his way to America with Mrs Helen Twomey from Tonbridge who had secured a new position with the Bishop of Indianapolis.

Among other Kent people feared drowned are Edward Colley of Hythe, a Gillingham lad named Beavan and Mrs L.V. Scape who until recently lived at *The Flying Dutchman* Inn at Hildenborough. Mrs Scape had been recently widowed at the age of 22 and had accepted a post on the *Titanic* to try and forget the tragedy that befell her husband Captain Scape in Hong Kong. She was the daughter of Mr and Mrs Ed Leppard of Cataract Cottage and the family is well known in Hildenborough.

The *Titanic*, on her maiden voyage, was speeding through the ice field hoping to win the Blue Riband for the fastest Atlantic crossing.

April 26th: Mr Norman Craig MP for Thanet has been favoured by a wonderful piece of luck. Having booked and paid for his passage on the *Titanic* for a holiday in New York, intuition suggested that he would be better advised to remain at home during the vital Home Rule debate in the House of Commons. He cancelled his passage hoping he could sail on the *Titanic* on another occasion. It is seen in Thanet as a providential escape and many people have congratulated the fortunate MP.

Another to escape is Miss Kate Buss of Sittingbourne who was put on a lifeboat.

The bitter irony of Sassoon's wireless bill

May: Two years ago the Unionist MP for Hythe, Sir Edward Sassoon, introduced a bill in the House of Commons urging that installation of wireless telegraphy should be compulsorily installed on all ocean-going steamers. The bill was given a First Reading, but to Sir Edward's chagrin, got no further. The bitter irony is obvious to all. The Titanic lies at the bottom of the ocean and the commission of inquiry into the disaster is recommending that all passenger ships should be installed with wireless telegraphy and a sufficient number of trained operators. There is also a plan for the establishment of a British-Atlantic Wireless Station and the man behind the scheme is Signor Guglielmo Marconi, the great wireless pioneer who lives in Essex. Sir Edward Sassoon died this year. It is expected that his son, Philip, will contest the seat for Hythe and Folkestone and take his father's place in the House.

Octavia Hill, the lady of green spaces, dies at 74

August 13th: Miss Octavia Hill, one of the founders of the National Trust and a lady committed to the ideal that green open spaces of Britain as well as our historic buildings, should be saved for everyone to enjoy, has died at her home in Crockham Hill. She was 74.

Her funeral service took place this week and she was buried in the village churchyard directly beneath a yew tree to the right of the gate. An effigy has been placed inside the church and the inscription reads: *"Noble in aim, wise in method, unswerving in faith and courage, she devoted her life to raising the bodily condition of her fellow citizens."*

It was in 1884 that Miss Hill met Sir Robert Hunter to discuss the idea of forming a national organisation for open spaces. She had already formed the Kent and Surrey Committee of the Commons Preservation Society and was anxious to control the ambitions of private speculators. In the same year a Mr Evelyn had attempted to give his Deptford estate, Sayes Court to the nation but discovered there was no legal provision for such a gift.

Sir Robert and Octavia looked for a solution and sought the advice of Canon Hardwick Rawnsley, another reformer, who was working in the slums of London. The trio hit on the idea of forming a Trust, Octavia set out the aims and, in January 1895, the National Trust was registered by the Board of Trade. Octavia would not accept a post with the new organisation but a friend with whom she has shared a house, Miss Harriet Yorke, is the treasurer.

Transport strike brings country to a standstill

July 29th: After just five days on strike many Chatham dockers have joined their London brothers and gone back to work. The national dock strike was called by the year-old National Transport Workers' Federation who demanded that employers recognise a union closed shop. It collapsed when talks with the Government broke down. All year there have been heavy clouds over the industrial horizon, starting with the great coal dispute in January and the transport strike in May. That intensified on the Medway when union leaders called for more support.

The transport strike has proved to be one of the longest struggles of recent years involving a vast amount of suffering among women and children. There have been open-air meetings, processions and the transport of food supplies to markets has been made under police protection.

Feelings in the Kent dockyards have been running high between those who chose to strike and those who defied union recommendations. Many fights have broken out between bargemen and mariners, particularly in the area around the Victoria pub in North Street and courts have dealt harshly with the offenders.

■ There is growing concern in Kent about the number of cars using very inadequate roads. On some of the major routes, tarred macadam has been introduced in place of waterboard macadam to make a firmer surface.

It is certainly needed as there are more than 11,000 car registrations now in the county. Compare that with previous years — 5,133 in 1910; 2,456 in 1906 and 1,305 in 1905. If the number of motor car owners continues to increase at this rate the towns will become paralysed with traffic.

The removal of the fountain from Olantigh Towers followed a great fire which devastated the house near Wye. The fountain had been one of the attractions at the Great Exhibition in Hyde Park in 1862

American woman flies the Channel

April 20th: Miss Harriet Quimby, an American aviator who is little known this side of the Atlantic, has become the first of the fair sex to make an aeroplane flight unaccompanied across the English Channel. She achieved the feat on Tuesday morning (April 16th) in a Gnome-Bleriot without any fuss or elaborate preparations. In fact only a few friends were present at the start.

On her arrival from America Miss Quimby stayed in Dover under the name of Miss Craig and took her place in the pilot's seat at 5.38 am. She took off from Whitfield and, steering a course by the aid of a compass, flew over Dover Castle at 1,500 feet. Rising to 2,000 over the Channel she arrived above the Griz Nez Lighthouse a little under an hour later, made her way to Boulogne and came down at Equihen by a spiral *vol plané* not far from the Bleriot sheds.

Miss Trehawke Davies, it will be remembered, was the first lady to cross the Channel in an aeroplane but she was a passenger with Mr Hamel in his Bleriot monoplane.

Tragedy behind the Olantigh fountain

August 12th: The townsfolk of Ashford are in a state of deep shock. The body of Mr George Harper — their greatest benefactor and a man who lived in the area all his life — has been discovered on the railway line running through the Warren. Suffering from neurasthenia and temporarily unhinged in mind by lack of sleep, Mr Harper had committed suicide by placing his head on the railway line just as an express train was approaching.

The pathos of the tragedy is accentuated by the fact that, as recently as last month, he presented a magnificent fountain to the town. This real art treasure was accompanied by two reclining statues and was purchased at the cost of several hundreds of pounds and removed from Olantigh, Wye to a site in the town centre at Ashford.

Mr Harper had a deep love of his town and an honesty of purpose. He felt Ashford should become a town attractive enough to lure people from all over the country. He was instrumental in the purchase of the gas works in 1897 and he helped to provide a good and cheap water supply, efforts which were frequently damped by opposition. More important he fought against local beauty spots being destroyed "in the name of progress".

The crowning feature of his generous regard for Ashford was the offer of the Hubert fountain from Olantigh, following the disastrous fire there several months ago. His gift was at first rejected by the local council and Mr Harper felt snubbed. He offered again to pay all the installation costs if the council would provide the water supply and make sure the fountain always played on his birthday. His motives were severely criticised and, being a person of a singularly sensitive nature, he suffered deep depression.

The offer was eventually accepted and the presentation of the spectacular fountain took place on July 24th, the day after Mr Harper's 71st birthday but the great man was not there to see the formal unveiling. He told the *Kentish Express* that he had found very little gratitude in Ashford, but a lot of abuse. "I'm giving the fountain to the town I love", he said. "I have been slighted because men who ought to know better have imputed all sorts of motives to me."

Three weeks later, came his untimely death.

October 14th: An airship, designed by the aristocratic German Count Ferdinand August Adolf von Zeppelin, yesterday paid a clandestine visit to north Kent sending shock waves throughout the land. The people of Sheerness heard the noise of engines in the sky and saw the large black monster approaching from the sea. Hundreds surged down to the water's edge while many others, terrified out of their wits, sought cover as the Zeppelin cruised menacingly over the town. It was a moonless night and the airship was soon swallowed up by the blackness. Word of the eerie sighting, however, reached London and questions are to be asked in the House of Commons. Why has a German airship travelled across the Channel on a reconnaissance visit to the Kent coast? How many more will appear in the future? It is all highly suspicious.

New naval bases in Kent to combat German threat

December 30th: A new hydro-aeroplane (seaplane) base has been commissioned on marsh land at Grain. For some months now workmen have been cutting a slipway on a large area of foreshore through to the sea wall. Almost £20,000 has been earmarked by the Admiralty for the building of sheds, and coastguards' cottages have been taken over. It is hoped, by next year, that Grain will be in a sufficiently advanced position to replace Eastchurch as the principal air station in the Sheerness Naval District charged with the responsibility of defending the Thames Estuary. Vital development work on hydro-aeroplanes will also be carried out.

Another hydro-aeroplane station is planned at Dover Marine Parade and an air station will be built at Guston Road, Dover about a mile and a half from the town centre.

There is growing concern about the continuing German naval build up in the Channel and the North Sea and Britain has already withdrawn her battleships from the Mediterranean and placed them on patrol in the North Sea.

This action follows the summer breakdown of the Anglo-German talks aimed at slowing down the rate of expansion between the two countries' navies.

Germany has asked for a mutual declaration of neutrality in case either side became involved in war with a third power but Britain, fearing it would harm relations with France and Russia, turned this proposal down.

Some weeks ago Winston Churchill, First Lord of the Admiralty, asked the Commons for an expanded naval budget, boosting the sum to be spent on ships and men to £45 million. Guston Road is among the new air stations planned. It will be needed to help defend the recently approved naval base in the harbour as well as provide a departure point for France.

Serbia's victory against Turkey in the recent Balkan war threatens Austrian and German predominance in the Balkans and the German Kaiser has already said that if Russia supports the Serbs then war would be inevitable. The situation is Europe is grim.

Oak telephone poles for new trunk route

Summer: Following the takeover of the National Telephone Company by the Post Office, new trunk routes are being established across Kent. A familiar feature on many main roads in the county is the sight of men erecting the tall wooden 'H' poles by using a derrick. The poles are extra thick and it is necessary for them to be braced together to form a rigid structure to withstand all types of weather conditions. In the great ice storm of 1908 many single poles were snapped in half under the pressure caused by the weight of snow on the wires. With 17 arms, made of oak, it would take a Caribbean-type hurricane now to fell the new monsters.

One trunk route runs from London to Tonbridge, via Sevenoaks, and this carries local lines which join and leave over shorter distances. The photograph above, taken at Watts Cross, near Hildenborough, a few years ago, shows the manpower necessary to erect the poles.

November 19th, 1912 — coal is raised at Snowdown Colliery

Snowdown wins the great coal race

November 19th: This has been a red letter day for Kent and a triumph for Arthur Burr, head of Kent Coal Concessions Ltd. Early in the morning the first bucketful of East Kent coal was raised at Snowdown giving that colliery victory over Tilmanstone in a race that began almost six years ago.

In fact it was on January 11th, 1907 that the first sod at Snowdown was cut by Mrs Western Plumptre, wife of the owner of the site. Colliery shafts were then sunk and, ten months later, two 18-inch seams were identified. Work has been slow and difficult but worthwhile because there is an abundance of good quality coal under East Kent.

One understandable grievance and a talking point in the local inns is the fact that no local labour has been employed, even on the surface. All the miners have been, and will be, imported from Durham, North Lancashire and Wales. These men bring with them great experience of mining and all those other delightful interests for which they are distinguished at home.

Mr A.C.Bradley writes: "In their hours of copious leisure these mannerless exotics, when not wandering around the lanes of rural Kent, fill the village alehouse. That time-honoured place of rustic rendezvous seems altogether at odds with the alien, harsh-throated crew. However, as they are here, and if the Kentish landscape is to be besmirched, let us hope they will some day provide us in the south-east with cheaper coal."

The next stage in the development of the collieries is the construction of an East Kent Light Railway to serve them all. A light railway order was granted in June last year for a track to connect Shepherdswell to Sandwich and Richborough, Eastry to Wingham, Eythorne to Guilford Colliery and Eythorne to Tilmanstone Colliery. The capital authorized is £240,000.

'The diseases of Ireland are many, and the sickness is grown to that contagion that is almost past a cure' — Barnabe Rich: *The Anothomy of Ireland*, 1615.

January 13th: The pioneer pilot Leslie McDonald and his mechanic Harry English died today when their biplane crashed into the River Thames. The aircraft was a Vickers No 6 monoplane which had been converted into a bi-plane. It is believed the engine suffered sudden loss of power. There will be an inquiry and an inquest will be held at Dartford.

January 31st: The Home Rule for Ireland Bill proposed by the Liberal Government has been rejected by the House of Lords. Voting was 326 against and 96 for. Under the 1911 Parliament Act, however, the Lords can delay, but no longer veto.

February 10th: Captain Robert Scott and two of his companions, Dr Wilson and Lieutenant Bowers have been found dead in a snow-covered tent returning from the

February: Mr and Mrs G.H.Dean of Sittingbourne have provided the town with its first motor ambulance. It can carry two passengers and an attendant and has a 15 hp engine capable of more than 30 mph. The previous ambulance was horse-drawn and the new one, says the specification, is "a miracle of modern mechanical wizardry".

April 25th: Nelly Ternan, of Margate, died today. It has long been an open secret that she was the mistress of Charles Dickens who left her £1,000 in his will.

May: Joseph Deedy of the Merrie England Society is delighted with

King's horse at the Derby has died from her injuries. She is now regarded as a martyred heroine by thousands of suffragettes all over the country.

June 6th: The German army is to be increased from 653,000 to 863,000 men. The Reichstag is concerned at the weakness of the Triple Alliance partners Austria and Italy.

July 11th: Rumania joins Greece and Serbia by declaring war on Bulgaria.

July: The world roller skating championships are to be held in

sea rescue by the Ramsgate lifeboatmen, the entire crew of the Ramsgate fishing vessel *Puritan* have been saved. The vessel sank after being rammed by the smack *Lizzie*.

December 16th: A report today shows that one child in 12 at Britain's state elementary schools is suffering from disease or the effects of a poor diet. The situation is particularly bad in the poorer areas of London.

November 19th: Dartford has a cinema at last The New in Lowfield Street, designed by Richard Lovell, opened today amid great acclamation. The foyer is paved in mosaic and a marble staircase takes patrons to the 995-seat auditorium. Meanwhile work is continuing on the building of a second cinema in Spital Street. The Gem Picture House with 750 seats (stalls and balcony) will open early next year.

November: A new organisation called the Association of Kentish Men and Men of Kent has been formed in Maidstone. It is hoped there will be branches established in most towns.

December: Work on the magnificent new iron bridge across the Medway at Rochester is almost complete. It will be opened early next year.

Following the raising of the first bucketful of coal at Snowdown Colliery last year, Tilmanstone Colliery is now in production for the first time.

August: Harry Hawker's Sopwith floatplane in Ramsgate Harbour during the Round Britain Seaplane Race.

South Pole in atrocious weather conditions. A diary left by Scott confirms the death of two more explorers, Petty Officer Evans and Captain Oates.

February: Among the exhibits at the Olympia Air Show this month is an Experimental Fighting Biplane or EFB1 for short. Built by Vickers of Crayford the appearance of this prototype has attracted a great deal of interest because it is armed with guns. It is nicknamed Destroyer.

the success of the May Queen of London pageant which he organised and then staged in the village of Hayes. More than 1,000 children took part in the "coronation" procession and the royal progress of the Queen united London with this small Kent village. Mr Deedy now hopes this Merrie England event will be held annually in this most attractive village

June 4th: Miss Emily Davison who threw herself under the

the Grand Pier pavilion rinks at Herne Bay.

September 29th: The Bill giving Home Rule to Ireland has become law. Ulster Unionists have set up a provisional government, their leader Sir Edward Carson declared: "We will scientifically work out a plan which will make it impossible for a parliament in Dublin to govern this province."

December 8th: After a dramatic

Following the death of Sir Edward Sassoon, MP, pioneer of wireless telegraphy and a strong advocate of the building of a Channel Tunnel, his son Philip has been elected Member of Parliament for Hythe and Folkestone.

Short Brothers have opened a new factory on the Esplanade at Rochester.

GREAT HITS OF 1913

Hello, hello! Who's your lady friend?
You made me love you.

101

Fire destroys Park Langley Manor House

Tuesday January 7th: The firemen of Beckenham, assisted by the Bromley and West Wickham Volunteer Brigades, have failed to save Park Langley the 15th century manor house. Despite the attention of four jets at full pressure for almost 12 hours, most of the historic building, together with valuable frescoes, old paintings and rare Italian marble pieces, have been destroyed.

The fire broke out on Monday evening in the fine old dining room and was discovered at 7.30 by the steward's boy, Lane. Mr Brett, the steward, called the brigade at 7.50 and Superintendant Gear and his team were on the scene by 8 o'clock. It took almost three hours for the men to get the engine in position by the lake and by this time flames had engulfed the whole building and further assistance was wanted. Bromley and West Wickham responded but, sadly, all attempts to check the flames proved unavailing and the main building was completely burnt to the ground.

Many Beckenham people, distressed by the loss of the old manor, are questioning the time it took to get a telephone message from the burning building to the fire station and the abortive attempts of the brigade to get their engine and hoses into position quickly. They may feel that the building could have been saved.

The Walmer lifeboat and crew who are so frequently called to the Goodwin Sands. It is such a treacherous area that it has been nicknamed by some, Calamity Corner.

Electricity — a story of breathtaking expansion

March: The most advanced form of lighting and heating is now spreading rapidly across Kent — arriving for most people like a fairy godmother. At the beginning of the century the spread of electric power in Kent was the piece-meal achievement of private companies who would build their own power stations and then connect the current to houses in the surrounding district. Many companies were established essentially to serve the tramways. Gravesend, for example, had electricity for its trams in 1902 and it was not available for general consumption until the following year.

Today, much of the electricity undertaking is controlled by municipal councils and is within reach of most towns although many large businesses, shops and even houses still have their own generating sets. At Sevenoaks, a large steam engine drives the dynamo which lights the great house of Knole while Sir John Laurie of Rockdale and Youngs Department Store in the High Street make their own current.

These generators will soon be in competition with the newly-formed Sevenoaks Electricity Company, due to open in a few weeks time. A public generating station is being installed in the old brewery buildings behind Suffolk Place and next year a larger plant will open at Sundridge and then connect to all Sevenoaks consumers.

The growth of demand for the electric current throughout the county is one of breathtaking expansion and we are constantly reminded that it is less than 30 years since hundreds of people from Kent travelled to London to see the first public building lit by electricity. It was, of course, the Savoy Theatre.

The "Squire of Kent" — why Cornwallis deserves this title

Colin Blythe, Kent's great spin bowler. He lives in Tonbridge.

September: With the fourth championship title in eight years, Kent Cricket Club is sailing along on the crest of the wave. By winning 20 out of its 28 games the county finished the season 11 points ahead of Yorkshire and, with so many outstanding players, the stage is set for many more honours to follow.

The most remarkable match was at the county ground, Tonbridge in June when Warwickshire were humiliated. They were bowled out for 16 in the second innings with Frank Woolley and Colin Blythe each taking five wickets for eight runs. The innings lasted 43 minutes and 62 balls.

Winning the title was essentially a team performance but there were some remarkable individual efforts. Blythe took 163 wickets for an average under 16, Woolley took 83 and scored 1,737 runs showing all-round form of the highest quality. Hardinge wrote his name in the club's record books by scoring four successive centuries, and Huish, now 42, claimed the highest ever number of dismissals in a season by a wicket-keeper — 102 (32 stumped and 70 caught).

There is one sad note. Edward Dillon, Kent's captain since 1910 who has played rugby three-quarters for Blackheath and England, has been forced to resign because of business commitments. He leaves the club in a very healthy state.

One man who is delighted by Kent Cricket Club's continuing success is Mr Fiennes Stanley Wykeham Cornwallis, a former president of the club who is also a member of the MCC, I Zingari, the Band of Brothers and the Free Foresters. Mr Cornwallis, who inherited the great estate at Linton Park while still training at Sandhurst, is known today as the "Squire of Kent" — a title he thoroughly deserves.

Since 1910 he has been chairman of Kent County Council and, in that capacity, he has overseen the completion of the Sessions House and Council Chamber next to the Maidstone Gaol. The opening ceremony took place earlier this year. He certainly enjoys public service for Kent more than parliamentary life, although he treasures many highlights during his ten years in the House of Commons as member for Maidstone where he was a tower of strength to the Conservative party.

He is also an active member of the Association of Kentish Men and Men of Kent and only recently in a rousing speech he appealed to the members to treasure Kent's immortal and invincible spirit, its cathedrals and stately homes, its castles, its beautiful views, its traditions and its inheritance.

Mr Cornwallis was born in 1864, educated at Eton and Sandhurst and inherited the Linton Estate soon after his 21st birthday. In 1888 he founded the Linton Beagles and still hunts the pack regularly. He is also an active Freemason and in 1905 was elected Provincial Grand Master of Kent in succession to his relative Earl Amherst.

The "Squire of Kent" has many more years of active service ahead of him and he is confident that the county club will win the championship on more occasions in the very near future.

Everyone's "smitten" by Gladys

Gladys Cooper, a beautiful 25-year-old actress from Lewisham, has successfully auditioned for the leading role in a revival of Sardou's *Diplomacy*. The news was broken to her this week by the director Gerald du Maurier. Miss Cooper is enjoying some wonderful successes on the stage. Two years ago she played Cecily in *The Importance of Being Earnest* and has since had major parts in the works of Shaw, Galsworthy and Arnold Bennett.

One night when she was 19, a 26-year-old Boer War soldier, Herbert Buckmaster, saw her dancing and singing as a Gaiety Girl. He was immediately "smitten" and arranged a meeting. Later that year (1908) they were married and they now have a little girl, Joan.

1913

These ladies of Folkestone may not throw bombs or start fires — but they would like the vote. In Folkestone, as in most towns, there are two " suffragette wings", the non-militant and the militants who are mostly young women of the middle and upper classes.

Suffragettes destroy pavilion at Tunbridge Wells

May 2nd: Following the destruction of the cricket pavilion at the Neville Ground, Tunbridge Wells by a group of suffragettes, a protest meeting has been held at the Great Hall with a view to denouncing the women who are violating the laws of civilisation. Among the speakers was the well-known author, Sir Arthur Conan Doyle, who said the meeting must differentiate between the home constitutional suffragist, who had a right to her opinion, and those female hooligans who debased themselves by crime.

Not only has the pavilion been burnt to the ground but, during a concert at the Opera House, two suffragettes, Miss Davison and Miss Olive Walton hid beneath the stage and at a crucial moment burst upon the performances with posters and cries of "Votes for Women".

It was, however, the pavilion fire which caused most outrage. A street lamp lighter on his rounds saw the building blazing but, by the time the brigade arrived, it was too late — only the brick walls were standing. On the turf in front of the pavilion the firemen found a portrait of Emmeline Pankhurst who was already on trial charged with wrecking a £2,000 golf villa at Walton Heath.

The structural damage at Tunbridge Wells is covered by insurance but lost in the fire are all the records of the famous Blue Mantles cricket club together with valuable sporting prints and engravings of Kent cricketers. The fire follows rumours in the town about bombs having been traced.

At the protest meeting the Great Hall was guarded by police and a collection made on behalf of the cricket clubs who had suffered losses. Generous donations came from Lord Amherst, Lord Camden and Captain Spender-Clay MP.

Sir Arthur Conan Doyle said he found the argument that every woman householder should be given the vote very strong, but if carried out to the full, such an electoral system would work out against the civilised law and even the laws of nature. "Two years ago", he said, "women might have won their cause but the method of advocating it has changed so much lately that I do not believe they would obtain the vote even in a generation (loud appalause)."

Meetings supporting the votes for women campaign have been held in towns all over Kent. At Tonbridge the Rev Llewellyn Smith said that women were led by more emotion, feelings and sentiment than men but, apart from this, he was convinced there was no fundamental difference whatever in the outlook. And if women were really like men there was no reason for disqualifying them from the vote. Other speakers said it would be good for men for they would have the opportunity of fighting side by side with the women for the great reform.

104

Now women can play golf at Sandwich

Summer: Women may not be allowed to vote but, thanks to the proprietor of the Prince's Links Club at Sandwich, they can now play golf. Dr Laidlow Purves, who laid out the links more than 20 years, ago recently saw his daughter practicing and noticed that she could hit the ball a long way. He has decided to open his club for female membership and so becomes the first to recognise the rights of women to play golf.

Good luck to them. They may never be as good at men at this noble game but they may share the facilities of one of the finest golf clubs in the land and one, of course, which used to be patronised by Prince Edward before he became King.

Ellen Terry, her son, Edward Gordon Craig and grandchildren at Smallhythe Place.

Smallhythe Place — where Ellen Terry wants 'to live and die'

Our most illustrious lady of the theatre, Ellen Terry, continues to enjoy her country retreat at the 16th century farmhouse, Smallhythe Place near Tenterden which she bought following a day in the country with her great friend Henry Irving. "This is where I should like to live and die" she cried. The house was originally the harbourmaster's house and serviced the one-time small port of Smallhythe which flourished between the 13th and 17th centuries. Smallhythe Place makes a perfect escape from the glamour and social whirl of London.

Today Ellen lives close to her son and daughter, Edward and Edith (Teddy and Edy) and her son's two children who she loves to entertain with recreations of her past performances. "In fact", recalls a friend, "if a midnight wayfarer passes the Smallhythe cottage window he will see a dim light in an upstairs window, and hear a woman's melodious voice mingling with laughter as her grandchildren roll with mirth in their blankets."

Ellen Terry has not retired from the theatre. She has enjoyed a wide variety of roles but, it is Shakespeare, which best matches her vivacious personality. Her greatest successes were in partnership with Henry Irving — as Ophelia and, to universal acclaim, as Beatrice in *Much Ado About Nothing*, opposite Irving's Benedict. Meanwhile, she continues to support the Suffragette movement with considerable vigour.

If there is a war it will be over by Christmas

May: As the grim prospect of war in Europe looms large, Kent's newspapers continue to publish details of the great arms race which, they say, threatens to run out of control. The First Lord of the Admiralty, Winston Churchill, who has spoken so often in the county, has presented a navy budget which shows his intention to put eight squadrons into service. However, there is a feeling in Kent that his attitude represents a real danger for the security of the country. The German navy is also growing fast. Armaments are being given precedence in Austro-Hungary. Russia intends to quadruple the size of her army. Many now believe that war will engulf Europe with astonishing speed and the era of peace and prosperity which Kent has shared with the rest of the country may come to an abrupt end.

The complexity of the political situation in Eastern Europe confuses the vast majority but most people understand that the root of the trouble is territorial greed. Italy has conquered Turkey and annexed Turkey's vast North African province of Libya. Bulgaria has beaten the Turks and acquired an outlet to the Aegean. Austria dominates Bosnia and the Dalmatian Coast. Land-locked Serbia, convinced that Austria is attempting to deny her access to the Adriatic, has occupied Albania. Austria has given the Serbs an ultimatum (successfully) to quit that country and Germany is delighted. Russia has said they will take any necessary action on behalf of Serbia. Britain and France will rally to Russia's aid.

A sense of instability hangs over the vast Austro-Hungarian-German structure now known as the Central Powers. Opposing them is The Entente — Britain, France, Russia.

If there is a war it will be bloody and many will die. But it will be over by Christmas or Easter next year at the latest and Britain and her allies will be triumphant. If fighting breaks out in Western Europe, Kent will be in the main line of communication and already there are signs that the county is becoming a vast military camp — preparing for the soldiers to sail from East Kent to do their duty for God and King.

An officer hangs on grimly as his mount rears. Here are the men of the 8th Middlesex Regiment marching through Sittingbourne town centre.

1914

January 3rd: The last horse-drawn bus has made its final journey through Beckenham.

January 15th: Winston Churchill, First Lord of the Admiralty has threatened to resign from the Government in protest against Ministerial opposition to higher naval expenditure.

February 9th: The wireless pioneer Marconi announces that he can light a lamp six miles away by wireless power.

February 25th: Ulster's opposition to Home Rule for Ireland as a whole means the country is drifting towards civil war. The parliamentary Ulster Volunteer Force (UVF) has 100,000 armed men and has warned there will be bloodshed if the Home Rule bill should ever become law.

April 13th: Mr Bernard Shaw's new play Pygmalion opened in London last night to great acclaim. Actress Mrs Patrick Campbell made a personal success as the Cockney flower girl who is taught to speak like a lady.

April: Cricket ball makers at Penshurst and Tonbridge are among thousands of workers throughout the country on strike for higher wages. Building workers came out in January followed by Yorkshire miners in March.

June 20th: The world's biggest liner, *The Bismarck*, is launched by The Kaiser in Hamburg.

June 28th: Archduke Franz Ferdinand, the heir to the Austro-Hungarian throne and his wife, the Duchess of Hohenburg have been assassinated as they drove through the streets of Sarajevo, the capital of Bosnia. They were killed by two shots from a Browning automatic.

July 28th: Austria declares war on Serbia.

July 30th The German Kaiser Wilhelm III warns the Czar of Russia that Germany will mobilise unless Russia withdraws the mobilisation orders of 1,200,000 troops.

July 30th: The Government agrees to shelve the Irish Home Rule bill in the face of the crisis in Europe.

August 1st: The Kaiser declares war on his cousin, the Czar. The Royal Navy is mobilised.

August 3rd: Germany declares war on France. Britain says it will stand by the 1839 Treaty of London guaranteeing Belgium neutrality and will protect French coasts.

August 4th: Germany invades

John French and his British Expeditionary Force land in France.

August 23rd: Russian troops penetrate 50 miles into Prussia. Japan declares war on Germany. Brussels falls.

August 31st: British troops are engaged in a bitter struggle for the town of Mons. Bloody battles are being fought in an ever-shifting line from Belgium in the north to Lorraine in the south. The Russian army have suffered a terrible defeat on the Eastern Front along the borders of East Prussia.

Kent volunteers receive the oath and the King's shilling before leaving for Dover and Belgium.

Belgium and Britain declares war against Germany.

August 6th: Austria declares war on Russia. Serbia declares war on Germany. Germany and Austria threaten to attack Italy if she refuses to renounce neutrality.

August 16th: Germany takes Liege after fierce Belgian resistance.

August 17th: Field Marshal Sir

September 9th: Herbert Asquith, the Prime Minister, has called for another 50,000 men to sign up for the army. The army's strength is now 825,000 and almost as many men are joining in a day as are normally recruited in a year. Thousands are coming from Kent.

September 12th: German troops take Ghent and Lille. Rheims has already fallen.

September 23rd: Zeppelin sheds

at Dusseldorf are bombed by British aeroplanes. Three British cruisers have been sunk off the Netherlands.

September 7th: The first bomb falls on London. The Royal Flying Corps are throwing steel darts out of their aircraft into the German trenches.

September 14th: Germans in retreat from Paris after decisive battles on the Western Front.

September 18th: Crayford inventor Hiram Maxim reveals his anti-Zeppelin incendiary bullet.

September 28th: Turkey attacks Russian ports.

September: Gravesend Grammar Schools for boys and girls are opened. Previously they had been educated in a co-educational school.

October 10th-17th: More than 5,000 Belgian refugees and wounded soldiers are brought into Dover.

October 28th: Police round up aliens across the country. Concentration camps are set up in Kent.

October 29th: The Ramsgate fishing vessel, *Our Tom*, is blown up by a German mine. All hands are killed.

November 26th: *HMS Bulwark* blows up in the harbour at Sheerness. 700 are killed. Income tax is doubled to pay for the war.

December 8th: *HMS Kent* sinks the German cruiser *Nurnberg* in the Battle of the Falkland Islands.

December 24th: An aerial bomb falls on Dover.

December 28th: *SS Montrose*, intended as a blockship in Dover Harbour has blown out to sea and been wrecked on the Goodwin Sands. No casualties.

GREAT HITS OF 1914

Keep the Home Fires Burning

St Louis Blues

107

Rochester Bridge opened by Lady Darnley 14.5.14 (886)

May 14th: *The handsome new bridge across the Medway at Rochester which took three years to build and cost £80,000 was opened today by the Countess Darnley of Cobham in the presence of an immense concourse of people. It is the fourth bridge constructed on or near this spot. The first, opened in 960, was made of wood and lasted 400 years. Next came a bridge of stone from 1388 to 1856 succeeded by the great iron bridge. Now we have this present handsome structure of steel and granite which gives a headway for navigation of 24 feet at high water.*

Thirty nine steps to Buchan's 'private cove'

June: Once again, the people of Broadstairs have welcomed a well-known author to their town. The 39-year-old Scot, John Buchan, famous for his exciting adventure stories, has been recuperating from indifferent health and, at the same time writing another book in which Broadstairs and the North Foreland are both prominently featured.

Some years ago Buchan, on holiday in Broadstairs, stayed with his friends, The Grenfells who had rented a small villa on the Foreland, the tenancy of which carried the privilege of a private beach. There were 78 steps down to that cove and Buchan, then in better health, remembers how he could take them two at a time.

With the house, cove and steps as a background, an exciting plot is developing — concerning an elaborate international conspiracy to invade Britain. The book will be called *The Thirty-Nine Steps* and it is due to be published next year.

The 2/1st Battalion Kent Cyclists enjoy an orderly rest during training in Canterbury. The Battalion was formed in Tonbridge in 1909 under Colonel C.E. Warner, joining two other territorial units in that town — The 4th Royal West Kent Regiment and the Kent (Fortress) Royal Engineers.

Kent Cyclist Battalion is ready for action

July: There has been a slow but steady build-up of military activity in Kent during the first six months of this year. "Britain's contemptible little army", as it has been described by the Kaiser, is certainly no match numerically for the vast war machines of Europe but the men are well-trained professional soldiers ready to be mobilised should that extreme measure be necessary.

Practically every week from January to August there has been a meeting somewhere in the county to talk about Britain's contribution to the great European struggle. At Maidstone in March hundreds attended a public meeting to discuss the case against compulsory military training. After many stirring speeches it was finally resolved that the time had arrived for every able-bodied youth to be compelled to receive a training in the territorial forces. It was the only way, the meeting decided, that peace in Britain could be maintained.

Throughout the year the strength of Kent's National Service League has been gaining momentum. Most towns now have branches and regular recruitment meetings are held. At a recent concert at the Corn Exchange in Maidstone 300 new members joined the League — and the following day that branch was accused of hindering recruitment for the territorial forces.

There have been scores of military exercises in the county. The latest was a "sham fight" at Penenden Heath. Apparently an "invading force" landed at Hastings and advanced to Smeeth where fighting was intense. The railroad between Aylesford and Maidstone had been destroyed so armaments could not be sent by rail. This enabled the "invaders" to proceed. The "defenders" consisted of members of the West Kent Yeomanry, the Army Service Corps, a half company of the Officers' Training Corps and a section of the 1st Home Counties Field Ambulance Corps and the "invaders" were a half company of the Offficers' Training Corps, the A and B sections of the Royal West Kent Regiment and the enthusiastic members of the Kent Cyclists' Battalion. The exercise showed in theory how Kent could respond to an invasion.

This week Kent County Council received a Home Office order instructing the county to strengthen its police force and it has been decided to free Boy Scouts from schools for possible police service. The council is also making preliminary plans to take over public buildings and turn them into hospitals. Red Cross detachments and the St John's Ambulance Brigade are stepping up their training procedures and the Kent Cyclists are still tremendously keen to demonstrate the value of two-wheeled marksmen capable of crossing virtually any terrain at eight miles an hour.

Assassination of Archduke puts Europe "on stand-by"

June 30th: The news of the assassination in Sarajevo of Archduke Franz Ferdinand, heir to the Austro-Hungarian throne, and his morganatic wife, the Duchess of Hohenburg, has put the whole of Europe into an advanced state of preparedness. Sketchy details of the murders came through on the wireless telegraph on Sunday evening followed immediately by a wave of horror and indignation.

Although a 19-year-old student fired the fatal shots from a Browning automatic pistol it is believed that the outrage was part of a carefully laid plot by Serbians who are taking revenge for the oppression of their people. The royal couple were driving in an open carriage through the streets of the Bosnian capital when the student darted out of the crowd. His first shot hit the Archduke in the neck

and his second struck the Duchess who died almost immediately.

The increasing tension in European affairs has meant the boom across the mouth of the Medway has

Long queues have formed outside many banks following the news that the Bank rate has risen to 10 per cent and the Stock Exchange is closed. This was the situation in Folkestone as men waited patiently for their turn with the teller, many wanting to exchange bank notes for gold.

been placed in position and all internal traffic through the port of Dover will be regulated.

A special detachment of police has arrived from London to guard the Ordnance depots. In Sheerness marines have been recalled to duty afloat. The notice was read from the stage of the Hippodrome and a search in working men clubs in the area has been made for bluejackets.

The five battalions of the Queen's Own are also on stand-by. In fact the 4th and 5th Territorial battalions are about to embark on their fortnight's training holiday.

The Times yesterday said the assassination in Sarajevo has shaken the conscience of the world. Certainly public feeling in Vienna is running high with anti-Serbian demonstrations. The Austrian Emperor, Franz Josef broke down when he heard the news and cried "No sorrow is spared me".

The likelihood of a European war is now even greater.

Meanwhile the men of the Green Street Green Fire Brigade have plenty on their hands as they race to another blaze. In fact they have devised a new method of speed and efficiency as this photograph clearly shows.

One of the airships based at Kingsnorth.

New airship base a tempting target — for Suffragettes

July: Work on the newly-commissioned airship base at Kingsnorth on the Hoo peninsula, is now underway and it is already considered to be the most important and largest airship station in the country. Under the control of Commander N.F.Usborne, the *Astra Torres* (Airship No. 3) stands by to defend Chatham and Sheerness from attacks by German airships; in fact airship patrols over the Thames Estuary have started.

The Admiralty, which took responsibility for the commissioning of these lighter-than-air craft some weeks ago, has recommended that regular daily flights should be made between Dover and Calais should it be necessary to send an Expeditionary Force to France.

A Royal Navy Air Service has also been created and will now absorb the Naval Airship Branch.

Construction work on the airship base has been long and tedious. It covers a large expanse of low-lying land two miles east from Hoo village and is conveniently close to the Chatham naval base and the new air station at Grain.

The next step is the construction of a large double-bay airship shed, a railway spur, a hydrogen production plant and wooden huts for personnel accommodation.

Despite its isolation security remains a big problem for the Admiralty — not necessarily protection from enemy attack, although that may follow, but from suffragettes with boxes of matches. They may consider the large wooden shed to be a tempting target!

Men of all ages are coming forward in great numbers in response to the crisis in Europe. Bicycles are being given to Boy Scouts in all areas of Kent, ambulance men are being drilled almost daily and scores are joining the police force as special constables with a brief to look out for aliens who might be spies. Here, at the top of Chelsfield railway tunnel are Special Constables Stone, Blackwell and Hatherill. Such posts are now found all over the county.

Kitchener calls London from the post office at Barham

August 2nd: As events in central Europe continue to unfold with bewildering speed it seems likely that Kent's 64-year-old veteran soldier Lord Kitchener will be summoned to join the Government. Last week Austria declared war on Serbia. Two days ago Russia, France and Germany ordered mobilisation of their armies and yesterday Britain angered the Kaiser by offering to mediate. A European War is inevitable and Britain may join the fight.

Herbert Kitchener, who was enjoying life in retirement on his 500-acre Broome Park estate, near Canterbury, had planned a Mediterranean cruise but instead he has accepted an invitation to meet Herbert Asquith amid rumours that he will be given the job as Secretary of State for War.

If Kitchener does accept, the whole of Britain will be grateful that there is a public telephone in the little Kent village of Barham. The former British Commander-in-Chief, during hostilities in South Africa, had actually booked his passage by train to Marseilles and then by cruiser to Alexandria. He was due to leave on Friday but decided first to use the telephone in the post office at Barham to get the latest news from London. He was told it was unadvisable to go on holiday to anywhere but Switzerland and that all Ministers had been told to return to their posts immediately.

A few weeks ago Winston Churchill, First Lord of the Admiralty, pointed out to Prime Minister Asquith the impossibility of his continuing to hold the seals of Secretary of State for War as well as his own supreme office, and advised that he should consider the appointment of Lord Kitchener to the former post. Mr Churchill said: "I could see by Mr Asquith's reception of my remarks that his mind was already moving, or had moved, along the same path."

Kent seaside resorts suddenly deserted as Britain declares war on Germany

August 4th: Britain has declared war against Germany and it is expected that an Expeditionary Force, under the command of Sir John French, will quickly be assembled and sent across the Channel to take its place in the front line. Already several million soldiers, who form the vanguard of many armies, are on the move throughout Europe; soon they will be joined by Kentish Men and Men of Kent.

The news of the declaration of war, which followed Germany's invasion of Belgium, has sent cheering crowds surging through most Kent towns. There is a great feeling of euphoria and, in Maidstone, hundreds of young men have been singing the National Anthem as they make their way towards the recruiting offices.

The Prime Minister Herbert Asquith today gave the House details of the ultimatum calling on Germany to respect the neutrality of Belgium, guaranteed in the Treaty of 1839. The Kaiser has already dismissed this treaty as a mere "scrap of paper".

Events in Kent have been moving fast. A week ago the seaside resorts in Thanet and along the east Kent coast were packed with the usual holiday crowds, determined that the European crisis was not going to spoil their fun. Scores of people in Hythe watched a runaway horse collide with a railway van opposite the Oak Inn, turning the wagon completely over and, in Folkestone, the newly introduced red bus service was attracting many customers. A concert in the Winter Gardens in Margate was as popular as ever and the sands at Broadstairs echoed with the voices of children happily playing with bucket and spade. The only real change from normal seaside activities was the fact that corporation bands have included, each day, renderings of the Russian National Anthem and the Marseillaise.

Now suddenly the people have gone, driven home by the fear of German naval bombardment and the desire to "show their loyalty to King and country". Emergency meetings have been held in many seaside towns to consider what steps can be taken to save the season. One London newspaper said that the Kent beaches had already become forbidden ground, a statement which prompted an immediate response. "It is utterly devoid of foundation", writes the *Folkestone Herald*. "Hotel, boarding house and apartment owners should do all in their power to make it known that our promenade and beach are as free and open to holiday folk as at other times."

Away from the coastal towns there is frenzied activity. The East Kent (The Buffs), the Royal West Kents, reservists and Territorials have already left for duty and their dependents have been asked to give their names to town clerks throughout the county. Just last week Tonbridge held a Territorial Week to stimulate recruiting. The Royal West Kents and the Royal Engineers were on the Castle Lawn with the Kent Yeomanry, the nurses, Tonbridge School Officers' Training Corps and the Kent Cyclists. The latter have now been told to patrol the sea wall at Reculver and watch closely for a German invasion.

In Tunbridge Wells there were stirring scenes as the Territorials (D and E Companies) marched from the Drill Hall to the station and then on to another destination. The approaches to the station were packed with people who sang *God Save the King* and *Rule Britannia*. Sir David Salomon, of Broomhill, the well-known scientist has offered himself for service and undertaken to equip 100 men. In Ashford the Territorials have had a rough time. After marching into the town, prior to their departure for Dover, they stood all night because the ground was too wet to lie upon, without food (except bread) and without tobacco. It's enough to damp the ardour of the best, although the Terriers look well and cheerful. There was no standing all night for the soldiers waiting in Maidstone as churches in the town offered the use of their Sunday schools as reading and waiting rooms for the military.

As men in their thousands surge heroically to their colours, to do their best in what may be the greatest and perhaps the most momentous struggle the world has ever known, one Man of Kent alone shoulders much of the burden of what lies ahead. Field Marshal Sir John French from Walmer will command the British Expeditionary Force when it is assembled. He has high regard for the French army and he is of the opinion that the war will be over by Christmas.

There are many who don't share that view. Sir Edward Grey has assured Parliament that there is no British commitment to send troops at all. He said that the British contribution to the European struggle could only be a small one — 50,000 men under arms compared with more than three million Austro-Hungarians, four million Frenchmen, four and a half million Germans and nearly six million Russians. "Britain is vulnerable."

In Ashford hundreds of employees from the Railway Works have joined the Naval Reserve. This means that extra labour has had to be occasioned for the fitting up of three special ambulance trains. Men have been working all day and night to get them ready in time.

Full pay for the papermakers

August 8th: There has been a wonderful gesture by the directors of Lloyds Papermakers at Sittingbourne. More than 100 men (Territorials and Reservists) have signed up and the company has agreed to pay the wages in full during the duration of the war to all men who have dependents.

At St Mary Cray Paper Works where £1 and 10 shilling bank notes are being manufactured there are armed guards composed of local residents on duty day and night. The building is also floodlit.

Brewers lose their best horses to the army

August 9th: Upwards of a thousand horses, as well as scores of waggons, have been commandeered by the military authorities in the Maidstone district. The four brewery firms of Messrs Esherwood, Foster and Stacey, Style and Winch, Fremlins Bros and Mason and Co have all lost their best horses.

While the brewers have been willing to make the sacrifice, farmers in Kent are not so keen. The Kent branch of the NFU has been told that the War Office is collaring horses in a very free manner and one farmer near Tonbridge who was over 80 had his only horse taken from him.

'Your country needs' another 100,000 men

August 7th: In an attempt to increase the number of British soldiers under arms, Lord Kitchener, now Secretary of State for War, has called publicly for another 100,000 volunteers. His patriotic plea has prompted enormous meetings throughout the county in which speakers have referred to Belgium's neutrality and how badly this little country has upset the German timetable. At Hythe, yesterday, a meeting at Moyle Tower was addressed by Henry Fielding Dickens QC, son of the famous novelist, who said the spirit of Nelson remains with us but his navy did not scatter mines on the open seas. "Lord Kitchener is a man we can trust. Let us do what he asks."

August 8th: A true spirit of loyalty has animated the people of Kent and the manner in which the members of the local Territorial units have responded to Kitchener's new call to join the Colours has been more than gratifying.

August 9th: There were touching scenes at St Mary Cray, Swanley and Orpington stations yesterday when a large number of reservists who had been called to the Colours said goodbye to mothers, daughters, wives and sweethearts, with promises that they would soon return.

VAD girls will tend the wounded

August 15th: All Kent branches of the St John Ambulance Society, the British Red Cross and the Territorial Force Voluntary Aid have been amalgamated and will work together under the title of the Voluntary Aid Detachment. Most of the members are women and they will staff voluntary hospitals throughout the county and tend to the wounded, including those of our allies. The president of the VAD is the Marchioness Camden of Wildernesse, Sevenoaks, the county director is the Earl of Darnley and the chief of staff is Dr J.H.Yolland of Bromley. It is hoped that VAD units will operate in every town and village.

Through the kindness of the Earl of Romney, Hayle Place, Tovil has been placed at the disposal of the VAD for use as a general hospital and a number of schools in Sittingbourne have been secured as hospitals for the naval wounded who may be landed at Sheerness. It is hoped that many more large buildings all over Kent can be converted into hospitals ready to care for the wounded.

At Beckenham, for example, Christ Church Halls and Balgowan School have been converted into military hospitals — the latter with an operating theatre and all the latest technology.

A civic welcome in Dover for these boat loads of refugees from Belgium.

Heartrending scenes as Belgians pour into Kent

October 14th: As more Belgian cities fall to German troops the number of refugees escaping into England continues to increase dramatically. Kent witnessed the first stirring scenes, before Britain entered the war, as smartly-dressed Belgians carrying whatever possessions they could arrived at Folkestone and Dover. They were warmly greeted. Today the refugees are homeless, bedraggled and, in some cases, badly wounded.

It was the third week of August that saw the biggest influx. Small fishing vessels, mud barges, sailing boats from Ostend were arriving at Folkestone every hour and close on a quarter of a million refugees were efficiently dealt with by the authorities and then found homes all over Kent. The really destitute people were sent to London with interpreters to help them understand what assistance is available. Heartrending scenes were witnessed by those who poured down to the harbour.

In early September Lord Gladstone visited Folkestone, spoke to the Committee dealing with the Belgians and suggested that a large house should be obtained and turned into a hostel with housekeeper and staff. The Bevan Home, Sandgate may be one such suitable place.

As the fighting in Belgium continued, soldiers cut off from the main body escaped to England — many arriving side by side with the first batch of the British wounded. Yesterday (Tuesday) saw one of the saddest sights when 2,000 Belgian wounded arrived from Ostend, the majority coming straight from the fighting line with their wounds roughly dressed. Hotels have been commandeered and the visitors in them have been given notice to leave immediately. Other buildings have been converted into hospitals while every motor car seen in the street has been ordered to assist in the transport of the wounded soldiers.

If Folkestone has opened the way for the whole of Britain in their thought and care for the heroes of a desperate nation, then other towns in Kent are not far behind. The village hall at Orpington has been converted into a hospital for the Belgians and 66 are due to arrive at Orpington station this morning. Tunbridge Wells has become another to hold out the hand of hospitality. 150 Belgians who arrived there have already been told they can stay until their repatriation.

The *Kent Messenger* is now finding it difficult to obtain any reliable war telegrams to satisfy the crowds of people who wait each week outside the offices in Maidstone. A reporter said: "It is now impossible to get any reliable news notwithstanding the fact that we have two telegraphic services and one telephone in operation!"

August 31st: The war is less than two weeks old and already there has been heavy fighting and hundreds of British casualties. Men from Kent, in action alongside French and Belgian comrades defending the town of Mons, are among those dead and a retreat has been ordered as German infantry battalions advance.

Led by Field Marshal Sir John French, the British Expeditionary Force — the finest army to leave these shores — sailed from Dover on August 17th in a secret naval operation. The 150,000 men of the BEF arrived in France amid scenes of great enthusiasm. Commanded by well-qualified officers the volunteers' orders were to halt the mighty German war machine already overwhelming France with a massive flanking movement through Belgium.

Official news telegrams show that the struggle is not going well for the Allies although one company of the 1st Battalion of the Queen's Own (Royal West Kent Regiment), under Lt-Col Martyn have helped to "knock out" the 3,000-strong Brandenburg Grenadiers. Sir John French intended to make a stand at Mons but the withdrawal of the French army gave him no choice but to retreat.

Kent newspaper editors, enthused by the success of the Royal West Kents but disappointed by the wireless telegraphy reports that the cavalry is already in retreat, hardly know how to be constructive. Certainly no-one is going to suggest that the whole of Sir John's army could be bottled up and captured.

Liege fell on August 16th, Brussels was taken two days later and, by the 23rd, Germans were engaged along a 150-mile front from Mons to Luxembourg.

Swimming pool 'gunsite' worries Sevenoaks

August 10th: One of Sevenoaks' greatest benefactors has left the area with his family amid rumours that he is a German spy and may even be planning to bomb London!

A few months ago the same man presented new swimming baths to the town. They are sited at Eardley Road and were opened in July. A commemorative stone records that they have been presented to the town by Edward Kay of Ashgrove, where he lived for a number of years. Mr Kay's real name is Kraftmeier and the fact that he has left the area suggests something suspicious. Some Sevenoaks people believe that the floor of the baths has been specially strengthened to provide a platform for German guns which would bombard London.

If Mr Kraftmeier does have German nationality he is not alone in wanting to be many miles away from England. Many have already fled, but those German cooks and waiters from Kent seaside hotels and boarding houses who were unable to find a passenger boat at Folkestone or Dover have been rounded up and sent to concentration camps. There have been arrests on espionage charges and hundreds of alien's homes have been ransacked.

There was great excitement in Chatham High Street last night. A man boarded the nine o'clock bus but did not wait for his change. He aroused the suspicion of the booking clerk, a message went through to Maidstone and when he arrived at that destination he was arrested. The former mayors of Gillingham, Aldermen Featherby and Swain have also been arrested for "suspicious conduct". They had landed at Sheerness after a cruise on the Thames and were immediately marched off to the guard room. When their identity became known the military authorities there laughed and apologised!

English holidaymakers in France, Germany and Switzerland are having their own troubles. There is so much congestion at sea and so many people returning that the situation is chaotic. On Sunday the turbine steamer *Victoria* left Boulogne with 1,000 passengers and another 400 left behind on the quay.

Many cricket matches have been suspended but Kent has decided to honour all their fixtures — one of the few counties to do so. One man who will not complete the season is Colin Blythe, the 35-year-old brilliant left-arm bowler. He has embarked on active service and the people of Kent wish him well.

October 15th: **The Royal Flying Corps, with seven squadrons, is playing a vital part in the war effort. Five of those squadrons are now in France having given aerial protection to the BEF. They crossed the Channel from a small landing ground near Dover and are currently flying over German lines on reconnaissance flights.**

Sadly there has already been one casualty, although not in combat, and there may be many more. Second Lieutenant Skene and his mechanic, Barlow, were killed when their two-seater plane crashed at Dover on its way to France. In another incident a German aircraft was shot down by machine-gun fire from a British plane.

November 11th: A British gunboat HMS Niger, engaged on patrol duty in the Downs off Deal, was torpedoed by a German submarine this morning and foundered. All hands were saved although two men are severely, and two slightly, injured. The crew of the Niger are lucky for the power of the German submarines is considerable. Less than a month ago the British cruiser Hawke was torpedoed in the North Sea and 525 sailors drowned.

Wounded Belgium refugees are in hospitals all over Kent including this one at Rolvenden.

'Boy Scout with a quarterstaff can hurt a German'

December: Volunteer units, made up mainly of Boer War veterans and a few patriotic teenagers, are springing up all over Kent. These spontaneous groups of dedicated men who are prepared to defend their county in the event of a German invasion have no Government recognition; in fact that has been refused, but they are training in arms and, on the North Downs, digging trenches to deter any advance towards the capital. The units have no proper uniform or name. In some areas they are called Volunteer Training Corps, in others The National Guard.

There has been a move in Hythe towards the formation of a local committee to watch for spies. At a recent meeting in the town, Captain Beauclerk suggested that Boy Scouts should be employed in a vigilante group. "They could guard the railway station", he said "and their signalling would be very useful." He said that the quarter-staff of a Boy Scout was a serious weapon if used on a German

but was told he should really leave matters to the local military or police. One councillor said: "Boy Scouts could easily mistake a Frenchman for a German with serious consequences."

There has been one piece of good news for the county to celebrate. *HMS Kent* was triumphantly involved in the Battle of The Falklands on December 11th when the Royal Navy sank

four German cruisers with no British loss. The battle was fought at night and the British victory means that the German fleet away from the Baltic and North Sea has been practically eliminated and the Atlantic is free again. *HMS Kent* played her part by engaging and sinking the cruiser *Nurnberg*. The King has sent his condolences to the families of the four Kent sailors who died on duty.

Pilot drops a bomb on British soil

Christmas Eve: The people of Dover, particularly those who live close to St James' Church, cannot believe their eyes, or their ears. A German pilot flying a seaplane from Belgium this morning dropped a bomb which landed harmlessly in a garden near the Rectory. It made a crater of about four to five feet deep, smashed some windows and the blast knocked the gardener Mr James Bank out of a tree he was pruning.

He wasn't hurt but, if such attacks continue, he will go down in history as the first casualty of a bomb dropped from an aeroplane.

The German pilot is Lt von Prondzynski and he was flying a Taube at an altitude of about 5,000 feet. It is believed his intention was to damage Dover Castle or the naval harbour. He had to lift his bomb in both hands, control the "joy stick" with his knees and then let go. It fell 400 yards from the Castle.

The Bulwark blows up in the Medway: 741 killed

November 26th: *The Bulwark*, one of the great ships of the Battle Fleet anchored in the Medway has been destroyed in a single explosion, killing all but 12 of the 741 officers and men on board. This dastardly crime is believed to be the work of a U-boat or enemy agents in the area.

Witnesses on the mainland at Stoke and Grain say the incident will for ever be fixed in their memory. There was a tremendous flash, accompanied by a blast and one of the ships was suddenly enveloped in a huge cloud of smoke. When that smoke cleared the vessel had gone. *The Bulwark* had simply just disappeared.

Admiralty divers are currently examining the wreckage in an attempt to determine the cause of the explosion. They are faced with a hopeless task for the upper deck of the ship has been ripped asunder and timber and metal strewn over an area of sea believed to be more than a mile in radius. Parts of the ship, including an officer's wardrobe, are lying on marshes on the mainland.

Meanwhile work continues in looking for survivors. A few were picked up by boats which went to the rescue in the wake of the tragedy. They were in the water surrounded by floating debris and corpses and were shouting hysterically for help. Other bodies were being washed downstream by a strong current and the rescue parties made the decision to leave the men in their watery grave.

An official enquiry will be held soon. The U-Boat theory may be dismissed as unlikely. That means the explosion was caused by an accident or sabotage — and the latter is strongly suspected. Some people in Sheerness have already reported the sighting in the area of a foreign-looking gentleman dressed like a farmer but having a military bearing. There are spies all around us.

The Bulwark moved to the Medway anchorage earlier this month with the Fifth Battle Fleet to combat any German moves to invade England. She was launched in 1899 as a flag ship and carried 11 magazines connected by a passage running through the entire ship. These ammunition passages were packed with shells and cordite.

The explosion was seen as far away as Southend and Sittingbourne where one man reported it as being just like a wonderful sunset.

'Patriotism is not enough. I must have no hatred or bitterness towards anyone' — the last words of Edith Cavell before her execution

January 1st: The strength of the British army stands at 720,000 men.

January 19th: A Zeppelin airship has bombed Great Yarmouth and King's Lynn. Bombs fall near the King's home at Sandringham. 20 are killed.

January 25th: A telephone call betweeen New York and San Francisco is made by Alexander Graham Bell.

Field Marshal Lord Kitchener, Minister of State for War, has been elected an Honorary Life Member of the County Society.

February 2nd: In a gamble designed to destroy the British economy, Germany have started a submarine blockade of the British Isles.

February 4th: The youth who killed Archduke Ferdinand and his wife in Bosnia escapes execution because he is too young. The other conspirators are shot.

The inquiry into the *Bulwark* disaster in November 1914 has concluded that there is no clear evidence to suggest the explosion was caused by the accidental ignition of ammunition on board.

March 21st: *HMS Kent* was present at the sinking of the German cruiser *Dresden* off Juan Fernandez Island.

March 26th: Sylvia Pankhurst is told by Lloyd George that women on war work will receive the same pay as men.

April 22nd: A War Office communique says British forces have been successful after a desperate

battle for a small hill around the town of Ypres. The position is known as Hill 60 and there have been casualties on either side.

April 22nd: The Germans have introduced a terrible new weapon — chlorine gas. Victims have fled from the trenches coughing, half-blind and panic stricken.

April 26th: Allied troops have positioned themselves along the Gallipoli peninsula after heavy fighting with Turkish forces. Churchill hopes to knock the Turks out of the war.

August 17th-18th: An airship crossed the coast at Herne Bay and came low over the pier. It was fired on by members of the 42nd Provisional Battalion but flew over Canterbury, Ashford, Faversham and Whitstable, spending two hours overland. The airships dropped 18 high explosive and 40 incendiary bombs — all in open countryside.

September: King

Capt D.R.Salomons of Broomhill, Southborough, son of the great motor pioneer, has been killed in Gallipolli. See page 130.

George V today arrived in Folkestone with Lord Kitchener to inspect the Canadian troops at Shorncliffe Camp.

September 27th: 600 Germans and Austrians arrested in England are taken to Alexandra Palace for internment.

October 12th: A British nurse, Edith Cavell, has been executed for treason. She was charged with

harbouring Belgians of military age and helping young English and French soldiers to escape to freedom across the Dutch border.

October 29th: 10,000 attend memorial service for Nurse Edith Cavell at St Paul's Cathedral.

November 11th: Winston Churchill has resigned from the Government and intends to rejoin his regiment in France. He was sacked from the Admiralty six months ago.

December 8th: New flags have been presented to *HMS Kent* by the County Society to replace those damaged in the Battle of the Falklands. The County Society has also opened a fund for prisoners of war in Germany.

December 15th: Sir Douglas Haig, First Army Commander in Flanders, has replaced Sir John French as commander of the British forces on the Western Front. The front runs from Ostend across Flanders and then assumes a deep salient above Paris before swinging east to the fortress town of Verdun. It has hardly changed position in more than a year.

December 19th: A major landslip on Folkestone Warren has closed the South Eastern and Chatham railway line between Folkestone and Dover. It may be closed for many years and there is a suggestion that explosives should be stored in the tunnels.

The last horse-drawn bus in Kent — Maidstone to Tenterden — has been replaced by more modern means of travelling.

There are now 162 VAD units operating in Kent. Number one is Dover. The Beckenham unit is Number 162 .

A branch of the Womens' Institute movement has been formed at Kemsing. It is the first in Kent.

GREAT HITS OF 1915

Pack Up Your Troubles in Your Old Kit Bag

Back Home in Tennessee

Great gale causes havoc in Thanet

January 1st: Two men have been killed by falling trees, a barge with all hands has foundered at Margate and the South Goodwin Lightship manned by men who formerly belonged to the Ramsgate Trinity House Station is missing, following one of the greatest gales ever known in the Thanet area.

The wind blew with hurricane violence and the Thanet lifeboats at sea experienced terrible weather. There have been countless cases of damage to property in Ramsgate and Margate and many have been hurt by falling tiles.

A liner with 12 hands is also stranded on the Goodwin Sands.

Ivor's great song was composed in a Romany caravan at Biggin Hill

January: The young man sitting on the steps of his mother's bungalow at Biggin Hill is David Ivor Davies, a 21-year-old Welshman who is now better known all over Britain as Ivor Novello. At the end of last year young Ivor composed a song which is bringing him fame and fortune. *Keep The Home Fires Burning* was written in Ivor's Romany caravan, situated in the grounds of his mother's bungalow in St Mary's Grove, Biggin Hill.

Many people are wondering how this young Welshman, came to live in a tiny village on the North Downs. Early last year his "mam", Madame Clara Novello Davies, founder and conductor of the Royal Welsh Ladies' Choir

decided to take her pupils — the Singing Colony — away from Cardiff to a place where clean air and fresh foods were readily available. She chose Biggin Hill, rented a bungalow, placed the caravans in the garden and then got to work training her pupils in voice production and helping Ivor with the words of his new song.

Today everyone is singing *Keep The Home Fires Burning* — especially in music halls, in cinemas and even by the soldiers encamped all over Kent. Few people had ever heard of Biggin Hill or Ivor Novello but his song is on course to become one of the most popular ever written.

Staff of the VAD army hospital at Tenterden. There are now more than 100 active VAD units operating in towns and villages throughout the county, including one at the village hall in Orpington. Canadian engineers billeted in that area have already suggested that they would be pleased to build a temporary hospital in Orpington if the land can be found.

West Kent soldiers blinded by chlorine gas

April 22nd: A terrible new weapon has been introduced by the Germans during fighting near the town of Ypres — a swirling yellow vapour which attacks the throat and eyes. The Allies have now said they will go into battle holding wet cloths to their faces hoping it will give some protection against chlorine gas.

The battle at Ypres is a desperate one with many heavy casualties on both sides. In a few weeks the French have lost 69,000 men killed or taken prisoner and British losses include many local soldiers who were serving with the glorious West Kents.

Among those who have come home suffering from the effects of gas is Private Edward Murphy, an old boy of Crayford School who joined Kitchener's army, came through the retreat of Mons and found himself in the thick of fighting near Ypres. He said this week that it was hell, with mines and shells exploding every few yards. "Although we were killing many Germans, they continued to advance", he said, "so the West Kents were given the order to charge with fixed bayonets. As I was running out of the trench a shell exploded close to me and suddenly I was blind. It contained gas."

Private Murphy said the gas caused him great thirst and he was foaming at the mouth and, although he couldn't see, it turned his clothes yellow. He said the enemy released their gas in three ways — by packing it into shells, by pumping it from their trenches or by carrying it in little boxes and then throwing it when charging.

The lad from Crayford will be spending a few days in the Orchard Hospital, Dartford where he has many wounded chums before rejoining his battalion in France.

In Kent many people are following the King's example and giving up drinking. George V is leading a government campaign to cut down heavy drinking among armament workers which is slowing vital production. In fact David Lloyd George, Chancellor of the Exchequer has described Britain's three enemies as Germany, Austria and Drink. Lord Kitchener has complained of slow delivery of arms and supplies to troops on the Western Front.

January 12th: The German submarines have not had things all their own way. The submarine U8 was sunk off Dover by a destroyer flotilla, having been picked out by the powerful harbour searchlights (see above and bottom right). In another incident all but one of the crew of U7 were drowned when their submarine was torpedoed by mistake by U22.

Steamer rescues 2,200 from torpedoed ship

March: The East Kent fishing industry, passenger boats and those bringing supplies of food to Britain are being terrorised by the presence in the Channel of mines and — an even greater menace — submarines. The German Imperial Navy has launched submarine warfare against all ships apparently in retaliation against the British hunger-blockade of Germany.

Extraordinary stories of drama and courage at sea are beginning to emerge. The captain of the South Eastern Railway Company's steamer, *The Queen*, totally ignoring the presence of a U Boat, dashed to the rescue of a French steamer which had been torpedoed. He brought his ship alongside the sinking vessel and kept the two boats interlocked while 2,200 Belgian and French refugees jumped aboard. The task was accomplished in just 20 minutes and *The Queen* made for Folkestone, its decks crowded with a complement of passengers which was double the ordinary capacity.

As the submarine warfare becomes even more intensive plans are afoot to fight the threat. Two lightships are being placed two miles off Folkestone pierhead and ships going up and down the Channel will have to pass between. It will be known as the Folkestone Gap. There will also be a special patrol from Dover.

On February 17th the submarine base at Zeebrugge was bombed by 17 aircraft and floatplanes which flew from the Admiralty air station at Guston Road, Dover. The largest bomb weighed 100 lbs but it is believed that little damage was caused to the dock installations. At Dover Marine Parade a slipway into the sea has been built enabling the two seaplanes stationed there to be manhandled up and down the beach.

The other threat in the Channel comes from mines. Following the loss of the Ramsgate fishing smack *Our Tom* in which all hands were lost, it is now feared that more fishing vessels have been sunk and time after time skippers have returned with dire stories; in fact many of them have now said they prefer to face bullets than mines and have enlisted in the army.

Last week one man escaped death in an explosion but sadly lost his mind and has been removed to the Chartham Asylum. This week comes the news of the hairbreadth escape of one of the trawlers in a mine explosion in the middle of the night. Frank Kemp, the skipper of the *Rhodera*, a 25-ton craft, said he and his two mates were thrown around the deck and when they recovered a wonderful sight met their eyes. "The water was a phosphorescent glow and the sea was bubbling like boiling water. We began to haul the trawl aboard but it appeared to be unusually heavy and then, to add to the horrors of the night, the glow of the lamps on deck revealed that we had fished another mine. We cut the whole lot away and saw the gear and the fish and the mine sink to the bottom."

The fishing industry is now paralysed but the ferry companies are continuing to sail as usual. A spokesman in Dover said today that the Germans do not have sufficient submarines to implement their threat.

Two more great disasters at sea

1,400 die as the Lusitania is torpedoed

May 14th: The famous Cunard liner *Lusitania,* on her return journey from New York to Liverpool, was torpedoed without warning on May 7th and sank off the Irish coast with the loss of more than 1,000 lives, many of them women and children. It is believed that the great ship took just 20 minutes to disappear beneath the waves.

Several from Kent are among those feared to be drowned The *Lusitania* was carrying nearly 2,000 passengers and among the 500 who escaped was Mr Hugh Whitcombe of Dudbourne House,

Eardley Road, Sevenoaks. Some passengers got a glimpse of the submarine's conning tower and thought they saw the track of the torpedo. There was a loud explosion, the ship lurched forward and pieces of hull were thrown into the air. The lifeboats were launched and the ship quickly went down. Many people spent hours in the water.

Among those who drowned were 128 American citizens including Alfred Vanderbilt, the yachting millionaire. Germany claims an advertisement in New York last week had warned Americans not to sail but the State Department in Washington is now wondering what effect the disaster will have on American neutrality.

The *Lusitania* with her sister ship, the *Mauretania,* was one of the finest liners in the world and it was thought that her speed made her safe against submarine attack.

Princess Irene, minelayer, explodes: 273 killed

May 28th: There has been another disastrous explosion on the Medway resulting in the deaths of 273 officers and men. *The Princess Irene*, anchored just off Port Victoria Pier in Salt Pan Reach, blew up with such force that the ship, a converted passenger liner, was hurled into the air and the pier itself badly damaged. Those killed include the crew of officers and men and 76 dockyard workers who were actually on the vessel. There is just one survivor.

Full details of the explosion have been heavily censored but the *Chatham News* today wrote: "The force of the explosion was terrific. To many it seemed louder than the *Bulwark* explosion and that shook houses to their foundations. The sight was terrific in its grandeur — one who has seen Vesuvius in eruption likened it to that great spectacle for a moment as flames and smoke belched forth in great volume. Then the flames were no more but over the spot where *The Princess Irene* had been moored hung a dense

pall of white smoke. Not a vestige of the majestic liner was visible when it dispersed — only the wreckage.

Rumours abound as to the cause of the tragedy. Many believe it was the work again of enemy agents who had somehow placed a time bomb on board the vessel but, on this occasion, it was more likely to be an incorrectly primed mine for *The Princess Irene* was in service as a mine-layer and there were almost 500 mines on board.

The ship was built as a passenger liner for the Canadian Pacific line and only completed last year. She was immediately commandeered for military purposes and packed with her explosive cargo. When she blew up pieces of the ship were thrown far and wide. Part of the boiler fell on a passing coal vessel and flying metal damaged the Admiralty oil tanks at Grain. Sadly a nine-year-old girl, Ida Barton who was in the garden of her home at Grain was killed by a piece of metal plate which struck her on the head.

1915

Sinister Zeppelins rain death from the sky

Summer: Life in Kent will never be the same again for death has rained from the sky. On May 17th just after midnight a Zeppelin passed over Ramsgate and hovered menacingly over the town at a height of about 2,000 feet. It was attacked by an Avro but climbed out of reach, dropped 52 bombs and killed one man. It then flew out to sea where it was fired on by a guardship in the Downs. The airship loitered in the area of the North Goodwins until 3.15 am and went back to Belgium passing over British lines at Armentieres where again it came under attack. The Zeppelin then slipped away as mysteriously as it had arrived.

Chief Inspector Paine of Ramsgate police said he had heard the Zeppelin come from the direction of the county school. He went immediately to see what had happened and found Queen Street ablaze and the Bull & George Hotel completely wrecked. The dining room floor had collapsed and two floors had gone through to the cellar. The staircase was blown out and John Smith was lying in the cellar, alive but badly injured. He died later in hospital.

At an inquest which followed, the coroner said that the deceased was killed by an act of war, in the way the German nation appeared to think that war ought to be waged. The jury returned a verdict of wilful murder against the Kaiser.

The commanders of this evil machine were lucky to survive the attentions of the Avro which was piloted by Flight Sub-Lieutenant R.H.Muluck from Westgate. Armed with two incendiary bombs and two grenades he courageously attacked the Zeppelin but it climbed out of reach.

There is now news of more attacks from this sinister new flying machine. Thanet has been repeatedly attacked and last week (August 9th) Dover Harbour was bombed. On this occa-

The Bull & George Hotel, Ramsgate, wrecked by Zeppelin bombs

sion, however, the unfortunate German wandered into the hornet's nest; he was hit by massed anti-aircraft guns and crashed into the sea near Zeebrugge. On the same night Flight Sub-Lieutenant R.Lord took off from Westgate in a Sopwith to intercept another German naval airship but lost it in the darkness and was fatally injured while attempting to land in fog.

Westgate airfield is playing a useful role in air defence against Zeppelins. Land was requisitioned from Mutrix Farm in April and wooden hangars and huts hurriedly erected. It is now the temporary headquarters of A Flight of No 2 Squadron with Avro 504s, Curtiss JN3s and BE 2Cs.

Brides-in-bath murderer hanged at Maidstone

August 14th: *Scores of disgruntled national newspaper photographers have been sent back to London. They had invaded Maidstone to take pictures outside the prison following the execution of George Joseph Smith, described as one of the greatest criminals of the century. Sadly for the cameramen Maidstone is a wartime prohibited area and it is an offence to take pictures.*

Smith (who used the alias of Williams) murdered his wife Bessie Mundy of Herne Bay in a zinc bath on July 13th 1912 and then, in the next three years, married three more times using an alias on each occasion. Within months of each "wedding" he had persuaded his wife to make a will in his favour — drowning two more in their baths. A sensational trial at the Old Bailey lasted nine days.

He was executed at eight o'clock yesterday morning at Maidstone. The Press were excluded, there was no traditional tolling of the prison bell and no hoisting of the black flag over the gates, but the Brides-in-the-bath murderer has had his just reward..

Gillingham's formidable force of road sweepers.

Women leave home to work in the factories

July: The women of Kent have responded enthusiastically to an appeal by the Government for all women to sign on for war work in trade, industry, agriculture and armaments. In Maidstone, where there has been an acute shortage of labour due to voluntary enrolment, the girls are taking on skilled male jobs and even heavy labouring.

The war is affecting the town's industries in many ways. Drake and Fletcher's hop-spraying machines have been adapted to War Office specifications for use against German gas, Sharp's toffee factory is now carrying out fruit pulping on a large scale to make jam for the army, Tilling-Stevens has gone over to munitions and Cliffords are making hop-screening cloth for use in the trenches for gun emplacements.

Women are employed now in all these factories and are earning higher wages than ever before — a situation welcomed by Emmeline Pankhurst, leader of the suffrage movement who has said that women can be employed in almost any capacity of intellectual or physical work. Sadly those in the paper industry are being paid at pre-war levels and that is leading to an increase in trade-union membership in the machine mills, particularly at Tovil.

There has been some controversy in Kent over the need for women to work in agriculture. At a special meeting in Sevenoaks a Miss Cohen said there were two centres where the girls could be trained, at Swanley and at Wye College. She said a badge or armlet and uniform will be given to those who volunteer to work in the fields. Mr Dyson Laurie recommended that the females should learn how to plough and lead horses and should be paid no less than 3s a day.

July: One young lady in the news is 17-year-old Enid Blyton, a pupil at St Christopher's Girls School, Beckenham who has won a prize for literature and says she would like to write for a living. Enid was born in Dulwich on August 11th, 1897 and soon moved to Beckenham. She has been attending St Christopher's since 1907.

Vita Nicholson (nee Sackville-West), daughter of Lord and Lady Sackville who accompanied her parents on that emotional journey to Knole in 1910 (see page 80) has moved into Long Barn, Sevenoaks Weald with her husband Harold. The 15th-century house is dubiously claimed to be William Caxton's birthplace.

June 5th: *Zeppelin raiders yesterday flew down the Thames and Swale Estuaries and attacked Sittingbourne. There were no casualties and military sources believe the Huns mistook Sittingbourne for an important military centre. Unity Street (above) and the upper end of Park Street (left) bore most of the damage and other bombs dropped in Milton. Mrs Marjorie Dean, whose husband, Donald, is with the 8th Battalion Royal West Kents in France said: "I saw the flash because one of the bombs fell on what was Billy Stevens carrier's yard next door. I think the Germans were just getting rid of their bombs in preparation for the flight back across the Channel. Park Road, of course, is open land right down to the High Street. There is nothing there but meadows."*

Chislehurst Lads Leaving For The Front, July 10th 1915.

All over Kent meetings have been held under the auspices of the Joint Parliamentary Recruiting Committee emphasising that England's honour is at stake and appealing for more men to come forward. Here are the lads from Chislehurst who volunteered to do their duty on the Western front.

Glorious West Kents capture famous hill at Ypres

July: Britain's New Army, recruited under Kitchener's scheme has been proving itself in the great autumn offensive on the Western front. Among them are the 10 battalions drawn from the young men of Kent who have distinguished themselves at such places as Neuve Chapelle and Loos in Flanders where massive blows have been struck against the German line. Sadly, however, the British death toll exceeds that of any previous battle.

Details are now in about the gallant action of the 1st Queen's Own East Kent Regiment (The Buffs) and Royal West Kent Regiment in capturing a vital German position simply known as Hill 60. The hill, the spoil of a nearby railway cutting is on the right flank of the 30-mile front held by the British around the town of Ypres. 'C' Company of the 1st Battalion RWK's supported by 'B' Company and two Companies of the KOSB's, who formed a working party, were the only troops engaged in the taking of this famous hill. Five mines were detonated, 'C' company stormed the German garrison, occupied the enemy trenches and took the summit with only seven casualties.

This means that the glorious West Kents have still never lost a trench during the war and probably never will. The Germans, who call them "Godfools" for their bravery, were certainly caught with their trousers down in the storming of Hill 60. They were, of course, unaware of the fighting record of the West Kents which has been a distinguished one ever since it was raised in 1740.

The Buffs, too, have played their part in this offensive but have suffered terrible losses — 300 at the foot of Hill 60 and more than 450 officers and men lost in seven days at Neuve Chapelle. Among the dead is Corporal Cutter of the 6th Buffs whose action during a German attack on the Hohenzollern Redoubt was so brave that he has been recommended for a posthumous VC. With one leg blown off and wounds in both arms Corporal Cutter crawled forward to an outpost and for two hours directed his forces against heavy attack while in terrible pain. He died from his injuries.

Altogether it is estimated that 385 officers and 7,861 men have been killed or wounded in the Battle of Loos and among the officers reported missing is Second Lieutenant John Kipling, only son of the author Rudyard Kipling of Bateman's, Burwash. It is believed he was killed by a German shell.

Hero's welcome in Faversham for Captain Philip Neame

July 17th: Faversham today gave a hero's welcome to Philip Neame, a son of the town, a captain in the Royal Engineers and a remarkably courageous man. Captain Neame comes home with the Victoria Cross, the highest honour for gallantry, which has been awarded to him by the King following the hand-to-hand fighting in October last year in the village of Neuve Chapelle when he stoutly resisted German fire and grenades and rescued many wounded colleagues.

It was at Neuve Chapelle that the enemy drove a gap through the British line and the Indian soldiers holding the village were driven back by savage German artillery and machine gun fire. More than 500 soldiers were killed in this battle including 25 British officers. Captain Neame, aged 26, was one of the lucky ones.

Among those in the welcoming party at Faversham were his parents, Mr and Mrs Frederick Neame formerly of Macknade, the mayor and mace bearer. The guard of honour was provided by the 3rd West Lancs stationed locally.

The names of officers, NCOs and men who have answered the call to serve in the armed forces are now being published in most Kent newspapers each week. There are amendments giving the names of those killed or wounded and, in the newspapers of the larger towns, it makes up several columns. We understand these roles of honour will be a continuing feature throughout the war.

Victoria Cross for the boy from Herne

December: Sergeant Harry Wells from Herne, of the 2nd Royal Sussex, has been awarded the Victoria Cross. Sadly, this 27-year-old will never have the opportunity to wear it — he died leading his men towards the German lines near the French village of Le Rutoire.

Sergeant Wells was taking part in the first joint offensive launch by the French and British and his division had been ordered to make the opening assault at Loos in September. A vile gas cloud was put down in front of them and many British soldiers were killed, including the platoon officer of the 2nd Royal Sussex.

Sergeant Wells took command and led his men forward to within 15 yards of the German wire. Half the platoon were killed or wounded and the remainder were shaken but, with the utmost coolness and bravery, the Sergeant continued to lead them forward.

Finally, when very few were left he stood up and urged them forward once more, but while doing so he himself was killed.

His citation said he gave a magnificent display of courage and determination.

Sergeant Wells was born at Hole Cottage, Millbank, Herne and left school at the age of 12. He took a job as a farm labourer, lost two fingers in an accident and enlisted at the age of 16 with the Royal Sussex Regiment at Chichester.

After seven years with the colours he joined the police at Ashford but rejoined the army on the outbreak of war.

The last-known photograph of WG Grace.

Cricket's finest — WG Grace dies in his garden

October 24th: Dr William Gilbert Grace, the finest cricketer ever known and the game's greatest figurehead, is dead. He collapsed yesterday in the garden of his house, *Fairmont* at Mottingham from a stroke and died almost immediately. WG, or "The Champion" as he was affectionately known had not been well for some months but he continued to work diligently in his splendid garden and give faithful support for war charities. He was 67.

For a man so fearless and determined in the face of the most hostile bowling, Dr Grace was frightened by the war and the noise of the Zeppelin raids. The German press, always on the look out for propaganda, true or false, have claimed him as an air-raid victim. In this country his untimely death has temporarily replaced war news in newspaper headlines.

With his bushy grey beard and large frame WG was the most recognisable Englishman and dominated the first-class and Test game throughout its formative years. He scored 126 centuries and took 2,876 wickets — a target that future players will have difficulty in beating.

Dr Grace's last appearance on the cricket field was at Eltham and his final appearance in public was at a match at Catford Bridge on Whit Monday this year in aid of war charities when, to the delight of the spectators, he walked round the ground with a collection tin.

He was depressed by the fact that cricket was still being played while men were losing their lives in France and Belgium and recently wrote this letter to *The Sportsman:* "The fighting on the Continent is very severe and is likely to be prolonged. I think the time has arrived when the county season should be closed for it is not fitting at a time like this that able-bodied men should be playing and pleasure-seekers look on. First-class cricketers should set a good example and come to the help of their country without delay."

In a tribute to his friend, Eric Midwinter, a former Test cricketer has said: "He was forcibly shaken by the immediacy of the Great War...It involved reported atrocities just across the Channel and the need to succour victimised Belgians through charity matches. So WG's last duty on cricket's behalf is to bring the game to a halt."

Dr Grace will be buried at Elmer's End cemetery in Beckenham. He leaves behind more than £10,000 and a game which is in good shape thanks to his supreme mastery and commitment. The Champion will never be forgotten.

Kent's survivors pull out of Gallipolli

December 24th: Surviving soldiers from the Royal West Kent Regiment and the Kent Fortress Engineers have successfully taken part in the evacuation of the Gallipolli Peninsula, right under the noses of powerful Turkish forces. It was an epic escape. 90,000 men with 4,500 horses, 1,700 vehicles and 200 guns were lifted off the beaches and, although 30,000 beds had been prepared for expected casualties in Mediterranean hospitals, not a single life was lost.

The men are part of the ill-fated Gallipolli campaign which was abandoned after months of indecision and what David Lloyd George describes as the "mocking spectre of too late". He told the House of Commons: "Unless we

British troops land at Gallipolli, among them Royal West Kents and Kent Fortress Engineers. The scene shows the fleet in the Dardanelles.

quicken our movements damnation will fall upon the sacred cause for which so much gallant blood has flowed."

It has certainly flowed on the Gallipolli Peninsula and Kent is counting the cost in terms of sacrifice. A few weeks ago 127 soldiers of the 1/3 Kent Field Company Royal Engineers were drowned when their ship collided at night with another vessel in Mudros Bay. For security reasons both ships were sailing without lights. Among those lost is Captain D.R.Salomons, only son of the great scientist, David Salomons of Broomhill. He stayed aboard his sinking vessel helping as many men as possible to escape.

Canadians killed at Otterpool

October: There have been many more attacks from Zeppelin airships in the past few months. The monsters approach with a weird humming noise which sends shivers down the spine of those who hear them coming. The worst attack was on Folkestone in the early evening when a Zeppelin dropped its deadly cargo on the Canadian Camp at Otterpool, not far from Westenhanger. Fourteen artillery men were killed and three wounded.

Other Kent men have been fighting alongside Australian and New Zealand troops with outstanding heroism and hundreds have been frozen to death, waist deep in their trenches in what the survivors describe as their worst experience of the war so far. The most tragic week began on November 27th when torrential rain swept men and animals along the gullies and trenches, drowning at least 100. There followed two days of ferocious blizzards with driving snow when another hundred men died of exposure.

The evacuation order came on December 20th when men from Tonbridge were among the Royal Engineer Territorials who rigged up an unmanned "firing line" and arranged realistic explosions to convince the Turks that the British trenches were still manned. The Australians who suffered so heavily exploded a giant mine by remote control a few hours before leaving, killing hundreds of the enemy.

Winston Churchill, as First Lord, played a crucial part in the Gallipolli campaign when he agreed that the Royal Navy should try to get munitions to Russia's Black Sea ports by forcing the passage of the Dardanelles. The land troops were sent ahead as a back-up force. Dardanelles casualties are 25,000 dead, 76,000 wounded and 13,000 missing. Many are blaming Churchill for the disaster.

'If this be the last song you shall sing, sing well, for you may not sing another' — Poet Julian Grenfell who has died of his wounds in France.

January: One man has been killed during a German seaplane raid on Dover.

January 27th: Royal assent is given to the Military Service Bill. A few cabinet ministers have resigned in protest.

Thomas Keeler a 31-year-old single man from Hythe has asked for exemption from military service as he is the owner of 14 donkeys who "are very necessary on the sands in summertime".

February: The blackout which has been in force in East Kent towns for more than a year, has been blamed for causing the death of a Canadian soldier who fell down a basement on Marine Parade, Hythe. The coroner said the early closing of public houses encouraged fast drinking and he felt the army should rescind this rule. Hythe, apparently, has a reputation for being the darkest town in Britain!

February 23rd: Well-off families have been urged by the National Organising Committee for War Savings to shut up part of their homes, close down their greenhouses and have simpler meals in order to release servants for more useful purposes.

March 21st: A special town meeting held in Ramsgate is today demanding adequate protection from German air raids. The meeting follows the devastating seaplane attack on Ramsgate a few days ago.

March 28th: Ramsgate fishing vessel, *Irene*, has foundered off Dungeness. Henry Morrall is the only survivor.

May 8th: **British Summer Time — by which all clocks are advanced by one hour from Greenwich Mean Time — has been introduced under the daylight saving scheme. The originator of the idea was William Willett of Chislehurst, an MP who campaigned furiously for daylight saving, having thought of the idea during a canter on his horse over a Petts Wood Common in**

September: There have been many more aeroplane raids on Kent and great damage has been caused but, considering the number of bombs dropped, few casualties. A soldier of the 3rd Battalion East Surrey Regiment has been killed and a seaman on a drifter badly injured.

The first attack was on the night of May 19/20th when five raiders dropped bombs on St Peter's, Broadstairs, near the Whitfield Monument, the Electric Tramway Depot, Rumfields Waterworks, a farm at Bromstone, Sholden (by the Chequers Inn) and Snargate Street,

---

Dover. Here a public house was badly damaged and a soldier killed.

The second attack was on August 12th when a Roland Scout plane dropped high explosives on the airfield at Dover. Seven RNAS machines gave chase but the raider escaped.

The third attacker was an Albatross plane which dropped three bombs on the Duke of York's School. The lack of warning as to its approach led to great dissatisfaction among the flying services but there was thick haze at 10,000 feet. Eight RNAS and two RFC aircraft chased the invader but lost him in the clouds.

1907. At the time, in the early morning, he noticed how many shutters were closed and realised that this was a dreadful waste.

Willett's Bill, which he called 'The Waste of Daylight' was introduced the following year and defeated. Willett, a builder with his father's firm, and well-known for the elegantly designed homes he built in the Orpington area, died last year.

April 1st: Anti-aircraft gunners from Dartford have played a big part in bringing down a Zeppelin L15 which fell into the Thames Estuary. The gunners are to be presented with a gold medal from the people of the town.

April 25th: Eleven men have been killed in Dublin during a rebellion against British rule. Rebels proclaiming an "Irish Republic" have seized control of the post office and are currently under attack from British forces.

July 1st: The County Society today organised a service in which the battle-torn flags of *HMS Kent* were laid up in Canterbury Cathedral. Dean Wace took the service.

July 6th: David Lloyd George becomes Secretary of State for War in succession to Lord Kitchener who has been drowned.

August 11th: A number of automobile companies have amalgamated to form the East Kent Road Car Company. They are Thomas Tilling, the British Automobile Trading Company Ltd, Margate and District Motor Coaches Ltd, Wacher and Co Ltd and Ramsgate Motor Coaches.

September 29th: Medical scientists have discovered a procedure by which internal organs can be photographed. They are calling the invention the X-Ray.

October 12th: The price of bread in most Kent shops is now 10d. Bakers blame the rise on the soaring cost of flour. Bread is the staple diet of the poor.

October: Whitefriars Press has bought the printing works known as Messrs Bradbury, Agnew and Co in Medway Wharf Road, Tonbridge and extended them considerably. This means they now have the capacity to produce the popular satirical magazine *Punch* and more than two million Penguin books every year. Tonbridge is on the road to being the headquarters of the printing industry in Kent.

October 31st: British casualties for the last three months are around 40 per cent of total war casualties — 350,000 men.

November 24th: Sir Hiram Maxim, the great inventor, died today bringing a very full life to a close. Towards the end of his life he was asked about the lack of monuments in his memory particularly at Baldwyns Park. He said that the authorities had demonstrated their appreciation by building the largest, finest and best-equipped lunatic asylum in the world there!

November 28th: Since the Battle of the Somme opened in July, 500,000 Allies and 650,000 Germans have been killed.

December 7th: After three days of plotting and controversy inside the coalition government, The King has appointed David Lloyd George to succeed Herbert Asquith as Prime Minister.

New church in Kent: St Augustine's, Gillingham.

GREAT HITS OF 1916

Take Me Back To Poor

Old Blighty

If You Were The Only Girl

In The World

Airship commander killed while testing anti-Zeppelin plan

February 3rd: Wing Commander Usborne, CO of the airship base at Kingsnorth was killed yesterday when his BE2C aircraft which he was attempting to attach to an AO1 (airshiplane) suddenly turned over and crashed into the goods yard of Strood railway station. His colleague Lieutenant Commander de Courcey W.P. Ireland also died.

The pilots were bravely testing an ambitious anti-Zeppelin fighter scheme in which the plan was to attach the aircraft to the envelope of an airship so it could be released quickly in the event of a Zeppelin raid. The AO1 had reached a height of 4,000 feet when onlookers saw the BE separate. Ireland was thrown out immediately and Usborne died on impact.

Despite the tragedy the Admiralty say the experiments will continue

The Royal East Kent Yeomanry Mounted Rifles at Somerhill Park, Tonbridge.

Too few volunteers

January 6th: Kent has responded positively to the intensive recruiting campaign, but elsewhere there are not enough volunteers and so military conscription has been introduced. The debate in the House of Commons lasted two days before Parliament voted overwhelmingly that there are too many men shirking their duty. It is anticipated that all men between the ages of 18 and 41 will be called up and that includes those who are married.

February 16th: The Ontario Military Hospital, at Orpington, reputed to be the largest and most up to date military hospital in the world was opened today by the Right Honourable Andrew Bonar Law, Secretary of State for the Colonies. Comprising long and sturdy pre-fabricated huts, it is situated on the Boundary Estate just south of the town. The people of this little Kent town on the fringe of London are delighted by this most generous gift because the entire cost has been borne by the Province of Ontario and the cost of maintenance will be provided by the Dominion of Canada.

The new hospital took four months to complete and will provide accommodation for just over 1,000 patients. It was the Canadians themselves who chose Orpington because the water supply is reputed to be the best in England and the district is "charming and healthy."

Wounded soldiers will soon be receiving the best attention. The hospital has been built just yards from the main railway line from London to Dover so we anticipate that soldiers on leave trains will give a special wave and cheer to their comrades below the embankment.

A few years ago these girls were at school with the probability of a domestically orientated future ahead of them. Today they are munition workers, doing a man's job in one of the greatest engineering factories in the country — J and E Hall of Dartford. The company is proud of its considerable female workforce and of the fact that its Hallford lorries are transporting the munitions to the Channel ports in order to keep the troops supplied with weapons and provisions.

Liner torpedoed off Dover: 155 drowned

The largest vessel of the P and O line, the *Maloja*, sank off Dover on Sunday morning after being torpedoed. More than 150 people were drowned but many were rescued by the Dover Harbour tugs, *Lady Brassey* and *Lady Crundall* which steamed to the assistance of the stricken vessel.

It was at 11 .30 on Sunday morning that the inhabitants of Dover heard an enormous report like that of a heavy gun. Those in view of the sea saw the liner just to the west and a column of water and debris rising up in the air from her stern. Trawlers, destroyers and smaller boats followed the tugs to the vessel which was already listing badly and sinking.

Unfortunately the damage caused by the explosion flooded the engine room and the vessel gathered stern "way" which meant the lifeboats could not be lowered and the rescue boats could not go alongside to take people off. The *Maloja* continued to go down by the stern and list to the starboard until it lay completely on its side and slipped under the water. The drama was watched with increasing anxiety by those on shore.

The majority of people saved were those who jumped into the icy water. Many were taken out nearly dead and hurried to the hospital ships, the *St David* and *Dieppe* where everything was done to try and restore life. Those who were alive were kept on the hospitals ships, suppplied with warm garments and then conveyed to the Lord Warden Hotel by naval ambulances.

Children die on their way to Sunday School

March 22nd: Four children on their way to Sunday School in Ramsgate have been killed by a bomb dropped from a German seaplane during a devastating raid on East Kent. A further 10 people have lost their lives and 18 are badly injured.

The raid began early on Sunday afternoon when two seaplanes from the direction of Belgium, flying at a height of about 6,000 feet, dropped six bombs on Dover harbour. The aircraft then parted — the first heading for the town and the second flying towards Deal. People in their homes in Dover heard the explosions, went outside and were presented with the fearful sight of bombs raining down from the sky. Twenty four bombs were dropped on the town and seven people were killed.

Several minutes later a second pair of seaplanes appeared over Ramsgate and dropped their bombs before parting, one hotly pursued by a pilot of the Royal Navy Air Service. In this raid five were killed and 10 injured.

Eye witnesses say that it was the bombs which fell near St Luke's Church which brought tragedy to the little group of schoolchildren. A brother and sister were killed outright and two more expired a moment or two after being picked up. A passing motor car was hurled against a tree and the body of the driver thrown across the road onto the opposite footway. Nearby windows of neighbouring villas were completely shattered.

Shocking stories have been told in Ramsgate of the suffering of the children. One woman said her husband carried a little girl into their home. She was barely conscious and her arm was terribly injured. Inside her muff she carried a bible. Another spoke of a small boy lying in the road but struggling to get up. He said his stomach was hurting badly.

The pilot of the RNAS who chased one of the seaplanes is Flight Commander Bone. He took off from Westgate in an FE2b and followed the raider towards the Goodwins. After an action lasting 15 minutes in which he killed the observer he forced the seaplane into the minefields off the Goodwin Sands.

Flight Commander Bone was originally a midshipman but the air service appealed to him so strongly that he took up that branch of the service in which he has now so distinguished himself. He trained at Upavon, served at Yarmouth and was transferred to No 4 Wing of the Royal Navy Air Service at Dover last year.

The vicar of Ramsgate, the Rev E.L.A. Hertslet alluded to the air raid in his sermon on Sunday evening. "We are living in a time when the whole world is mentally and physically shaken to its foundations and in agonised convulsions, plunged into a maddening whirlpool of blood, fire and tears. Landmarks have been swept away. Frontiers have been obliterated. Values have been changed. And now little children have been brutally murdered."

A correspondent from Kingsgate has written to the *East Kent Times* suggesting that the country needs a Compensation MP. "No compensation is given by the Government for loss of life or injury from aircraft, even though such losses subsequently fall upon the poor and struggling classes. The Government is legally and morally responsible for all the damage sustained."

Other correspondents are urging the Government to appoint a Minister responsible for air defence. One suggested that the Thanet MP Norman Craig should get the job but others pointed out that Mr Craig is no longer active in the House, having thrown up a large and lucrative practice to undertake sea patrol work. There is no doubt that Lieutenant Craig, by patrolling the dangerous Channel waters, is setting a fine example to every man in his constituency.

Every local minister in Faversham helped the Archbishop of Canterbury with the burial service.

Faversham explosions kill 105 workers

April 3rd: In one of the biggest disasters in the history of the British explosives industry, almost 100 people were killed at Faversham yesterday when 200 tons of TNT blew up followed by a number of smaller explosions in a nitroglycerine washing plant some 150 yards away. Within minutes fires were raging throughout the factory complex and the dead and dying lay everywhere, many with their clothes still alight.

In conditions of immense danger, rescue workers and firemen rushed to the scene only to be killed and badly injured themselves as two further TNT stores blew up setting off new fires in the munitions factory where mines were also being made. The final death toll, believed to be 105, includes every member of the works fire brigade.

The full horrors of the afternoon — the first explosion occurred at 1.20 pm — are gradually unfolding. Faversham is headquarters of the Explosive Loading Company which is situated at Uplees Marshes and it was in these premises that someone noticed that sparks from a boiler house had set fire to some empty sacks piled against a shed used to store TNT and ammonium nitrate. The factory fire brigade with their manual engine were helped by staff who formed a bucket chain; in fact a force of more than 200 were involved in efforts to stop the fire spreading but, as it gained hold, the factory manager, Mr George Evetts ordered the attempt to be abandoned and the area cleared.

The shed blew up as they were leaving the site making a crater 40 yards across and 20 deep and setting fire to the entire complex. One witness, Mr George Goldfinch said he was running alongside a dyke towards the blazing shed when the explosion occurred. "The next thing I remember", he said, "was finding myself on the other side of the water with all my clothes blown off. I had broken my arm and I was partially deaf."

Mr Sidney Wilson, a volunteer firemen said: "We had a horse-drawn petrol engine but on this occasion we lashed it to the back of a Shepherd-Neame lorry and set off for Uplees. As we passed through Oare village a second explosion occurred and my only recollection is of seeing a fan of flame."

continued

continued

In fact it was not one explosion which Mr Wilson heard but three, simultaneously. The damage was so extensive that, of the five buildings which blew up, no trace is left.

Staff of the ELC showed great courage in trying to control the fire while explosives were removed and the 29 members of the three Faversham fire brigades remained all afternoon in the danger zone as explosions rattled around them. Nearby, fighting other blazes, were men of the Kent and Norwich Insurance brigades, units from the armed forces including the Kent Royal Garrison Artillery, engineers from the anti-aircraft battery at Oare and men from the West Lancashire Brigade.

It is a huge setback for the explosives' industry. Faversham's first gunpowder factory was established almost 300 years ago and there have been many disastrous explosions but nothing on this scale. The Cotton Powder (as it is known locally) occupies a 500-acre site and its range of products includes guncotton, distress signals, detonators, nitro-glycerine compounds and other munitions. Workers come from Faversham and the immediate area and also from Margate and Herne Bay.

Explosion victims buried in mass grave

April 6th: The funeral of the victims of the Great Explosion took place at Faversham Cemetery today. Forty people have been buried elsewhere but the rest were interred in a huge mass grave, hurriedly prepared in the cemetery at Love Lane. Joining the solemn procession from the Market House was Dr Alexander, the mayor and military guards of honour. The service was conducted by the Archbishop of Canterbury, Dr Randall Davidson.

It is now believed that the death toll is 116 but there is doubt even over that figure because of the mutilation of the bodies. So gruesome was the catastrophe that only half the victims could be definitely recorded by name.

Despite the fact that gunpowder explosions have occurred in Faversham before, the town was completely unprepared for a tragedy of this nature. There were only 10 beds in the Cottage Hospital in Stone Street in the town centre, usually enough for a small town of 10,000. Fortunately, two local mansions, The Mount, near Ospringe and Lees Court at Sheldwich are in use as military hospitals and there is an infirmary at the workhouse in Lower Road.

There have been many brave deeds and many medals and commendations will be earned by those who came to help. The importance of the fire-fighting work can be measured by the fact that there were another 3,000 tons of guncotton in store and if that had gone off it would have wiped out the complete Faversham complex and killed everyone on the site!

Preparing defences for the invasion —volunteers follow the instructions from officers of A Company dig trenches at Wrotham.

Kitchener — hero of the people — dies at sea

June 13th: More than 5,000 mourners crammed into Canterbury Cathedral today for a memorial service to Field Marshal Lord Kitchener who died at sea last week. The Secretary of State for War who lived at Broome Park, Barham, near Canterbury was travelling to Russia aboard the cruiser *HMS Hampshire* when it was struck by a German mine off the Orkneys. Few details are' available of the tragedy as there were no survivors.

The news of Lord Kitchener's death has been received in Kent with grief and dismay and memorial services have been hurriedly arranged in towns and villages across the county. This great soldier, who came to Broome Park to enjoy a life of retirement but instead responded to a call to rally the country in the face of the greatest crisis, remains a true hero of the people. He represented strength and stability at a time when it was so badly needed and was almost alone in seeing the need to prepare for a long conflict.

Herbert Kitchener was born in 1850 and came to public prominence in 1885 when he failed to relieve Gordon at Khartoum and became determined to avenge his death — an ambition achieved in 1898 at the Battle of Omdurman. From November 1900 he was the British Commander-in-Chief in the Boer War.

Following his appointment to the cabinet in 1914, Kitchener appealed vociferously for volunteers to come forward. His face was used on the the the recruiting posters pointing imperiously at the viewer with the statement 'Your Country Needs You'. The boys came forward in their thousands and, thanks to Kitchener, Britain has an army of considerable strength on the Western Front.

More than 80 members of Kitchener's army were in Canterbury Cathedral yesterday. All of them were wounded having been sent home from the fighting near Ypres. They occupied seats in the choir facing the large congregation which consisted of more than 3,000 officers of the King. The service was a moving one starting with the appropriate hymn *Abide With Me* and ending with *The Last Post* which reverberated through the imposing vaulted edifice like a bell.

There was also a memorial service in Barham church in which the employees of Broome Park Estate were present and also members of the Royal Flying Corps. The congregation here was reminded that Lord Kitchener was delighted with his mansion home on the Downs. He made the oak door himself, put the big knocker on with its curious figures and filled the great hall with treasures. He was designing the coat of arms on a panel when a messenger arrived with the news that he was required to join a delegation on a mission to Russia. He never returned.

Construction of airships (now known as Blimps) has been switched from Kingsnorth to Capel, near Dover and already the station has been subject to a seaplane raid in broad daylight. No damage was caused but there was damage to this Airship C21 during the deflating procedure!

Kent cricketer killed in action

September 4th: The county is in mourning again, this time for the Kent and England cricketer Kenneth Lotherington Hutchings who died yesterday after being hit by a shell in the fighting on the Western Front.

Hutchings, 34, was a soldier with the 4th battalion of the King's Liverpool Regiment. He will be remembered as a dashing batsman who made his debut for Kent aged 19 in 1902.

He played 163 matches for the county, hit 19 centuries and scored 7,977 runs. His highest score was 176. Born at Southborough in 1882, Kenneth Hutchings was a brilliant schoolboy cricketer at Tonbridge. He played seven times for England.

Sevenoaks hears gunfire from Battle of the Somme

July 2nd: Every morning just after dawn a loyal band of residents from Sevenoaks gathers around the fountain at the junction of the High Street and London Road to hear the buglers of the units stationed in the town sound *The Reveille*.

Yesterday, however, those waiting for the call, heard another noise — the sound of thunder rumbling somewhere in the East. It was quite loud and increasing in its intensity. It faded and then started again and they realised they were hearing, not thunder, but gunfire. It was the first day of the Somme campaign — the Anglo-French attempt to break through the German lines by means of a massive infantry assault.

In just over an hour, a quarter of a million shells were fired at German positions and so intense was the barrage that it could be heard on high ground even further away than Sevenoaks. This was the biggest British army ever sent into battle, 26 divisions on a 15-mile front and every man a volunteer. Among them were the boys from the Buffs and the Royal West Kents.

The artillery barrage was lifted at 7.30am and the British went over the top in waves. Each man carried 70 pounds of equipment including entrenching tools, two gas helmets, wire cutters, 220 rounds of ammunition, two sandbags, two Mills bombs, groundsheet, haversack, water bottle and field dressing.

A bloody month we will never forget...

August 1st: July 1916 has been one of the blackest months in the history of Kent. Hundreds of local lads have been mown down by German machine guns and shells in the Battle of The Somme, the bloodiest ever known — a battle for woods, copses, valleys and villages taken and lost, retaken and lost again. Still the carnage is not over.

The British infantry moved into the attack on July 1st and by the end of it there were 60,000 British casualties, 19,000 of them dead. On that day the 7th Battalion of the Queen's Own (Royal West Kents) lost a few men in the action at Montauban but they helped to capture the village. Two days later the 6th Battalion joined the fray at Ovillers and La Boiselle and of the 617 men who bravely started the day only 242 were alive at the end of it. The dead and the wounded with bursting entrails and torn limbs were littered around the trenches, still wearing the badge of the white horse.

The Buffs (East Kent Regiment) have also suffered crippling losses in the struggle for high ground — 400 casualties in the offensive at High Wood, more than 600 at Delville Wood and Pozières. The fight for Delville Wood began on July 15th and lasted 15 days with hand-to-hand fighting and ferocious artillery bombardments. One soldier who returned home wounded said: "On one occasion we moved forward through an orchard led in single file by the platoon officer. Smith, the Second Lieutenant got through but the next seven who followed were shot dead in a circle of a few yards. I was one of the lucky ones". The assault for a ridge at Pozières was renewed again and again with little ground gained on either side. The Buffs went down gallantly in No Man's Land — among 14, 691 killed on that ridge.

The poet, Siegfried Sassoon, born in Paddock Wood, "passed three badly mangled corpses lying in a communication trench". Then, at noon, closer to the front line he "passed 30 of our own laid out by the Mametz-Carnoy road, some side by side on their backs with bloody clotted fingers mingled as if they were handshaking in the companionship of death."

The RWKs and the Buffs have pushed forward, marching day and night in heat and dust. On the night of July 13/14th the 7th Battalion held Trench Wood against repeated German attacks and, on the 22nd, the 1st Battalion took and occupied some 40 yards of German trenches largely through the leadership of Lt Scott and the bravery of Private Butlin and Sergeant Taill. But their position was hopeless for there was an enemy machine-gun post nearby and in four hours of savagery the whole of the battalion's front line was killed or wounded.

On this night stretcher parties worked ceaselessly under artillery fire and when they could go no further Corporal Hatch crawled out and for hours on end moved the wounded into the cover of shell holes. Alone he carried back 50 wounded men and has been recommended for the VC. The battalion medical officer Captain Baines worked all night long and far into the next day under constant fire. Once when he had his fingers on a severed artery his trench was knocked in and although partly buried he maintained his hold.

When the battalion was withdrawn it was found that just 250 men could be mustered. Nearly two-thirds had gone.

The first of the wounded from the Battle of Somme began to arrive at Folkestone on July 4th. Convoys carried the men across Kent without cessation for about a fortnight and delivered them to whatever hospital had available beds. Many went to the Orchard Hospital, Dartford.

July2nd: The front line at Ovillers where the Buffs and the Royal West Kents fought so bravely.

July14th: Boys from the local battalions were among these troops sitting outside their dugouts at Bazentin-le-Petit.

Wounded, shell-shocked and gassed men who are too ill to be treated in the special centres and field hospitals around The Somme are coming home in droves. Many are without limbs and cannot return to the front. Sadly some men have been executed for desertion including 19-year-old John Bennett who panicked when he heard the "gas gong" and fled from his trench to the rear. When he returned he found seven colleagues had been killed and 46 wounded. He was arrested, charged and later shot for "misbehaviour before the enemy." Picture left shows some of the wounded arriving at Tonbridge station and, below, stretchers are carried into Fort Pitt Hospital, Rochester.

Silver cigar in the sky was a burning airship

September 10th: Thousands of people, gathered on rooftops and in the streets, looked at the sky in astonishment as a burning Zeppelin slowly fell out of the sky and crashed in countryside north of London. The airship was the first victim of a new incendiary bullet and it was fired by Lieutenant Leefe Robinson of the Royal Flying Corps who has already become a national hero.

The incident happened last week but those who witnessed it say it will make a lasting impression on them for the rest of their lives. So bright was the glow from the burning airship that it could be seen by those on the Downs as far away as Boxley and Stalisfield. One man said: "We couldn't tear our eyes away from the blazing hulk. It hung motionless in the sky like a big silver cigar before sinking nose-down and finally disappearing from view."

As the news of the Zeppelin's demise reached Folkestone and Ramsgate pandemonium broke out as people rushed out on the streets, singing, clapping and cheering. In the days that followed hundreds travelled by train to the scene of the crash.

The excitement of the crash is also accompanied by disgust that the 16-man crew of the Zeppelin should be given a military funeral with buglers of the Grenadier Guards sounding *The Last Post* in their honour. Townsfolk of East Kent are writing angry letters to their newspapers pointing out that Zeppelins have dropped scores of bombs on the county and killed many people.

Lt Leefe Robinson has been recommended for a VC, the first for an exploit on (or above) British soil.

With the Zeppelin attacks and the growing demands on the Royal Flying Corps, there is to be reorganisation among the Home Defence squadrons which will now be split into three flights and permanently detached to Class One Landing Grounds. Among those in Kent are Bekesbourne, Detling and Throwley — all assigned to No 50 Squadron.

The once-successful motor transport firm of London and South Coast Motor Service Ltd has been forced to close. It started life in 1902 as J.W.Cann of Folkestone and was based at Cheriton Road and Bouverie Road West. The company made several moves but, by the beginning of this year, it was no longer viable. Photograph shows employees and customers in happier days outside the Harbour Hotel.

1916

Germans blow up a heroine of the seas

October 26th: Two divisions of German destroyers (six boats each) made a daring simultaneous raid on both Dover and Dunkirk today, sank six drifters and a trawler, damaged three other ships, killed 45 officers and men and returned to Belgium unscathed.

One of the ships lost was *The Queen*, the South Eastern Railway Company's turbine steamer which had played such a crucial role in bringing Belgian refugees to Kent at the start of the war. The Germans, intent on striking a blow at the English transport service, attacked *The Queen* near the Varne Bank, then surrounded it and ordered the captain to stop. Officers and men from the German destroyers then boarded the ship and ordered the crew to take to the boats.

Bombs were placed on *The Queen* which was so damaged that after drifting beyond Dover it sank near the South Goodwins. Admiral Reginald Bacon, commander of the Dover Patrol said the enemy also sank *HMS Flirt*, a small torpedo destroyer and *HMS Nubian*, another destroyer. He also warned that the next time a strong raiding force ventures in the same waters they will pay dearly for their bravado.

Douglas Haig in his office on a train taking him to France.

Sir Phillip Sassoon, member for Hythe and private secretary to the Commander in Chief, Sir Douglas Haig. In 1914 he received a commission in the Royal East Kent Yeomanry.

No casualties as another gunpowder mill explodes

There has been yet another dramatic explosion in Kent but on this occasion, thankfully, no-one has been killed. The big bang occurred at Ramhurst Mill, Leigh — better known in the locality as the Powder Mills where gunpowder has been made and stored for many years.

It was on Sunday that the mill blew up with an explosion that was heard for miles around.

Houses in the neighbourhood lost their ceilings and windows, pieces of metal landed in Tonbridge and the following morning trees were festooned with rags and pieces of paper. Fortunately there were no workers in the mill at the time.

'To these I turn, in these I trust — Brother Lead and Sister Steel. To this blind power I make appeal I guard her beauty clean from rust' — This Kiss by Siegfried Sassoon

January 1st: William Waldorf Astor who converted Hever Castle into such a splendid house has been given a peerage following generous munificent gifts to war funds and British charities. Astor, of course, is also the owner of the *Pall Mall Gazette,* the *Pall Mall Budge*t and he founded the *Sunday Observer.*

January 11th: The Prime Minister, David Lloyd George and the Chancellor, Andrew Bonar Law have appealed for the entire nation to subscribe to the new War Loan. The issue is to finance the staggering cost of war now running at £5.7 million a day.

February 14th: The Royal Flying Corps' wireless testing park has moved from Joyce Green to a new airfield at Biggin Hill. The transfer of officers and men was completed yersterday, a canvas hangar has been established and a childrens' home has been commandeered for a Mess.

March 16th: A provisional government has taken over power in Russia. The monarchy fell today with little bloodshed as Czar Nicholas II signed the form of abdication on the Imperial train. It follows months of turmoil over the Czar's approval of the war which has resulted in enormous casualties.

March 24th: Three smacks from Ramsgate have been sunk by German submarines.

April 6th: American President Woodrow Wilson today signed the declaration of war which had been passed by his Congress, after a 17-hour debate, earlier in the week. In his speech to the House the President said the world must be made safe for democracy.

May 25th: A Zeppelin drops a bomb in St Leonard's churchyard, Hythe and kills the verger Daniel Lyth. The vicar who was standing near him later found a piece of shrapnel lodged in his pocket. There has also been a fatality in Ormonde Road and a stampede of horses in the Canadian camp at Otterpool near Lympne.On this day Folkestone was also bombed.

In tribute to the girls who work at the explosives factories in Faversham, local printers F.Austin and Sons have issued a postcard with the following poem:

The guns out there are roaring fast; the bullets fly like rain;
The aeroplanes are curvetting, they go and come again;
The bombs talk loud; the mines crash out; no trench their might withstands.
Who helped them all to do their job? The girls with yellow hands

The boys out there have hands of red; it's German blood and warm.
The Germans know what's coming when the English swarm —
Canadians and British and the men from Southern lands.
Who helped them all to do their job? The girls with yellow hands.

The boys are smiling though they rush against a barbed trench.
The girls are smiling though destruction hovers o'er their bench;
And when the soldiers sweep along through lines of shattered strands,
Who helped them all to do their job? The girls with yellow hands.

It should be explained that the yellow hands are caused by the nitric oxide present during the manufacture of TNT which often seeps through protective gloves.

June 7th: New offensive in Flanders. The British under General Haig capture territory held by the Germans south of Ypres.

June 13th: Twenty Gotha twin-engined bombers reach London in perfect weather and return to Belgium unscathed. They dropped 72 bombs which killed 162 and injured more than 400.

June 26th: The Royal Family have dropped their German titles. Saxe-Coburg-Gotha becomes Windsor and Battenberg becomes Mountbatten.

July 3rd: Lieutenant Bill Hicks, the schoolmaster who founded one of Kent's first scout troops, the 1st Sevenoaks, has died from his wounds in France. Only a few weeks ago Mr Hicks returned home on leave and was met at the fountain in Sevenoaks by his scouts who bore him shoulder high and carried him down the High Street. He was their hero and will always remain so.

July 5th: Additional wards have been added to Orpington Hospital by the Government of Ontario. Today the new wing was opened by the Rt Hon Walter Lond, Secretary of State for the Colonies.

July 17th: Winston Churchill is back in the Cabinet again — this time as Minister of Munitions.

July 27th: Loyal East Kent Yeomanry and Queen's Own Royal West Kent Yeomanry have been combined as the Kent Yeomanry.

July 28th: The Sheerness electric tramway has become the first tramway in Britain to be replaced by buses. The services, run by the Sheerness and District Electrical Power and Traction Company, has been unique in Britain for using German equipment which is no longer available. Standen's Sheppey fleets have taken over the route.

Sept 11th: More than 200,000 women are now working on the land.

September 30th: Russia's former Czar, Nicholas II and his family have been moved to Tobolsk in western Siberia to protect them from the Bolsheviks whose leader is Vladimir Lenin.

September 30th: 56 Squadron, back in France after a few weeks defending the Kent coast, has claimed its 200th victim and celebrated accordingly. Major General Trenchard, Commander-in-Chief of the RFC has sent a telegram of congratulations.

October 19/20th: Four German airships, out of 17, have been lost in the sea following terrific gales encountered at 16,000 feet. One of the airships dropped bombs near Maidstone and Leeds.

November 7th: Russia's Bolsheviks overthrew the provisional government in Petrograd today in a sudden coup bringing Vladimir Lenin and Leon Trotsky into power.

December 3rd: Britain refuses to recognise the Bolshevik regime in Russia.

December: Among the many Russians to flee the country when the monarchy collapsed early this year was Prince Belosselsky, an aristocrat and colonel in the Czar's army. The Prince has now made his home in exile in Tonbridge and the townsfolk are making him most welcome. The Prince is a fine horseman and plays polo. He also enjoys a drink in the Rose and Crown in the High Street.

An attempt by the crew of an armed trawler to salvage a Gotha which was brought down in the sea not far from Folkestone Harbour, has failed The bomber was fitted with a time fuse which one of the crew set off just a few minutes before he was rescued.

GREAT HITS OF 1917

Goodbye-ee
For me and my Gal

Railway abandoned but work on secret port continues

February: Work has been abandoned on the construction of the East Kent Light Railway which was planned to serve the coal mines but an army of men are busy on another project at Richborough, the former Roman town, which lies near the coast between Sandwich and Ramsgate.

The men are deepening the River Stour in order to build a canal, reclaim land and fit up a great wharf for sending material to France and men to the front. Full details about the mystery port are strictly classified but it is believed it will be used for assembling the enormous consignments of shells which are so desperately needed by our boys in France. Meanwhile soldiers are moving into camps on both sides of the marshes.

The East Kent Light Railway Company had hoped to link the collieries with the main line route and the new port at Richborough with extensions eventually to Canterbury, Deal and Birchington. However, the Company has opened one coal line with a terminus at Shepherdswell. It has been built to the standard gauge of 4 ft 8.5 inches and the first passengers travelled on it a few weeks ago.

March: A light railway and station has been built for the hundreds of gunpowder and munition workers who daily travel from Faversham to the site of the factories on the mouth of the Swale. The station is called Davington and is sited a little north of the town centre. It has come as a blessing to those who walk or cycle from their homes to the explosives factories.

Kent battalion's great role in the battle of Gaza

April 29th: The 2/4th battalion of the Royal West Kents have played a major role in the two great battles of Gaza. On March 26th, as part of General Sir Archibald Murray's army advancing towards Jerusalem, the battalion had to battle through treacherous quicksands with a special force detailed to make a demonstration to distract the Turks along the coast on the extreme left of the attack. There was a dense sea fog and much confusion but Murray's troops inflicted heavy losses on the enemy.

In the second campaign which ended yesterday (April 28th) the 2/4th took a strenuous part in the fighting for a hill known as Samson Ridge. The objective was taken and there were many courageous feats but Gaza remains unconquered and the British have withdrawn. Many Kent men are among the 6,000 British soldiers to die in the desert campaign. The Turks have lost 2,000. There are now rumours of General Murray being relieved of his command and General Sir Edward Allenby taking over.

The Kent Fortress Company of the Royal Engineers who fought so bravely at the Dardanelles are also in Gaza on the borders of Jersusalem but, as yet, they have been unable to break into the city.

Gotha bomber — a name that strikes terror in Kent

June 2nd: The Germans have introduced a new type of warfare — the Gotha bomber. This enormous aircraft is powered by two Mercedes engines, has a wing span of nearly 78 feet and can carry a 300 pound bomb load. Last Friday evening 23 Gothas took off from two airfields in Belgium but, because of low cloud, only two reached England. They dropped their bombs on the Folkestone area and returned. One of the bombs fell on the military camp at Shorncliffe and 16 Canadian soldiers were killed. The others caused an even greater death toll in the town centre. See full story over page.

As far as these British and Canadian officers are concerned the real war is in Europe, and especially on the Western Front where they will soon be fighting. At the moment, however, the men are relaxing in the lounge of the Shakespeare Hut in Shorncliffe Military Camp unaware of the new terror in the sky — the Gotha bomber.

Dover shelled by destroyers — but the plan backfires!

April 22nd: An attempt last night by German destroyers to shell Dover has backfired, very badly. About 100 shells were haphazardly fired and fell mostly in rural areas with no casualties. But as the Germans withdrew, Commander Evans of the Dover Patrol chased the raiders with his own destroyer *Broke* and another named *Swift*. Today the Commander and his gallant crew are the heroes of England.

The Dover destroyers attacked the enemy with torpedoes — and then by ramming. Two German ships immediately sank and three more were seriously damaged. Commander Evans ordered his men onto the damaged ships with cutlasses and, after hand to hand fighting, returned to Dover with 105 prisoners. He was met by hundreds of grateful people at the harbour. Fifty were killed in the skirmish, including 28 German sailors.

The enemy destroyers have returned many times to shell the Kent coast. Margate and Broadstairs were their first targets and then Ramsgate on several occasions. With the plans going so badly wrong at Dover it is unlikely they will attempt this method of attack again.

Meanwhile the Dover Patrol continues to protect the vital military lines of communication between England and France. The Dover Patrol regulates all the sea traffic and provides a convoy across the Straits.

Commander Evans, the famous Antarctic explorer, was the last man to see Scott alive in 1913.

Daylight raid by Gotha bombers deals death and destruction on Folkestone

June 2nd: Folkestone is sorrowing under the greatest and direst tragedy experienced in the history of the town. On Friday evening (May 25th) it was savagely attacked by a fleet of German Gotha bombers dealing out death and destruction in nearly every quarter of the town. It is believed that more than 70 have been killed, including 16 soldiers at Shorncliffe.

No less than 17 of these machines had flown almost to London and then swung around to return home. They followed the main line to Folkestone and there carried out the first big daylight raid of the war, dropping 51 bombs on the borough. One fell in Tontine Street which was crowded with people engaged in shopping.

There is now strong feeling in the town on the question of local defence against air raids and there is also indignation with regard to aliens of enemy origin. The mayor has opened a relief fund to which Sir Philip Sassoon MP has donated £100.

The *Folkestone Hythe Sandgate and Cheriton Herald* reported the incident in today's newspaper. "It was at about a quarter past six when the sounds which were the prelude to the bombardment were first heard in Folkestone. It was an exquisite Spring evening, calm and quiet, and ten minutes before the full fury of the bombardment was experienced there was not the slightest reason for anticipating the ghastly catastrophe which converted the glory of a perfect May evening into sombre tragedy.

"The people of Folkestone are used to the sound of guns in the distance but on this occasion the detonations grew louder and more insistent. As far as the borough was concerned the raid lasted no longer than 10 minutes but the havoc caused was appalling. It was in Tontine Street that the greatest loss of life occurred. This is a big shopping centre especially for people of the industrial classes and the streets were crowded with women and children making their purchases for the weekend. Hence the fact that out of the 72 persons killed all but 13 belonged to the female sex.

"A bomb dropped on the pavement outside Messrs Stokes Bros greengrocer's stores demolished the entire premises and other shops in the vicinity. Mr W.H.Stokes was killed by the fall of the roof and the staff, nearly all women and girls, were killed on the spot. In the vicinity, women and infants in perambulators were dead or dying and others terribly maimed.

"In other parts of the town shops were reduced to ruin but the loss of life was nowhere near so great. The work of removing the dead and conveying the injured to hospital

---

Bombarded by a fleet of aeroplanes

Greatest Calamity in Town's History

APPALLING DEATH TOLL

Seventy-Two Victims — Many Others Injured

HEARTRENDING SCENES AND INCIDENTS

The Town in Mourning

Questions of Aliens and Defence

BIG INDIGNATION MEETING

Some of the headlines in the Folkestone Hythe Sandgate and Cheriton Herald.

---

was expeditiously carried out by the local ambulance workers and Red Cross contingent. The Canadian Army Medical Corps, the fire brigade and special constables also gave valuable help."

The inquest on the victims was opened at Folkestone Town Hall on Saturday followed by a public meeting at the Hippodrome on Monday in connection with the alien question. It was proposed that "the residents of Folkestone call upon the Prime Minister the Rt Hon David Lloyd George to order immediately the removal from the district and internment of all aliens of enemy origin."

Messages of sympathy have been received from the King and Queen, from Queen Alexandra, from the Lord Mayor of London and from the Bishop of Southwark. A relief fund has been opened by the mayor with big donations from Sir Philip Sassoon, the Earl of Radnor and Mr J. Sainsbury.

There will be a memorial service in place of a public funeral at the parish church on Saturday when the Archbishop of Canterbury will give the address.

June 8th 1917: *Gravediggers in Folkestone cemetery are preparing for the burial of the children killed in the raid last week.*

Aces of 56 Squadron are told to defend Kent

June 14th: Folkestonians, like other vulnerable residents of east Kent, have reacted violently at the inability of anti-aircraft gunners or the pilots of the Royal Flying Corps to deal effectively with the speedy Gothas. They are also incensed by the absence of air-raid warnings and have sent a deputation to London to meet Field Marshal Lord French, Commander-in-Chief of the Home Forces, on the subject of defence against attacks from both aeroplanes and airships.

The deputation, which included the mayors of both Folkestone and Hythe, Sir Stephen Penfold and Cr W.R. Corbay, were told by Lord French that it was not possible to stop the bombers coming but measures were being taken to make any future raid a very risky operation, despite the great height at which they flew.

These measures, it is believed, include the recall of the already-legendary 56 Squadron from France, the introduction of searchlights and sound locators and more accurate barrage fire and the formation of an additional squadron, No 141, to be based at Biggin Hill — a new airstrip 600 feet high on the North Downs and just 17 miles south of London Bridge.

The recall of 56 Squadron is particularly satisfying. The average age of the young pilots is just 21 and the average period of life expectancy on the Western Front is just 11 days. They will be pleased to be based at Bekesbourne, the large sloping field just four miles south of Canterbury from where they can lie in wait for the Gothas of Kagohl 3.

One pilot who is making quite a reputation for himself is Captain Jimmy McCudden of Gillingham who is currently a fighting instructor with the 6th Training Wing at Maidstone. He has arranged for modifications to be made to his Sopwith 'Pup' which includes the mounting of a Lewis gun on the upper wing. He has also visited the Vickers factories to try out some of the newly designed machines. Among his favourite is the Vickers F.B.16D which has a speed well ahead of any contemporary fighter.

Folkestonians will be reassured by the measures being taken on their behalf.

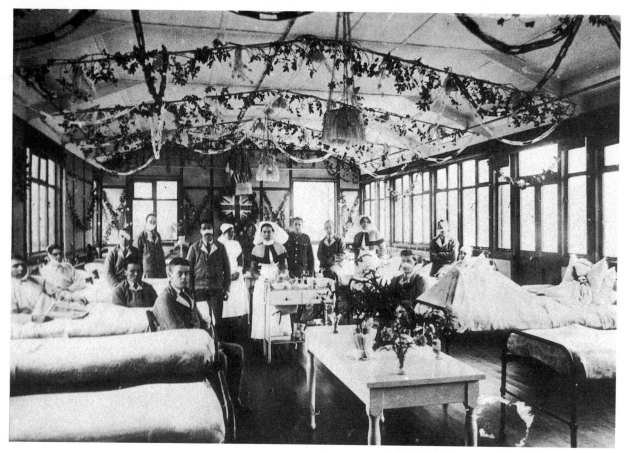

Christmas 1917 on Ward 10 of The Queen's Hospital, "Frognal", Sidcup.

Plastic surgery unit opens in new Sidcup Hospital

July 26th: A collection of pre-fabricated huts, built in the grounds of Frognal House, Sidcup, has been opened as a hospital by the Home Secretary, General Sir Francis Lloyd. Under the leadership of Sir Harold Gillies, the Queen's Hospital Frognal — as it will be known — will specialise in disfigured war casualties. Thousands of soldiers are returning from the front badly burned with horrific facial injuries and they will be treated by the surgeons in the special plastic surgery unit which is the first of its type in the country.

Large sums of money have been raised by the Red Cross, St John Ambulance and other charities and a recreation hall, cinema and canteen have been built with money given in response to an *Evening Standard* appeal. There are 560 beds in Queen's Hospital.

Frognal is the oldest house in Sidcup, parts of it dating back to 1200. It was rebuilt in 1670 and again in the 18th century. It has now been taken over by the War Office and becomes a residence for staff of Queen's Hospital.

Dartford's entire tram fleet destroyed by fire

August 10th: The tram shed and the entire fleet belonging to the Dartford Tram Company were destroyed by fire in the early hours of last Tuesday morning. The Fire Brigade arrived within four minutes of a call being made but there was little they could do to save the building or its contents. The whole place with 13 trams inside was a blazing mass and the neighbourhood brightly illuminated. The roof crashed in shortly after their arrival and, by the time they left, all that remained were three tottering walls, twisted and distorted metal work and sundry wheels and axles.

Many superstitious people believe that 13 is an unlucky number and the Dartford Company should have acquired at least one more tram. Others point out that the cars were totally overtaxed in an endeavour to cope with the Bank Holiday traffic and may have overheated.

The mangled wreck of tramcar number 20 at the foot of Crabble Hill.

Eleven killed as tramcar overturns on Crabble Hill

August 20th: Eleven people were killed and more than 50 injured yesterday when tramcar number 20, proceeding from Dover to River, ran away down the steep hill leading to Crabble, collided with the walls of Crabble Mills and overturned.

The car was crowded with passengers, undoubtedly considerably over the complement, and very few escaped without some injury. Ten were killed or died immediately after the accident, one died a few days later and many are in hospital with terrible internal wounds.

It appears that the car, having reached the top of the hill where Crabble Road meets the London Road, did not stop due, it is said, to its back brakes being partly on and preventing the front brakes being applied. The car at once gathered pace and took the curve at such a speed that those in the car were thrown about in all directions.

The driver, realising that he stood no chance of escaping death, jumped off. Two brave attempts to stop the car were made by a trooper gunner and a naval pensioner. Neither were successful. At the bottom of the one in 10½ gradient the car struck the wall of the Crabble Paper Mill and overturned. The scene was terrible and those who escaped serious injury were those who had jumped off.

The tram system began in Dover in 1897 and the extension to River was introduced in 1905. It is believed that the tramcar is repairable and will possibly now run on the more sedate Buckland-Pier service.

Bogged down in the mud of Flanders

August 4th: Will the rain ever stop? Between July 29th and August 3rd an incessant tropical downpour flooded many areas of east Kent. At one time it rained for 54 hours non-stop and Canterbury has recorded 10 inches. Detling, Chilham and Bicknor have been cut off by the torrents.

On the Western Front where the Third Battle of Ypres has just begun there is a new hazard facing the soldiers — mud. Those who have returned say the quagmire is worse than the German machine gunners.

Field Marshal Haig is talking of successful operations and of the capture of a series of strong points but the lads say the ground gained is a mere few hundred yards. The launching of the latest offensive has been accompanied by the firing of four million rounds from 3,000 British guns. The bombardment, accompanied by treble the average rainfall, has wrecked the network of streams and dykes which make up the Flanders drainage system.

1917

More raids on Ramsgate: Gotha bombers brought down

August 23rd: The townspeople of Ramsgate know more about this terrible war than many other communities in Kent. On June 17th two Zeppelins paid a clandestine visit to the town, dropped their bombs on an ammunition store, killed three, injured 16 and escaped before the defences could be organised. Yesterday it was not an airship but a Gotha which harrassed the Kent coast all the way from Margate to Dover and killed 12 people in a series of bombing attacks, paying particular attention to the military hospital at Ramsgate.

The June attack was intended for Dover but the airship crew made a geographical error and bombed instead the ammunition store at Ramsgate's fish market. The explosion wrecked 700 homes and shattered a further 10,000 windows. Personnel from Ramsgate Naval base were the first on the scene followed by the town fire brigade with its gleaming new engines which had just been donated by Councillor Janet Stancomb-Wills. As the fire caught hold the intense heat set off shells, ammunition and mines. Further assistance was forthcoming from Margate and Broadstairs brigades.

The defences were far more successful yesterday. Five naval machines from Manston, three from Eastchurch, six from Walmer and two from Dover attacked the raiders over Thanet and then pursued them to Dover. Two Gothas were brought down — one by anti-aircraft fire and the other by Flight Sub-Lieutenant J.Drake of 46 Squadron in a Sopwith Pup.

There have now been almost 100 separate raids in the Ramsgate area and the townspeople owe a debt of gratitude to the gunners, the pilots of the Royal Flying Corps and the fire service for their skill in dealing with the enemy. Chief Officer A Johnson of the Ramsgate Fire Brigade has been particularly courageous.

Gillingham's famous pilot, Major Jimmy McCudden is back in France as a flight commander with 56 Squadron. He is seen here in his SE5a which has a Lewis gun installation on the top wings and a Vickers gun with telescopic sights mounted on the left side of the fuselage. The pilot sits in a warm and comfortable cockpit well aft of the wings and enjoys an excellent all-round view.

136 naval ratings die in night raid on Chatham

September 4th: Once again a defenceless Kent town has suffered disastrously from a raid by Gotha bombers. Just before midnight last night four of these monsters took off from an airfield near Ghent, each with a 300 pound bomb load, intent on causing as much destruction as possible. They succeeded. Damage was caused at Margate and Sheerness and, at Chatham, a bomb fell on the barracks, killed 136 naval ratings and injured many more. The Gothas then returned to Belgium without opposition.

The full horror of the night is beginning to unfold. The bombers crossed the Channel when the home defences had organised a practice alert to test night defences and many of the gun crews were unaware of the real situation. No night fighters were available, the anti-aircraft guns were badly sited and the searchlights completely missed their targets. In fact so successful was the raid that there is real fear they will now return again and again.

It was at 10.30 pm that Margate was attacked with little damage and no loss of life. The four Gothas — one had turned back with engine trouble — altered course for the naval town of Sheerness and several more bombs were unloaded. Soon after 11 pm they were heard over Chatham and the first bomb fell on the naval barracks with horrifying results. More bombs fell — on the inner Lines, on Trinity School, on the burial ground and the High Street. Damage was vast but the loss of life was confined to those unfortunate ratings in the barracks.

The rescue squads were quickly on the scene and in the moonlight carried bodies into a room which had been converted into a makeshift mortuary. The seriously wounded were taken to the hospital.

September: The line of tents strung out on the Common at Tunbridge Wells is proof indeed that the Royal Spa town has become the headquarters of one of the new armies. Soldiers from all parts of the country are drafted to Tunbridge Wells ready to be transported to the battle front where the Third Battle of Ypres is well under way. Empty houses have become billets and some of the great homes have been requisitioned under the Defence of the Realm Act. The transformation of Tunbridge Wells into a military centre has meant that streets have had to be darkened at night, businesses closed and evening church services curtailed. In fact some older professional men have claimed they have nothing to do and are bored. Not so with the younger people, many of whom are in France or special constables or members of the Civil Guard. One Zeppelin airship has managed to wander inland as far as Tunbridge Wells and drop three bombs on Calverley Park where hundreds of soldiers are encamped. Fortunately no-one was injured but the blast broke all the windows in the vicinity.

December 1st: Gordon Bell, a Royal Flying Corps test pilot with Vickers, yesterday flew a prototype twin-engined bomber from Joyce Green airfield. It was so successful that the Crayford-based aircraft manufacturer hopes the bomber will be operational within a few months.

Although the aircraft is an FB 27 (Fighter Biplane 27) the production staff refer to it as the Vickers Vimy. The prototype was achieved by utilising designs produced in 1915 by Rex Pierson who worked in the drawing office.

Vickers will now test various types of engine, including the Rolls Royce, before a decision is made about which to use.

Coal for the poor: meat for the wealthy

October 20th: With another wartime winter approaching there is growing concern in Kent about the widespread shortage of domestic fuel despite the fact that the Government has taken control of the coal industry and set up regional coal control committees.

Last week 200 tons of coal were stored in the Tithe Barn (the Archbishop's stables) at Maidstone for sale to the poor when the need arises. This will be organised by the local coal committee who will also fix retail prices with the coal merchants in the area.

The poor may get their coal but there is great controversy in Maidstone and other towns in Kent about the activity of grocers and butchers who are delivering to wealthy customers while their shops remain closed to others. Food Control Committees have been told to stamp out this practice.

Other consumer news concerns the "indigestibility" of "war bread" and the long, long queues outside the few shops which are open. This, of course, is an ever present feature of wartime life in the county and the public will just have to remain patient. Kent MPs are to raise questions in the House following revelations that the war is now costing the UK some £7 million a day.

Kent's Charlie Blythe is killed at Passchendaele

November 9th: The whole of Kent is mourning the news that the county's greatest left arm spin bowler, Sergeant Colin Blythe has been killed in action on the Western front. A member of the Kent Fortress Engineers, Blythe died yesterday in the fighting at Passchendaele after being hit by a shell.

Colin, better known among his team-mates and all Kent supporters as Charlie, was one of the first professional cricketers to join up during Kitchener's recruiting campaign. While Kent was still playing first class matches in 1914 he went to France as a volunteer showing that he was prepared to fight for England with the loyalty he had given to his county on the cricket field.

Charlie Blythe lived in Tonbridge and was first seen in the nets at Rectory Field, Blackheath by senior Kent cricketers who were impressed with his gentle easy run up, the beautiful full swing of his arm and the deceptive flight. He made his debut against Yorkshire, took a wicket with his first delivery and never looked back.

The hero of Kent, who was in three championship-winning sides, took 2,509 wickets at an average of 16.80 and 10 wickets in a match on 56 occasions. He even topped the first-class bowling averages in 1914 — the season he joined up!

Of course Charlie Blythe is not the only Kent man to be killed at Passchendaele. Since the start of the offensive on the last day of July, Haig's forces have gained four and a half miles of ground losing 62,000 killed in the procedure. A further 164,000 have been wounded.

A few weeks ago Charlie Blythe said that when the war finally ends he intended to retire from county cricket. He then announced that he had been appointed cricket coach at Eton.

Canterbury rector arrests bomber crew

December 7th: A Canterbury Red Cross official was held at gunpoint yesterday by a German aviator while his comrade set fire to their Gotha bomber which had just crashed. It came down in the marshes adjacent to Broad Oak Road, injuring two of the crew who were eventually taken into custody by the Rev Philip Somerville, acting in his capacity as a special constable. Before the arrest, however, a most dramatic scene unfolded.

The Gotha of Bogohl 3 was on a raid of the area when it was hit by anti-aircraft fire and subsequently crash-landed in a field after just missing a mill and several houses. First on the scene was Mr J.B. Wilford of Mandeville Road, Canterbury, an orderly in the Red Cross. He noticed that two of the three German crew were injured and offered to render first aid. One of them promptly produced a revolver and held Mr Wilford at gunpoint while his comrade fired the aircraft. He is almost certainly the first man to face a German at gunpoint while on English soil.

The Gotha, now used extensively for aeroplane raids on England.

Mr Wilford was joined by the Rev Somerville, Rector of St Stephen's Church and another special, Mr G.W.Haimes from Sturry who said: "The plane was alight when we arrived. The Germans were not hostile and one was able to understand some English. They surrendered their equipment and arms to the Rev Somerville without protest."

The Rector said when he arrived on the scene the men were standing by the wrecked aircraft which was in flames with machine gun cartridges exploding right and left. "They asked me in broken English for a policeman to whom they could surrender and I assured them I was a special constable. An ambulance waggon conveyed the men to Canterbury police station and the two who were injured were then taken to hospital where they were well treated and most profuse in their thanks to the hospital authorities for the attention they received."

During the day the burnt-out Gotha was inspected by thousands of people who flocked to Broad Oak. The Red Cross took full advantage of the situation and made a collection; £32 was realised.

Knockholt major wins VC as Jerusalem falls

December 9th: The announcement in Maidstone today that Jerusalem had surrendered to General Allenby has been greeted with great jubilation. The Kent Fortress Company of the Royal Engineers, part of Allenby's Empire forces, were among the first units into the city. They advanced from Bethlehem while London infantry and yeomanry completed the encirclement.

The fall of Jerusalem marked the climax of a bloody offensive against the Turks which began last October. For the first time since the war church bells are ringing in Kent and the Jewish community are talking of the landmark "as glorious as any in the history of mankind."

One man who lost his life in Palestine in heroic action was Major Alexander Maline Lafone of Court Lodge, Knockholt, near Sevenoaks, an officer in the Middlesex Yeomanry. He has now been awarded the Victoria Cross and the full story of his courage is beginning to emerge.

Major Lafone held his position for over seven hours against superior forces and consistently drove the enemy back on every occasion the cavalry charged his flank. In one charge the Turks left 15 casualties within a few yards of his trench and one man who reached the trench was bayoneted by the Major himself.

When all his men with the exception of three had been hit and the trench was so full of wounded that it was difficult to move and fire, he ordered those who could move to retreat and from his own position maintained a most heroic resistance. When finally surrounded and charged by the enemy Major Lafone stepped into the open and continued to fight until he was mortally wounded.

The Victoria Cross will be presented to Major Lafone's parents by the King.

Old Hop Kilns are being used in a new village industry in mid-Kent. A vegetable drying factory has been organised by the Ministry of Food where women have been taught to dry all sorts of vegetables in case of food shortages during the war. Nothing wasted — the piles of vegetable peelings are used for pig swill.

German submarines will enter the light barrage at their peril

November: At last a bold but effective measure may have been found to defeat the German submarines in the Channel which have been causing so much havoc. Special ships (similar to lightships) have been placed in a long line across the Channel from Folkestone to Cape Griz-Nez and another line seven miles westward. Within this oblong drifters and destroyers will maintain a ceaseless patrol.

It is a simple and quite courageous plan. The ships are designed to outride the heaviest gale at anchor and each carries a searchlight, so powerful that no submarine could possibly slip into the oblong without being seen.

There will be other searchlights from the shore at Folkestone and Cape Griz-Nez and a million candle-power flares will burn on trawlers within the area. This means there will be continuous illumination of the Channel — almost as if it were daylight.

If a raider is seen, the patrolling ships will either drop depth charges or drive it into the mine fields.

The Admiralty believes the Light Barrage, as it is being called, will be more effective than the steel net or the Folkestone Gate which consisted of just two lightships.

'They shall not grow old as we who are left grow old. Age shall not weary them or the years condemn' — Lawrence Binyon.

January 2nd: Lord Rothermere has been appointed head of the Air Council.

January 8th: More trees are to be planted in Kent under a state-sponsored forestry scheme to ensure that Britain in the future will have sufficient home timber for military and commercial needs. Altogether, two million acres in England will be planted.

January 22nd: Government orders restaurants and all eating houses not to serve meat on two days each week. The food shortage is now acute.

February 8th: The Representation of the People Act receives Royal Assent giving the vote to married women over 30.

March 9th: New Military Service Bill has raised the maximum conscription age to 30.

March 20th: Coal, gas and electricity have been rationed. Theatres have been told to close at 10.30 pm.

March 25th: No details have been given but all traffic to the East Kent coast has been suspended. It is assumed that a big raid is being planned.

Vita Sackville-West, daughter of Lord and Lady Sackville of Knole, Sevenoaks, is enjoying a spring holiday in Cornwall accompanied only by her childhood friend, Violet Keppel. Vita's husband Harold Nicholson has told friends that he is rather distressed at his wife's "tremendous friendship with V.K" and says she is trying to destroy their love and home life by turning it constantly into ridicule.

April 22nd: Manfred von Richthofen, known as the 'Red Baron' and Germany's most feared pilot, has been shot down in flames and killed during the Battle of the Somme.

An exploding mine has completely destroyed Ramsgate Pier

July 1st: Dr Marie Stopes who lived at the Mansion House in Swanscombe for many years has

January: Despite the brave words of the Generals about the success of the British advance on the Western Front and the heroism of the West Kents many of the young volunteers aged 18 and 19 are returning home wounded with horror stories about the slaughter around them, particularly at Passchendaele. Some are in hospital suffering from "definite hysterical manifestations". Others are at home complaining they were given impossible tasks to accomplish and that they had not been fed. They say it is not a war of rapid movement but a struggle for the struggle for villages, hills, roads and even copses. Many have laid down their arms in the countryside around Ypres and, in their honour, a Canadian medical officer has written a poem. Here is the first verse.

In Flanders fields the poppies blow
Between the crosses, row on row,
That mark our place; and in the sky
The larks, still bravely singing, fly
Scarce heard amid the guns below.

written a book called *Married Love* which discusses a topic, rarely before mentioned in public — sex! In her book Dr Stopes calls for contraceptive advice to be made more available.

July 16th: Russia's Czar Nicholas II and his family have been massacred by Bolshevik rulers. They were shot and bayoneted to death in a cellar in Ekaterinburg in the Urals.

July 23rd: Heavy fighting has been resumed on the Western Front following a long lull caused by an influenza epidemic. Von Ludendorff's offensive across the Marne has already been halted and the tide appears to be turning for the Allies.

August 13th: The Goverment recognises the state of Czechoslovakia.

October 1st: A young British officer, Major T.E.Lawrence, has led an Arab revolt against the Turks and captured the most famous city in the Arab world, Damascus. Multitudes are now celebrating liberation from the Ottoman Empire.

October 23rd: Hundreds of schools in Kent have been forced to close as the worldwide influenza epidemic hits England with a vengeance. The outbreak has devastated Maidstone and those who are suffering the most are the people who live roughly in the crowded and sordid courts and alleys which have long been a blackspot in the county town. In London more than 2,000 deaths have been reported. Worldwide the total is some 53,000.

October 31st: Germany has appealed for an armistice as the shadow of defeat for that country and her Allies grows longer.

November 11th: The Armistice is signed today at 11 am in a carriage in the forest of Compiegne. Public revelry and rejoicing in Britain has marked the end of the war.

November 27th: A memorial was unveiled today in Gillingham Cemetery in memory of the men killed in the raid on the Royal Naval barracks in 1917.

Francis Bennett-Goldney, former MP and mayor of Canterbury has died in an American hospital in Brest following a motor accident. He was the Honorary Military Attaché to the British Embassy in Paris.

GREAT HITS OF 1918

Till we meet again

After you're gone

January: Strange to think that the men working among the coppices of Kent are helping the war effort. Charcoal made at Arketts Farm, Stalisfield Green, high on the Downs, is being sent to France for use as a fuel in the battle areas. It has many advantages. Being smokeless and odourless it does not give away the soldiers' positions and it provides plenty of heat. The Stalisfield charcoal also goes to the gunpowder makers at Faversham, where a new factory will soon open. Negotiations are taking place to create a holding company, Explosives Trades Ltd. When this is finalised all major business in the area will amalgamate.

Deep in the heart of Kent members of the Women's Forestry Corps are felling trees for the war effort. Here, two girls sharpen an axe on the grinder. It is backbreaking work.

Roman port back in business — but sshh, it's a secret

February 6th: Amidst the most utmost secrecy, Britain's first-ever port is back in business again — nearly 2,000 years later! Today the new cross-Channel train ferry from the old Roman base at Richborough will open by sending troops, stores and munitions to the French ports and then on to the Western Front. The opening of the service follows many months of frantic activity in which the River Stour has been deepened, a canal built, land reclaimed and the great wharf created. The new port will relieve the war traffic through Dover. Thousands of soldiers will now pass through, by day and night, until the war is over.

Drifters v destroyers — another story of courage at sea

February 15th: Dover was bombarded by five German destroyers in the early hours of this morning — one shell landing as far away as the Alkham Valley. There were no casualties on land but, at sea, there was appalling carnage. Eight patrol boats were sunk, 36 seamen died and many more were wounded. The story of the night, told by survivors, shows that the drifters put up a brave fight but had little chance against such mighty opposition. It was one of the most serious raids of the war.

Among the drifters badly hit was the *Violet May.* During the attack two sailors, Enginemen Ewing and Noble, managed to launch a boat and lowered into it the mate and a deckhand, both badly wounded. The remainder of the crew were dead and lay entangled in the wreckage. The survivors paddled clear, waited until the firing stopped and then returned to the drifter which was blazing. By this time the mate had died but the three men fought the fire and somehow managed to get the boat back into port.

The *Cloverbank* was another drifter hit. Here just one man, Deckhand Plane (RNR) survived and bravely continued to serve the gun single-handed. The whole of the crew of another drifter was rescued but the others were sunk.

Of the 39 bodies that are now laid out at the Market Hall, seven will buried at Dover, and the rest sent to their respective homes..

A Bristol Fighter (F26) of 141 Squadron on the ground at the new airfield, Biggin Hill. There's been a lot of activity on the site as can be seen by the new buildings in the background.

Rationing bites and the slaughter continues

February: "The Great War has entered its fourth year and there is still no sign that the tragedy will end. Something more potent than the force of arms must intervene to bring the conflict to its desired end." So wrote the editor of the *Sevenoaks Chronicle* this week who also pointed out that the lack of street lighting is causing accidents but more serious to the populous is the shortage of meat and the daily news of continuing slaughter on the Western Front.

In Hythe, the mayor has established a fund to help the families of those who have been killed and the returning wounded. He has set a target of £2,000 by June and has been given a donkey on which to travel around the locality. This week he pointed out that the town had sent over a thousand men to war and every week more were registering to help swell the numbers in France.

The county town of Maidstone continues to be a transit camp and a clearing house for aliens under the National Service Scheme. As a military base some 2,343 officers and 70,848 other ranks have been billeted in public buildings, schools and private house and accommodation has even been found for 3,000 horses.

Elsewhere in Kent, Food Control Committees are doing their best to make sure of fair distribution. The shortage of meat, butter and margarine is serious but, in the countryside villages of the Weald, pork is in plentiful supply thanks to the number of pigs kept in back gardens.

The tightening of the belts is now affecting rich and poor. In Tenterden two ladies watching the W.A.A.C. women marching through the town were heard to comment on the difficulty of finding domestic servants caused by so many girls going into the Forces.

It's now the RAF: Biggin Hill celebrates and so does Major Mac

April 1st: Following the devastating Gotha air raids on East Kent and London and the cries for help which followed, it has been decided to merge the Royal Flying Corps and the Royal Navy Air Service into a new Royal Air Force. The RAF, as it will be known, is formed out of a desire for revenge and the obvious lack of co-ordination by the previous services.

The Chief of Air Staff Lord Trenchard has told the Cabinet not to be too optimistic about the capabilities of the combined service but he is secretly hoping that 39 Squadron at Hornchurch and 141 Squadron at Biggin Hill will help to restore national pride.

May 21st: There was a great celebration last night in the Mess at Biggin Hill as the men of 141 Squadron celebrated their first "kill" — a Gotha bomber brought down in the countryside at Frinstead, south of Sittingbourne. The Squadron had been ordered to intercept an attacking force of 38 Gothas — the biggest raid of the war — and Lieutenants E.Turner (pilot) and H.B.Barwise (observer) in a Bristol Fighter successfully splayed incendiary tracer bullets into one of the raiders from nose to tail.

During the celebrations at Biggin Hill the men heard that more Huns had perished — three to the guns, two more to fighters, another down from engine failure and three had crash-landed in Belgium. For the first time the defences have really mastered the bombers. The Germans may now decide that it is too dangerous to continue with any more attacks on the civilian population.

June 4th: The Freedom of the Borough of Gillingham is today conferred on Major Jimmy McCudden, VC, DSO and Bar, MC and bar MM, the town's most famous son, who has now accounted for 58 enemy aircraft. A street is also to be named after him.

The storming of Zeebrugge — death and glory on St George's Day

April 24th: Winston Churchill has described it as one of the finest feats of arms ever known. Others will see it as the bloodiest, and most questionable, action of the Great War — the assault last night on the Belgian ports of Zeebrugge and Ostend. In little more than an hour of fighting, 200 men were killed and more than 400 wounded. The 4th Battalion of the Royal Marines was almost wiped out, ships were battered beyond recognition and at least eight heroes have been recommended for the Victoria Cross.

Admiralty sources say the raid has been a success, even if it did not achieve its object of blocking the harbour entirely to German submarines, "but it was a magnificent feat of arms, a great morale booster for Britain and there should be a respite for merchant ships carrying food across the Channel". Certainly Zeebrugge may never again be used by the Germans as a naval base.

The plans for the raid, drawn up by Admiral Sir Roger Keyes in command of the Dover Patrol, were to close canal entrances at the two ports by blockships and, at the same time, storm the Zeebrugge mole and cause as much damage as possible. The armada assembled in the Thames Estuary and at Dover. It was led by the 5,750-ton cruiser *Vindictive* from Chatham, followed by two former Mersey ferry boats *Iris* and *Daffodil*. Three old cruisers, the 3,600-ton *Thetis, Intrepid* and *Iphegenia* — their hulls filled with 1,500 tons of concrete — were behind the ferries. Straddled across the black water were a further 160 ships.

From Deal, where they had been training for weeks, came the 700-strong 4th Battalion of the Royal Marines (previously stationed at Chatham, Portsmouth and Plymouth), accompanied by 200 Royal Navy seamen in naval assault parties.

The raiding party left on April 22nd, the eve of St George's Day with Admiral Keyes on board the destroyer *Warwick*. His message signalled to the armada — "St George for England" brought this instant reply from the *Vindictive* — "May we give the dragon's tail a good twist."

The German battery crews on the Belgian coast saw the *Vindictive* emerge from the fog and smoke screen and began to fire. The action which then took place has been described as "heroic" by the officers who returned because the *Vindictive*, seriously hit, continued to approach the mole at Zeebrugge with the intention of putting its guns out of action. Storming parties assembled on the deck were mown down by shells. Some men landed on the mole and were killed immediately. A howitzer crew was wiped out so the replacement crew took their place. They, too, were all killed. A shell landed on the ship's foretop and killed everyone but a marine sergeant who continued firing. The dead and dying lay on the mole, or in the water, others were killed striving to jump the gap from the ship but they still inflicted great damage to the Belgian port.

Three of the blockships also ran into trouble. The *Thetis* failed to reach the lock gates, the *Intrepid* was sunk on the western bank of the canal entrance and the *Iphegenia* was grounded. A submarine, C3, managed to demolish an iron viaduct forming part of the mole and the crew made their escape in a skiff just seconds before the submarine was blown up by explosives.

The return of the expedition to Dover was an event always to be remembered. Twelve times the *Iris* was hit with heavy loss of life but the real heroine of the night was the *Vindictive*. She berthed at Dover, so battered, that she was almost unrecognisable. On board sailors were still wearing lifebelts and others were badly wounded. The landing of 151 shell-mangled bodies was a saddening sight. They were taken to the Market Hall while the wounded were taken to Naval hospitals.

Today King George and Queen Mary visited the hospital at Chatham and were told by one sailor: "It was bad, very bad, but it was worth it".

The Royal Marines are now on their way back to their respective ports. From Deal they marched from the depot to the railway station with heads bandaged and arms in slings, watched by hundreds of cheering people. Their rifles were decorated with flags. They were in high spirits despite the fact that their numbers had been reduced by more than half. As a mark of respect the 4th Battalion will now disband and it is unlikely that it will ever be reformed.

Sadly the Ostend force was not able to achieve its aim, the ships having been grounded before reaching the canal entrance but, despite the loss of life, the Zeebrugge raid is seen as one of the most brilliant actions in the history of the Royal Navy.

April 30th: The people of Dover witnessed a sight today they will never forget — a great stream of men marching from the station to the harbour — many of them singing. This is the United States army who have come to join the great Allied offensive. By the end of May there may be as many as 650,000 American troops in Europe to help send the Huns reeling. Meanwhile column after column of Yankees keep on coming.

10b. ZEEBRUGGE, SOUVENIR DE LA GUERRE. 1914-18. OF THE WAR.

Gros canon boche sur le Môle.
Big German Gun on the Mole.

December: The big gun at Zeebrugge which caused so much havoc is now in Allied hands. This postcard has been produced as a souvenir and is on sale in Belgium and England

"Entrepid"   "Arthemisia"

The canal entrance to Zeebrugge Harbour shows some of the blockships in place.

One million wounded men have landed at Dover

July: A few days ago the millionth wounded man landed at Dover, having gone through the casualty clearing station on the Western Front. He crossed France on one of the hundreds of hospital trains and was then taken to a hospital in Kent. Many men are dying from the effects of German mustard gas and the *Kentish Express* in Ashford described this week how one soldier arrived home suffering from severe conjunctivitis and superficial burns of face, neck and scrotum. Respiratory symptoms then developed and he died some days after his exposure to gas.

One British officer who has returned home badly wounded is Siegfried Sassoon. He said: "There were 500 other men on the hospital train. Many of us still had the caked mud of the war zone on our boots and clothes and every bandaged man was accompanied by his battle experience. As we bumped along, the bludgeoning reality of the Front Line diminished with every mile."

Sassoon has now written to the newspapers saying he has seen and endured the suffering of the troops and can no longer be a party to ends which he believes to be evil and unjust. He has handed back his Military Medal, resigned from the army and says he will continue to speak out against what he regards as a "wrongful war."

Gillingham's great hero is killed in France

July 10th: Major Jimmy McCudden, the leading British fighter pilot of the war, was killed yesterday at Auxi-le-Chateau in France. He was taking off in his S.E.5a biplane when it struck trees bordering the aerodrome. McCudden was thrown from the machine fracturing his skull. He did not regain consciousness and died two hours later. The people of Gillingham, his home town, are deeply shocked and saddened.

Major McCudden's achievements are already legendary. In his incomparable fighting scout (S.E.5a) and as commander of B Flight of 56 Squadron he came into combat on numerous occasions with the German machines of Manfred von Richthofen's "flying circus" — shooting many of them down in flames.

By November last year McCudden's tally of "kills" had risen to 23 but in December, by a combination of intelligent tactics, skilful flying and acute marksmanship, he registered 14 more victories and made aviation history on the 23rd by shooting down four enemy aircraft in one day. He was awarded a DSO in that month and a congratulatory letter from Major-General Trenchard.

Strangely at that time his achievements were unknown and the British press campaigned vigorously to establish the identity of the "nameless aerial hero". After demanding that the Royal Flying Corps should "tell us his name", the *Daily Mail* was eventually able to say that Jimmy McCudden was the crack flier upsetting the ambitions of "The Red Baron" (von Richthofen).

By February this year B Flight of 56 Squadron had accounted for 77 victories, 52 of these being credited to McCudden and that led to the award of the Victoria Cross. He was gazetted on March 29th and the citation stated that the award was "for most conspicuous bravery, exceptional perseverance, keenness and very high devotion to duty". King George V presented him, not only with the VC, but also with his DSO and bar and bar to his MC. He had already won the Croix de Guerre.

Jimmy McCudden was due to visit Gillingham on June 13th to be admitted as an Honorary Freeman of the Borough but

was posted to France and the event had to be cancelled. He was then instructed to take command of 60 Squadron and was actually on his way when he lost his bearings and landed at Auxi-le-Chateaux. After obtaining directions from the duty flight airmen he took off again. Then came the fatal crash.

May 10th: In another highly secret but risky naval operation, the battle-scarred cruiser, Vindictive was today taken to Ostend to be sunk in the mouth of Ostend Harbour. Unfortunately after another dramatic night the ship ran aground at the last moment and only partially blocked the harbour. This meant that U-boats could still squeeze past to attack Allied shipping. Photograph shows the Vindictive at Ostend.

Dover saved as burning ship is torpedoed

September 17th: *HMS Glatton*, a newly-commissioned monitor and one of a great fleet assembled at Dover Harbour for the final offensive on the Belgian coast, blew up last night with the loss of more than 100 lives. For over an hour following this tragedy the town itself was under the threat of being completely wiped out by a far more terrible explosion — for there was not one ship in the harbour that wasn't carrying a deadly load.

In an atmosphere of unbearable tension, Admiral Sir Roger Keyes ordered *HMS Glatton* to be torpedoed after the two magazines of live ammunition on the ship had been flooded. He reckoned that if flames reached these vulnerable positions, not only the rescue parties, but the town of Dover itself would be blown to pieces.

Many people watching from the harbour with bated breath recalled the shocking catastrophe nine months ago when a French munitions ship collided with another in Halifax harbour, Novia Scotia causing loss of life estimated at 1,500.

Captain W.J. Pearce, skipper of the Dover tug *Lady Brassey* said today: "I was on the deck when the calm September night was torn apart by the roar of an explosion that reverberated against the towering cliffs in the background and shook Dover to its foundations. When the great pall of white smoke abated the sight that met our eyes was appalling. On the *Glatton*'s deck were dozens of officers and men, terribly wounded. Many were naked for they had been bathing when the explosion occurred.

"The flames rose high with a terrible roar. The heat was intense. Someone then shouted. 'For God's sake, flood the magazines'. I ordered my men to get out the fire-fighting apparatus and we forced our way through the scorching, suffocating barrage of smoke and scrambled on the *Glatton*. Vague figures kept looming up — wounded men struggling to escape but everyone was now aware that at any moment she might blow up."

A band of ratings volunteered to open the seacocks or try to flood the magazines and bravely achieved the latter. Sir Roger Keyes then made the decision to torpedo the *Glatton*. All ships were moved out of the harbour and the ship was blown up. It was a heartrending scene because many men were trapped alive in the fore part of the ship and rescue parties had been unable to reach them. But Dover was saved from what undoubtedly would have been the greatest calamity the town had ever known.

"We must fight to the end", says Haig...

Troop ship Victoria leaves Folkestone with more men to face the renewed German assault in France. Ludendorff has said he can now drive the British from the Somme and Haig is ordering more and more reinforcements. Every day this month 10,000 men have been shipped across the Channel.

October: The boys from Kent have rallied strongly to Sir Douglas Haig's stirring call to all ranks. "Every position must be held to the last man", he said. "With our backs to the wall and believing in the justice of our cause each one of us must fight on to the end." This special "Order of the Day" was then handed to Philip Sassoon, his secretary, and MP for Folkestone and Hythe.

The Royal West Kents and The Buffs have done just as instructed. As heavy fighting resumed in the face of von Ludendorff's latest drive hundreds have been killed but the enemy is now retreating fast.

All along the ruptured front, pockets of Germans are being found hiding in shell holes and ruined buildings. They are offering no resistance but surrender at once and a steady stream of prisoners is being led back to the British camps. The battlefield is littered with abandoned weapons.

Although the Allies have lost more than 500,000 men this is Haig's final push. The attacks are spearheaded by more than 400 tanks and the gallant men of the new RAF are daily machine-gunning the German infantry columns.

In the first phase of Haig's Amiens offensive, the 1st, 6th and 7th Battalions of the RWK's were promi-

nent. August 8th was, according to Ludendorff, "the black day of the war for the German armies". On that day the 6th and 7th Battalions took Albert, crossed the Ancre, ploughed their way through the the battlefields and after a stern battle at Epehy drove the enemy back to the Hindenburg Line.

At one stage the Germans blazed away with machine guns hidden in the standing crops and Lt Col Dawson who commanded the 6th went into battle on horseback but it still appeared the Battalion would be halted. Sergeant Tom Harris then set the tone for the whole offensive. Three times he assailed the machine gun post on his own to silence it but was killed on his third charge. Sgt Harris's astonishing ferocity has been rewarded with a posthumous Victoria Cross.

At the end of August another member of the Regiment was to die earning that most illustrious award. Lt C.H.Sewell, attached to the Royal Tank Corps, crossed open ground under heavy shell and machine-gun fire to rescue the crew of a light Whippet tank which had side-slipped into a large shell hole, overturned and taken fire, with the door jammed against the ground. Sewell calmly dug clear the door of the burning tank and rescued the crew in full view of the enemy. This done, he went to the assistance of the driver of his own tank who was lying

...our boys follow the general's command

wounded. He was hit but still managed to reach the man and was in the act of dressing his injured colleague when he was hit again and killed.

Meanwhile on the Lens-Ypres front the 8th and 10th Battalions were briskly engaged. For three days at the end of September 2nd Lt Donald Dean of the 8th defended an advanced post against repeated attacks, refusing to be relieved. Early on the morning of the third day an intense bombardment forced him and what was left of his men to retire some 50 yards. Dean, supported by 2nd Lt Cambrook, then launched a spectacular counter attack. This feat of sustained heroism has earned Dean the Victoria Cross.

His recommendation says: "Lieut Dean worked unceasingly and with utter contempt for danger in an exceedingly difficult situation. His garrison was suffering casualties continually but he himself bore a charmed life. Five times he was attacked by a resolute enemy and each time the attacks were thrown back. Throughout he inspired all his men with his own contempt for danger and, in the consequences, they all fought with the greatest bravery though most of them were very young soldiers".

Throughout this month (October) the boys have continued to fight their way through the main Hindenburg Line defences. The end is in sight but most of them are far too dazed to grasp its full significance.

It is not only the soldiers being awarded the Victoria Cross. Lt Gordon Steele RN of Hythe has been recommended for the award — fighting the Russians, our former Allies. In a torpedo boat attack on Kronstadt harbour in the Gulf of Finland, Steele retaliated and sank two battleships which had just been taken over by the Bolsheviks.

Lieutenant William Rhodes-Moorhouse of the Royal Flying Corps No 2 Squadron has posthumously gained the Victoria Cross for his part in the daring raid on Courtrai.

Lt Sewell VC rescued the crew of a blazing tank in full view of enemy.

Captain Donald Dean VC of Sittingbourne was given an ecstatic welcome when he returned home. Hundreds of people lined the route from the station and a great reception was held at the town hall.

Sergeant Tom Harris won't be coming home to Snodland. He has been awarded a posthumous VC for his furious attack on a German machine gun post during an offensive in August.

The scene of this great dinner is the drill hall, Lowfield Street, Dartford held to celebrate the signing of the armistice and to welcome the return of West Kent volunteers from their ordeal in France.

Jubilation marks the end of the Great War

November 15th: Unprecedented scenes of rejoicing and revelry have broken out in every town, village and hamlet in Kent. Today is Victory Day. Church bells are ringing, Boy Scouts are cycling through streets shouting the news, the All-clear is sounding for the last time and the entire population, it seems, are on the streets. The great explosive factories at Faversham have closed, munition workers at Canterbury have the day off, shop girls from Maidstone are cheering on the pavements, effigies of The Kaiser and "Little Willie", the German Crown Prince are burning in Ashford, there are schoolchildren everywhere — and flags and bunting and soldiers. The greatest war that mankind has ever known is over. Never again will there be such conflict in Europe.

The end came quickly following Haig's "final push". At the end of September the Allies attacked simultaneously with 200 divisions right along the whole Western Front and the Germans made "stands" only to cover retreats. By October, in the shadow of defeat, Germany appealed for an armistice. Her allies — Bulgaria and Turkey — had already quit the field and the Austrian empire was disintegrating.

At dawn on the morning of November 11th, a party of German politicians and army generals entered a guarded railway carriage at Compiègne. A few hours later, at 11am, the Armistice was signed and the guns fell silent on the battlefields of Europe.

Ever since the Allies had broken through the German lines, England had been waiting anxiously for news of the surrender. It came in the most unexpected way. A wireless operator at Aperfield Court, Biggin Hill, seeking news from France accidentally picked up a message from Marshal Foch to all C in C's. "Hostilities will cease on the whole Front as from November 11th at 11 am (French time)."

The operator told his commanding officer who alerted the local padres and within minutes the church bells at Westerham and Cudham were pealing. They were the first bells in Britain to proclaim peace. Within minutes they were joined by the bells of St Nicholas, Sevenoaks, then St Stephen's, Tonbridge, All Saint's, Maidstone...from church to church, from bell to bell, from village to village the great news swept through the county and then the rest of the country.

continued

continued

As the lights come back on again and the rejoicing begins, memories of the carnage remain vivid among those who have survived and those who are bereaved. The statistics tell the story. Three quarters of a million men from Britain have died, plus a further 200,000 from the Empire. France, with a population smaller than Britain's, has suffered a death toll twice as high. People are already talking of a "lost generation".

In many towns in Kent the percentage of men killed is one in ten. They are divided among 13 battalions of the Buffs, the East Kent Regiment and 18 battalions of the Queen's Own Royal West Kent Regiment and other Regiments throughout the country. These soldiers have served in various theatres of war in France, Flanders, Italy, Mesopotamia, Gallipoli, India, Palestine and Germany. In addition four battalions of Volunteers have been attached to each regiment for home defence.

In Tonbridge, for example, out of a population of 14,000, some 2,500 men and women served in the Great War. More than 50 decorations for bravery were won including Miss Margaret Waite of Postern Farm, who has been awarded the Belgian Order of Leopold II for her courage as a front-line nurse in France. Another award winner is Thomas Dewey, former mayor of Bromley, who has won the Medaille du Roi Albert, for his services to Belgian soldiers evacuated to Britain.

Now the armistice has been signed the time has come to welcome home the prisoners of war and the other heroes and consider raising money for memorials to honour the dead. Already, in Gillingham, money has been raised by the officers and men of the Royal Naval Depot and a memorial

Thousands of ships and millions of men protected by the Dover Patrol

November 20th: Four years after its seizure by the Germans, the Allies have regained possession of the Belgian coast and all further fear of hostile action has been removed. No longer are soldiers, in their thousands, crossing to France and the battlefields. No longer are the wounded coming home in troop ships — to be transferred to hospitals all over the county. In their place now comes a great stream of returned prisoners of war and they are receiving a great welcome in East Kent as they march to the rest camps to be refitted.

When the history of the Great War comes to be written, much will be made of the part played by the ports of Folkestone and Dover. Folkestone was the main feeder to the British Army in France as far as men were concerned. Day after day troop ships left the harbour and by the end of the war more than 10½ million men and Red Cross workers had passed through the port. During the great German offensive of March this year when reinforcements were so badly needed, more than 10.000 men were taken over every day. Up to the Armistice no less than 10,686 crossings were made by troop ships and a further 8, 032 by vessels carrying stores and mail.

Escorting the ships to Calais and Boulogne — and back again with the wounded and those on leave — were the destroyers of the Dover Patrol, which not only protected the vital military lines of communication between the two countries but also all the traffic east and west through the English Channel. Add to this the barge transport and train ferry which passed through the newly-created port of Richborough and the importance of the Patrol becomes clear. In fact 125,000 vessels passed through the Straits under its guardship and, incredibly, only 73 were lost.

Admiral Reginald Bacon, commander of the Dover Patrol before Sir Roger Keyes said this week: "Not only was the sea traffic of the Downs, the transports between Folkestone and Boulogne and Southampton and Le Havre convoyed and guarded across the Straits but there fell upon us a leading share of the offensive work in checking the attempts of the enemy to push forward along the Belgian coast towards Dunkirk and Calais.

"The great ships of the British Navy", he said, "such as the super Dreadnoughts and the big Battle Cruisers never came near Dover Harbour. The Grand Fleet remained far away. In no section of the Navy were more constant vigilance and endurance required than from the ships of the Dover Patrol."

erected in the cemetery in memory of the 100 men killed in the bombing raid of September 1917.

All over Kent the heroes are being honoured but the Roll of Honour carried by all county newspapers shows no signs of fading. This week the *Tunbridge Wells Courier* announced the good news and in the next column reported the death of Captain Ben Buss who died in Wandsworth Military Hospital during an operation to remove

shrapnel from his brain. "Captain Buss came from Horsmonden and was a pioneer of the old Territorials. It was due to his efforts that Horsmonden provided such a fair quota of men at the start of the war and most people will remember the emotional scenes at the station as they left for the Western Front."

A few of those men from Horsmonden have returned home. Just a few.

December: All over Kent German prisoners-of-war are still working on the farms. This photograph was taken during the early summer this year showing a party helping with the haymaking at Marden.

Warm welcome at Dover for President Wilson

December 26th: President Woodrow Wilson today became the first President of the United States to set foot on English soil. He landed at Dover, where an enthusiastic crowd had gathered, and said: "The war has almost justified itself because it has brought together great communities with a common object, the permanent maintenance of right."

Mr and Mrs Wilson then took the train to Charing Cross where they were met by King George V and Queen Mary. Today the President will have lunch with the Prime Minister David Lloyd George and tomorrow there will be a state banquet at Buckingham Palace.

The American President is just one of many important world leaders who have landed at Dover and then spoken briefly before moving on to London. Earlier in the month Marshal Foch, Commander of the French Army arrived with M. Clemenceau and Signor Orlando, Prime Ministers of France and Italy. A few days before Christmas General Haig landed with all his army commanders, General Horne, General Plumer, General Byng, General Rawlinson and General Birdwood. They were received by the mayor, the Archbishop of Canterbury, the Lord Warden and a great concourse of people.

The greatest receptions, however, were reserved for Admiral Sir Roger Keyes, Commander of the Dover Patrol, who has been made an Hon Freeman of Dover, and two victims of German barbarity — the bodies of Nurse Edith Cavell and Captain Charles Fryatt.

'I want to make it possible for the humblest woman to follow the precedent I set' — Lady Nancy Astor on her selection as Britain's first woman MP.

January 1st: *HMS Kent*, now an old lady of the seas who has seen distinguished action in the Falkland Islands, the Pacific Coast and China, is now in Vladivostock, supporting the loyal Russians against the Bolsheviks.

January 23rd: Miners in the Kent coalfields have joined their brothers throughout the country in striking for a shorter working week. More than 150,000 men are in dispute.

February 14th: Delegates from 27 nations at the Paris peace conference have agreed to President Wilson's proposal for a League of Nations to prevent war.

February 9th: Passengers (all military) flew between Paris and London for the first time today. They took off from Kenley airport in a Farman F90 and took three hours and 30 minutes to arrive at Versailles. Experts hope this historic flight will lead to a real passenger service when civil flying is resumed.

March 10th: Talks about a proposed tunnel under the English Channel have resumed once again. The Government is in favour.

March 11th: Famine is sweeping Germany and much of Eastern Europe. The Allies have reached a compromise agreement to supply their former enemies with food relief.

March 19th: The influenza epidemic has hit England and Wales so badly that deaths exceeded births for the first time on record during the last quarter.

April 13th: The price of petrol has increased to 3/6d a gallon.

April 17th: Four American movie stars have teamed up to form their own film-distribution company, United Artists. They are Mary Pickford, Charles Chaplin, D.W.Griffith and Douglas Fairbanks.

Queen Mary has visited the wounded soldiers at Orpington Hospital and is both delighted and

Fashion editors are commenting enthusiastically about the young woman of today who is trying to emulate men by strapping her breast to give a flat appearance and wearing straight clothes and short hair. Letters to the newspapers, however, show that many more are displeased with the attempt by women to wear clothes that reflect their new freedom. A letter in the *Tunbridge Wells Courier* says that the styles encourage loose behaviour such as smoking, drinking and wearing make-up and the short frocks which reveal the calves of their legs are "totally inappropriate". For the benefit of those who prefer yesterday's fashions here is Hettie Backhouse, a fashionable young lady, who has not yet graduated to the rising hemlines.

July 18th: Sir Edward Lutyens' new war memorial, the Cenotaph, is unveiled in Whitehall.

Quebec House, Westerham, the former home of General James Wolfe and a square-built brick house of great distinction, has been given to the National Trust.

July 19th: Peace parades take place today in every village and town throughout the country. The celebrations follow the German signing of the Treaty of Versailles.

September 27th: Sugar and meat rationing have been reintroduced in the wake of a national rail strike.

December 15th: Sir Hugh Trenchard, Commander of the RAF has presented proposals which will make the force permanent.

December 22nd: The partition of Ireland has been announced. The country will have self government with two Parliaments, one for the north, one for the south and the whole country will remain part of the United Kingdom. Announcing this in Parliament today, Lloyd George said he knows the scheme is not generally acceptable.

December 23rd: Royal Assent is given to the Sex Discrimination Bill opening professions to women.

GREAT HITS OF 1919

I'm forever blowing bubbles

Don't dilly-dally on the way

amused to receive a copy of the hospital magazine which is called *The Ontario Stretcher*.

May 27th: A United States seaplane, piloted by Lt Commander A.C.Read and Lt Stone has made history by flying across the Atlantic. The crossing was made in three stages, the biggest being the 1,200 miles from Trespass Bay, Newfoundland to The Azores.

June 15th: Less than a month after the seaplane triumph, a Vickers Vimy flown by Captain John Alcock and navigated by Lt Arthur Whitten Brown has completed the first nonstop flight across the Atlantic.

Remember the Penny Bazaars?

The chain of shops known as Marks and Spencer no longer have a penny limit on their haberdashery and other clothes — but the success of the company is shown by the rapid expansion. Several new shops have opened in Kent since the war.

This impressive enterprise began in 1882 when Michael Marks began selling haberdashery from a tray around his neck with the slogan: "Don't ask the price. It's a penny". This led to a small chain of

shops and stalls and he went into partnership with Thomas Spencer in 1894 and the Penny Bazaars flourished.

Also flourishing in Kent is the international chain, F.W.Woolworth, whose first shops in Kent were opened before the war with a top price of 6d.

Marks and Spencer and Woolworth have a dominant position in most major High Streets and there are plans to open many more shops.

Years of military use mean the end of some great country houses

January: Will life in Kent ever be the same again? In the wake of the Great War and the suffering by thousands of wounded men a gratitude linked with sadness has settled on the county. The most obvious and dramatic sign of the new times is the physical destruction of some of the great houses, many of which had been commandeered for the accommodation of the troops and have suffered years of robust usage. Practically every community in Kent is about to experience the demolition of what, before the war, were large family homes.

Elsewhere improvements are being planned. The South Eastern and Chatham Railway is speeding up its services, cricket weeks are being planned again for the summer, tramways are being overhauled and arrangements made for a special Peace Day

July: Steam threshing has begun again on the Isle of Thanet as farm life gets back to the old routine. Thrashing or threshing is the act of separating the grain from the straw and chaff and it is a long and arduous process — dusty, repetitive and noisy. Here at Garlinge Farm on the Isle of Thanet there appear to be plenty of willing hands but elsewhere farmers are having some difficulty in recruiting labour. One farmer said: "Now the war is over the farm hands won't work. They are some of the laziest whelps you ever did see, almost too tired to eat their dinner.
But the rough old chaps, well they'll work all night and day. If they'd been drunk and laid out all night, they'll work the next day, no bother. 'Let's get 'em wheels going', they say. 'You don't earn nothin' if they don't go'".

Women vote for the first time: Coalition triumphs

January 10th: With all the results now in, the Coalition Government led by David Lloyd George has triumphed in the General Election, held in the period between Christmas and the New Year. The majority of Kent towns have provided a coalition member and Labour is challenging the Liberal Party as the county's main opposition to the Conservatives. Women have voted for the first time. Those aged over 30 who are householders, or wives of householders, put their vote in the ballot box with little opposition.

Women deserve this new recognition. During the war thousands of Kentish ladies took a great interest in local administration by serving on committees and their hard work and devotion throughout made their case for enfranchisement unanswerable.

Apart from the political aspirations of women, the main talking point in every town concerns the provision of war memorials. Committees are being formed to look at possible sites and ways of raising the money. Extensions are being added to existing hospitals in memory of those who gave their lives.

Sevenoaks is anxious to secure a war trophy and the editor of the *Chronicle* fully supports the Urban Council's request for a German field gun to be sited in front of the council offices. "Sevenoaks has done its share in the winning, not only on the field of battle, but in the way in which it has backed up the fighting man", he wrote. "It is only right that Sevenoaks should have a fair share in the distribution of these spoils of conflict."

March: Blinded by gas in the Somme and Passchendaele, these soldiers are now trying to cope with life without sight by learning poultry farming at Fawkham. Many are refusing to talk about the horrors they experienced on the Western Front but one soldier remembered. *"In the Battle of Lys on April 9th, 1918, terrible panic was caused when the Germans discharged mustard gas, phosgene and diphenylchlorarsine against the British forces. Something like 8,000 men were incapacitated and many died. I lost my sight, but I am alive."*

Sassoon's bitterness dims the patriotism

March: Siegfried Sassoon, the first to publish his disillusionment with the way the war was being run, has expressed his anger again in a new poem entitled *Aftermath:*

Have you forgotten yet?
Look down, and swear by the slain of the war that you'll never forget.

Do you remember the dark months you held the sector at Mametz—
The nights you watched and wired and dug and piled sandbags on parapets?
Do you remember the rats; and the stench
Of corpses rotting in front of the front-line trench —
And dawn coming, dirty-white, and chill with a hopeless rain?
Do you ever stop and ask, 'Is it all going to happen again?'

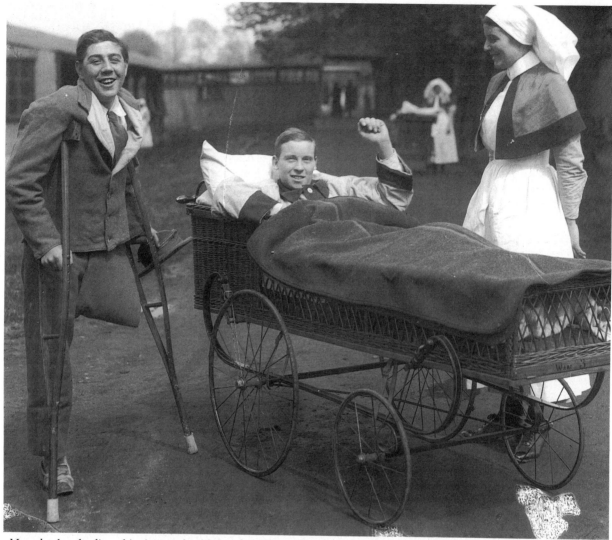

More broken bodies, this time at the 4th London Hospital in Denmark Hill. One soldier has written in his diary of a discharged colleague. "He has lost both legs and propels himself about in a mechanical chair. The other evening he was sitting talking to his bride when the kettle started to boil over. He forgot he had no legs and jumped up to seize the kettle only to fall into space on his sore stumps."

Memorial service for 'Captain Courageous'

July 11th: The body of Captain Charles Fryatt, the former captain of the South Eastern Railway Company's steamer, *Brussels*, who was shot by the Germans for having dared to ram a submarine, was brought home to Kent today. A memorial service will be held in London tomorrow.

In 1916 Captain Fryatt achieved national fame when he saved his ship by turning on his attacker and attempting to ram it. The submarine fled but the Captain was caught on another crossing to Holland and court martialled for being a non-combatant who attacked a vessel which, the Germans claimed, was against international laws. Shortly after his trial a message was received from Berlin that it would be an ille-

gal act to have him executed. The message was too late. Captain Fryatt had already been shot.

This German savagery caused great shock in Britain and there has been a campaign to have the Captain's body returned. He was brought over on the destroyer *Orpheus* and, on the way, the ship passed the wreck of the *Brussels* which is now sunk at the end of the Mole at Zeebrugge

August 23rd: Lord George Hamilton today unveiled a memorial at Canterbury to the memory of Colin Blythe, the cricketer, who was killed in action at Passchendaele in November 1917.

Vimy flies non-stop across the Atlantic

June 16th: The entire workforce of the Vickers aircraft factories at Crayford, Bexleyheath, Dartford and Erith are elated by the news today that Captain Jack Alcock and Lieutenant Arthur Whitten Brown have completed the first non-stop flight across the Atlantic in a Vickers Vimy. The biplane, flown by Alcock, who is British, landed in a bog yesterday on the Irish coast at Clifden.

The Rolls-Royce powered bomber, fitted with long range fuel tanks, took off from Newfoundland on Saturday (June 14th) and completed the 1,900-mile flight in 16 hours 12 minutes averaging 120 mph. "It was a terrible journey", said Jack Alcock. "We flew through fog and sleet storms, and all we had to sustain us was coffee, beer, chocolate and sandwiches."

The success of the Vimy and its triumphant crew has highlighted the possibility of organising scheduled flights to far-off lands and already a civilian version of the Vimy has been tested with a larger capacity fuselage than the military version. One director of Vickers has described the new aeroplane as an "airliner" as it can carry 10 passengers.

There are some criticisms. The prototype left the drawing board with an enclosed cockpit but the test crew objected to this idea; they said it would impair their vision and deprive them of fresh air so the Vimy Commercial, as it will be called was fitted with the usual kind of open cockpit for the first test flight from Joyce Green on April 13th.

More exciting plans are in the pipeline. Brothers Ross and Keith Smith are confident of flying a Vimy to Australia before the end of this year but by this time Vickers will have transferred their aircraft operation to a new site at Weybridge, Surrey where an adjacent airfield, Brooklands is available. It will be a sad day for Joyce Green and the employees who feel they cannot leave the Dartford area.

August: The Princess Theatre, opened for Vickers Munition workers at Crayford less than a year ago and destroyed by fire, has been rebuilt. The new opening ceremony was performed by Prince Albert, Duke of York in the presence of many civic dignitaries. The Theatre was first opened by Princess Christian in 1918 and few will forget the stirring performance of Miss Edith Evans who was on the opening bill. Photograph shows the Duke of York with Sir Trevor Dawson, managing director of Vickers and Lady Dawson. The company chairman, Douglas Vickers, is in the centre.

July 20th: Memories of Ypres and the Somme, Delville Wood and Hill 60 were temporarily forgotten yesterday as the Royal West Kent Regiment led a great procession of servicemen and women (military and civilian) through the streets of Bromley. This was not a recruiting parade like the many marches of the previous four bleak years. This was the official Peace Parade, held in every town and many villages throughout the country. Bromley did not shirk in its duty of providing men for the Great War but, sadly, more than 800 of them paid the supreme sacrifice. In Maidstone, Ashford, Canterbury, Gillingham and, of course Folkestone and Dover, the streets were packed and celebrations went on throughout the day.

It was on June 28th — just 22 days ago — that the Great War officially ended when the Germans at last signed the Treaty of Versailles. For several months they had refused to sign and gave in only at the threat of military occupation. The treaty is 200 pages long. It calls upon Germany to make a provisional payment of 20 million gold marks and surrender territory totalling 87 square km, with a total population of 7,000,000 to other states. The left bank of the Rhine is to be under Allied occupation for 15 years.

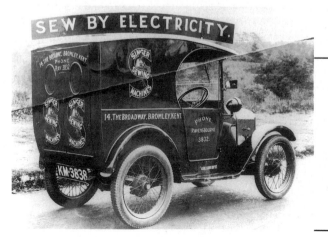

It is not clear whether this little trade van took place in the Bromley peace parade. It is more likely the driver was on his rounds, delivering sewing machines, which had been repaired, or collecting weekly payments from those who have bought on the "never-never". Bromley's most famous son, H.G. Wells, predicted in 1900 that carrier's trucks would be plentiful in years to come — and so they are . Every trader, it seems, has his own van with the name fixed above or on the side. They certainly outnumber private cars.

January 10th: 35 people drowned today in the English Channel when their steamer *Treveal* was in collision.

January 16th: America has passed an amendment to its constitution prohibiting the manufacture and sale of alcohol. The mayor of New York says he will need 250,000 police to enforce the new law in his city alone.

February 11th: The Council of the new League of Nations met for the first time today in St James' Palace, London.

May 21st: The Government has proposed a car tax of £1 per horsepower.

June 4th: With the Treaty of Trianon, signed today, the map of Europe has been redrawn. Hungary is a quarter of its old size, Germany gives territory of Poland and Lithuania, North Schleswig to Denmark and Alsace-Lorraine to France. Two new empires have been created in Yugoslavia and Czechoslovakia.

Gillingham Football Club, formerly New Brompton, has been accepted as a founder member of Division Three (South) of the Football League. The club has played in the Southern League since 1894, reaching Division One by sheer merit. Supporters at Priestfield Stadium are confident that Gillingham will earn promotion to Division Two and then perhaps Division One to compete with the footballing giants of Burnley, Liverpool, Newcastle and Tottenham.

July 20th: An inquiry opened today in the town hall Folkestone concerning an application from the council for sanction to borrow £10,000 for work on improving the Leas and the Cliff, including the building of a zigzag path.

August 14th-30th: Albert Hill, who runs with Herne Hill Harriers in South London has won the gold medal in both the 800 metres and the 1500 metres at the Olympic Games in Antwerp. Hill who served with the Army

Little Lost Bear. By MARY TOURTEL

No. 1.—Mrs. Bear sends her little son Rupert to market.

November 8th: A lively and delightful new friend, who has appeared for the first time today in the cartoon section of the Daily Express newspaper, is the creation of Mary Tourtel, a 45-year-old housewife from Canterbury. Rupert Bear, wearing check trousers, jumper and scarf, should prove very popular among children along with his mates — Algy Pug, Bill Badger and Edward Trunk.

Mary Tourtel was born Mary Caldwell in Palace Street, Canterbury in 1874 and was a pupil at the Simon Langton school where she excelled in art. Some years after leaving school she had several sketches published in the Express thanks to the fact that her husband was (is) night editor. For some time now Herbert Tourtel, and Express proprietor Lord Beaverbrook, have been concerned that their newspaper has nothing for young readers — like the Daily Mail, with Teddy Tail and the Daily Mirror, with Pip, Squeak and Wilfred. So he asked Mary to create a character that children may take to their hearts.

Well here he is. Little Rupert Bear — a fellow, say the editorial staff of the Daily Express, that will do wonders for them in the circulation war currently raging.

We shall see.

and Royal Flying Corps during the war actually ran in five races in five days.

Samuel Whitbread, the London brewers have purchased from E.A. White and the Draper's Company a large acreage of land in the Yalding, Paddock Wood area comprising Beltring, Brookers and Lily Hoo farms. Whitbread has sent letters to the well-established hoppers informing them of the take-over and also of the times of the hop pickers' train from London Bridge to Paddock Wood.

November 16th: Bolshevism has triumphed in Russia. The final battle between the Red Army and the Whites has ended in the Crimea with defeat for Baron Wrangel. It has been a long, bloody and chaotic civil war.

December 5th: Scotland has voted against prohibition. After a fiercely fought campaign between the non-conformist church, which claims that drink is the curse of Scotland, and whisky distillers, a referendum has come out in favour of the "wets".

Maidstone and District has introduced a new bus, the Leyland N. The company also continues to extend its services across Kent.

GREAT HITS OF 1920
Avalon
Margie

Introducing — The Orpington

November 6th: An exciting new car of high quality, first introduced at the Motor Show a few weeks ago, will soon be on sale from the sole concessionaires in London. It is called The Orpington built by Frank Smith and Jack Milroy at their Pond Garage, opposite Priory Road in Orpington. The Orpington is a two-seater with dickey seat capable of accommodating two small people behind the driving wheel and a 10 horse power engine and will cost £495.

A test run was performed today by the *Light Car and Cyclecar* magazine which reported that The Orpington had no difficulty whatsoever in surmounting the first hill on Ranmore Common which has a gradient of one in six.

Smith and Milroy are well-known in northern Kent. They went into partnership at the turn of the century with a bike-repair shop and then turned their attention to cars. They now hope to enter The Orpington in the London to Lands End motor rally.

Donald Clark, aged 62, has toured the Kent seaside resorts looking for "proper women's wear". He has found little to please him.

Unknown soldier comes home

November 10th: The body of an unknown British soldier arrived in Dover today. He was one of the unidentifiable soldiers from the Western Front and he will be reburied in Westminster Abbey where his grave will become a focal point for prayer and contemplation for the hundreds of thousands of widows, children and parents whose loved ones have no known grave.

The coffin, made of a British oak tree from the Royal Park in Hampton Court, was escorted through northern France by French cavalrymen and came to Dover on the French destroyer, the *Verdun*. The funeral and burial of the Unknown Soldier will take place tomorrow at the Abbey when a Guard of Valour will be formed by holders of the Victoria Cross.

War memorials have been appearing this year all over Kent. In the last month alone hundreds have been erected, all paid for by public subscription and unveiled by distinguished soldiers, bishops, mayors, rectors or the Lords of the Manor. At Matfield, for example, there is a simple memorial cross of Portland Stone — at Petts Wood, a memorial hall — at Judd School, a memorial organ in memory of the old boys and masters who lost their lives — and at Sittingbourne, an Avenue of Remembrance.

Sevenoaks lost 225 sons and, like many towns of a similar size, plumped for the memorial of the unknown soldier. The unveiling ceremony took place in late October when the Union Jack was taken off the tall figure with thousands looking on.

Mixed bathing decision shocks Boer War hero

August: Many councils throughout Kent are allowing couples to swim together, both in the sea and swimming baths but the Government recommendation that the sexes need no longer be kept apart is having a mixed reception in some areas.

One man from Tonbridge, incensed by the relaxation of the old laws, has earned the title of "Britain's Mixed Bathing Censor". Encouraged by the editor of the *Tonbridge Free Press* and the *Daily Mail*, Donald Clark, a former Boer War hero, is touring the Kent coast looking for the areas where the sexes are still apart and where women have proper swimming wear.

He said this week that he had seen more potential partners lost on the beaches — "the result of a young man's shock on seeing his pretty dance partner of the night before looking ridiculous in a scanty bathing costume with her hair drawn up under a horrible rubber hat."

Mr Clark, aged 62, has found little to please him. "Mixed bathing", he said, "will always have a debasing influence by lowering the respect that should obtain between the sexes."

War leaders enjoy hospitality at Port Lympne

June 20th: Sir Philip Sassoon is seen above (far left) with some of the many war leaders who arrived this weekend at his new home, Port Lympne, completed just after hostilities ended.

During the lengthy negotiations which led to the signing of the Peace Treaty and the formation of the League of Nations, Sir Philip — a bachelor — has entertained lavishly and continues to do so. Yesterday's peace conference was held in the Octagonal Library and among those who attended were Generals Weygand and Foch, Marshal Millerand, the Prime Minister David Lloyd George, Austin Chamberlain, Sir Henry Wilson and Maurice Hankey.

The elegant Port Lympne has particularly pleased the French contingent who can take advantage of the direct telephone line to the Quai d'Orsay. No doubt they also enjoy the brandy, the sumptuous menus and the availability of five of Sir Philip's Rolls Royce motor cars standing in the drive ready to whisk them through the countryside.

It is interesting that Lloyd-George, who is a Liberal, should be such a good friend of the Unionist MP for Folkestone and Hythe. He will shortly appoint Sir Philip as his private secretary, whose fluent French will be useful in the forthcoming Anglo-French meetings at Port Lympne to discuss war reparations and to decide how best to carve up the Turkish Empire — a matter of considerable interest to the Sassoon family.

Politicians have found Port Lympne a convenient and welcome rendezvous but so have soldiers and film stars. Mountbatten was a recent visitor when the guest list included Charlie Chaplin.

Mrs Amelie McCudden, the mother of England's flying hero, the late Major Jimmy McCudden has been invited to represent the Mothers of Britain at the inauguration ceremony for the Tomb of the Unknown Warrior at Arlington Cemetery in the United States. Amelie has been hailed by the American press as Britain's "Gold Star Mother" and, of course, she is delighted by the honour. Amelie is well known in Gillingham, not only as Jimmy's mother, but also as the daughter of the former landlord of the Shipwright's Arms. She and her husband, William, had four sons and two daughters. Three of the boys were killed in action with the RFC or RAF.

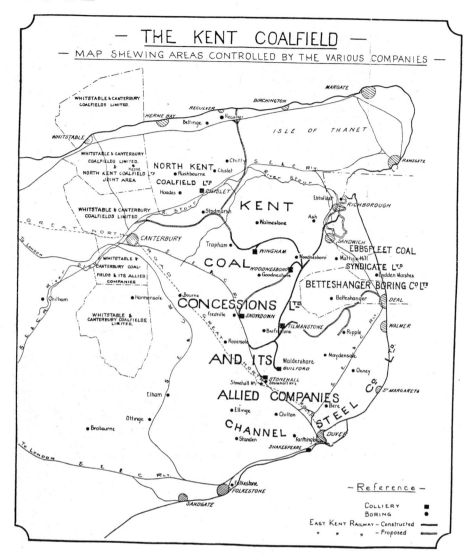

— THE KENT COALFIELD —
— MAP SHEWING AREAS CONTROLLED BY THE VARIOUS COMPANIES —

This map of the Kent coalfields shows the areas controlled by the various companies. The Betteshanger Boring Company gave an option to Messrs Dorman, Long and Co of Middlesborough two years ago. They are now exercising that option for a payment of £30,000 in cash and a royalty of 1½d per ton raised, for the western area and £15,000 in cash and a royalty of 2d per ton raised for the eastern half.

Coal mines to be extended under the sea

July 21st: Prospecting in East Kent has revealed the presence of extensive deposits of rich coal believed to be the best in the world for iron-smelting purposes and work has already begun on sinking an option owned by Messrs Dorman, Long and Company, the great Middlesborough iron firm.

This news was broken today by the Deal correspondent of the *Daily Express* who says that south eastern Kent is not likely to remain the Garden of England much longer as excavation activities will soon transform it into a vast coalfield.

He writes: "I was this afternoon informed by Colonel Standen, an authority on Kent coal, that new collieries with an output of one million tons have been planned. Further pits are to be sunk in the neighbourhood of the old Chequers Inn in the sandhills midway between Deal and Sandwich from which workings will be carried out under the bed of the sea in the Downs towards the famous Goodwins. Immense deposits of the most valuable steam coal undoubtedly exist under the Downs from the northern end of the roadstead to somewhere near St Margaret's Bay. It is understood that Messrs Dorman, Long and Co have set aside the sum of £7,000,000 for the development of their holding."

The company has already bought a number of huts from the Admiralty yard at East Cliff and erected them at Finglesham, near Betteshanger where preparatory work is under way. A railway connection is to be made from the proposed colliery at Betteshanger to Deal but nothing has been done yet apart from the marking out of the course. A colliery under the sea was to have been undertaken by the Downs Colliery Company in which Messrs Schneider, the cement firm, was interested.

'I see nothing but ill-clad figures, all hurrying, all carrying loads...as though the entire population is setting out in flight' — H.G.Wells writing of his trip to Moscow in 1920.

1921

January 20th: The Royal Navy submarine, K5, sank today in the English Channel with the loss of 56 crew members.

February 16th: The Government is to increase unemployment benefit from 15 shillings to 18 shillings as those out of work tops one million for the first time ever.

March 31st: Winston Churchill, now Colonial Secretary, tells Jews in the UK that Britain will abide by the Balfour Declaration and find them a homeland in Palestine.

July 2nd: Four Irishmen, members of Sinn Fein, the political wing of the IRA, have been sentenced to long terms in prison — up to 12 years — for the attempted murder of two policemen in Bromley. The Kent Assizes were told that they have been involved in a campaign of violence and sabotage.

July 14th: The young Duke of York visited Sittingbourne today for a whirlwind tour of farms and industry. His first stop was at Rainham and on the road to Sittingbourne he was cheered by fruit pickers and schoolchildren as he passed through the villages. At the town hall the Duke saw a sale of work which is raising money for disabled soldiers.

July 22nd: A truce has been declared in Ireland following three months of the bloodiest fighting ever known.

Storey's, the motor manufacturers of Tonbridge, has produced a four-seater saloon called The Tonbridge. It is priced at £1,200.

August 30th: The Cenotaph in Brenchley Gardens, which is a smaller replica of that erected in Whitehall, London, was unveiled today in memory of the Queen's Own West Kent Regiment soldiers who died in the Great War.

September 2nd: Folkestone's new Zig-Zag path which leads from the Leas to the Lower Sandgate Road below the West Cliff is proving more popular than anyone had imagined. The results of a survey, published today, show that on one day in August 2,630 persons and 37 prams had used the path downwards and 2,324 persons and 19 prams had returned back up! The Zig-Zag path was built earlier this year by a London company which specialises in rockwork.

December 7th: An agreement has finally been signed giving independence to Ireland. Twenty six southern counties will be known as the Irish Free State and six of the counties which form historic Ulster will remain part of the United Kingdom and continue to send MPs to Westminster. At one stage during the talks the Prime Minister, David Lloyd George threatened to "put down" the Irish rebellion if the treaty was not signed.

GREAT HITS OF 1921

The fishermen of England

Three o'clock in the morning

Springfield, a large house close to the river in Maidstone, has been purchased by the Kent Education Committee and will be used as its new headquarters. The county has also set up a library service and chosen, controversially, a woman as the first county librarian.

This is an interesting appointment. Before the war the only women employed by Kent County Council were teachers and nurses and domestic staff at the various institutions. Women now are filling many vital jobs and it is just as well for the KCC is becoming a large-scale employer, responsible for mental institutions, industrial schools, police and roadmen. In fact the headquarters staff is in excess of 300.

All set to go. Tenterden day trippers look forward to their journey.

Bank Holiday crowds break records in rush to the seaside

August 2nd: Following two of the most memorable summer months ever known, thousands of Britons have packed excursion coaches and trains and headed for the Kent coast — breaking all records on the fiftieth anniversary of the first Bank Holiday.

The approach to the Isle of Thanet yesterday was jammed by charabancs and trains were arriving at Margate at 10-minute intervals.

The summer of 1921 will always be remembered thanks to a wedge of high pressure which has stretched from the Azores and refuses to budge.

June was almost rainless and by July the countryside was so dry that thousands of fires broke out, particularly on the railway embankments and at Seal Chart, Dartford Heath, Hothfield and other open spaces.

If the dry weather continues, 1921 may well go down in history as "the desert year". Since last October only half the annual rainfall has been recorded and both farmers and anglers are suffering greatly.

July 27th: *Kent gave a rousing welcome to the Prince of Wales on Wednesday and Thursday (July 22nd and 23rd) when His Royal Highness attended several public functions throughout the county. From Dover, Folkestone, Sandgate and Hythe to Maidstone, Aylesford, Greenhithe and Dartford, the path of the royal visitor was thronged with cheering people.*

One of the Prince's duties was to unveil the obelisk to the men of the Dover Patrol and in a speech he said that the work of the men who served with the Patrol would serve as an inspiration for generations to come.

The Prince of Wales moved on to Folkestone (see photograph) where he met scores of ex-servicemen and mentioned the fact that the Port saw the arrival and departure of some 11,000 combatants during the war. He visited the Royal Victoria Hospital, Folkestone where 1,963 wounded soldiers were admitted as well as the 265 civilians injured in the disastrous air raid of May 1917.

At Aylesford he opened Preston Hall, one of the stately ancestral landmarks of Kent which has been transformed into a colony for the treatment, training and care of ex-Servicemen with tuberculosis.

Migration responsible for Kent's population increase

August 27th: First results of the Census taken in June shows that Kent has a population of 1,118,127, of whom 531,284 are males and 586,843 females. With the exception of seven towns, including Maidstone, every Kent town shows an increase in population, giving the county second place in this particular league (to Middlesex) with 97,164 more people since the last census. There is only one county borough in Kent, which shows a decrease and that is Canterbury which is down by 888.

With over 55,000 more women than men it might seem that the war, or the "lost generation" is a key factor to the inequality in numbers, but the ratio has not changed dramatically. The growth is almost entirely due to migration and the movement of population towards the more prosperous south-east and away from the depressed areas of the North and Wales. For the first time in the county's history lilting Celtic strains and full-blooded northern vowels can be heard in every Kentish town.

There are five towns in Kent with a larger population than Maidstone, the County Town — Gillingham, Margate, Chatham, Dover and Folkestone.

The census shows an increase in the population of Great Britain of almost two million since 1911, making a grand total of 42,767,530. Of these, some 7.4 million live in London.

City and County of Canterbury 23,738

Municipal Boroughs & Urban Districts	Population	Municipal Boroughs & Urban Districts	Population
Ashford	14,355	Sidcup	8,940
Beckenham	33,350	Sittingbourne	9,339
Bexley	21,463	Southborough	7,104
Broadstairs	15,465	Tenterden MB	3,438
Bromley MB	35,070	Tonbridge	15,929
Chatham MB	42,065	Tunbridge Wells	35,568
Cheriton	6,995	Walmer	5,354
Chislehurst	8,980	Whitstable	9,842
Crayford	11,924	Wrotham	4,240
Dartford	26,005		
Deal MB	12,990	**Rural Districts**	**Persons**
Dover MB	39,985		
Erith	31,568	Blean	8,682
Faversham MB	10,870	Bridge	11,228
Folkestone	37,571	Bromley	26,018
Gillingham MB	54,038	Cranbrook	12,909
Gravesend MB	31,137	Dartford	37,612
Herne Bay	11,872	Dover	8,871
Hythe MB	7,764	East Ashford	14,853
Lydd MB	2,256	Eastry	13,433
		Elham	7,910
Maidstone MB	37,448	Faversham	14,301
		Hollingbourne	13,163
Margate MB	46,475	Hoo	4,815
Milton Regis	7,481	Isle of Thanet	14,081
New Romney MB	1,605	Maidstone	16,986
Northfleet	15,719	Malling	25,351
Penge	26,178	Milton	13,997
Queenborough MB	3,073	Romney Marsh	3,158
Ramsgate MB	36,560	Sevenoaks	23,861
City of Rochester MB	31,261	Sheppey	4,591
Sandgate (part of)	2,243	Strood	16,279
Sandwich MB	3,161	Tenterden	5,852
Sevenoaks	9,058	Tonbridge	17,399
Sheerness	18,596	West Ashford	7,740

Ambitious scheme in Whitstable to build "council houses"

April 7th: Lord Harris, the former Kent captain, showed today that he is just as competent with a spade in his hand as he is with a cricket bat. With a grace that reminded a large gathering of his sweetly struck cover drives, His Lordship deftly turned over the first sod of earth at Whitstable where the local urban council plans to build 51 houses in connection with the National Housing Scheme. When the small estate at Teynham Road and Railway Avenue is completed they will be the first council-owned homes in the country — a unique first for Whitstable. The "council houses", as they are called, are designed for those earning less than £250 per annum and the total cost of buildings will be less than £40,000 including sewerage and roads. Mr Pratt Scott, Minister of Health, has been invited to open the estate, when completed.

July 30th: The Cenotaph in Brenchley Gardens, Maidstone was unveiled today to commemorate the men of the Queen's Own Royal West Kents who died in the Great War. Their achievements during the long struggle are legion. Apart from their two Regular Battalions and their two existing Territorial Battalions they put into the field at the beginning of the war, they raised a further 13 Territorial and Service Battalions, between them fought on every front and won some 70 Battle Honours, including the three Victoria Crosses. The Regimental Memorial clearly shows the scale of their achievement for it commemorates nearly 70,000 officers and men lost. The names of The Buffs who made the great sacrifice are inscribed in the Books of Life kept in the Warriors Chapel of the Cathedral Church of Christ, Canterbury. The Cenotaph was designed by Sir Edward Lutyens, pictured above, a close friend of Lady Victoria Sackville-West of Knole, for the past few years. He has given her his first sketch for the Cenotaph. It is understood that Lord Sackville has long sought a divorce but that Lady Sackville has turned down the idea, no doubt fearing to lose her title.

'In the twinkling of an eye I found myself without an office, without a seat, without a party and without an appendix' — Winston Churchill after his defeat in the November general election.

January 1st: Four fire brigades, from Margate, Ramsgate, Broadstairs and Birchington were called to a massive conflagration in the hangar at Manston in the early hours of this morning. The hangar was saved but an instructional aircraft was destroyed.

January 5th: Sir Ernest Shackleton died today of a heart attack in South Georgia on his fourth expedition to the Antarctic.

January 21st: The provisional Irish parliament has approved the treaty with Britain which sets up the Irish Free State. Eamon de Valera has refused the presidency of the Dail. Ireland's political future is still uncertain.

February 7th: The outbreak of Foot and Mouth disease has hit Kent badly and hundreds of head of cattle, sheep and pigs will be slaughtered.

A new paper mill at Aylesford has been opened. It is called Reed's.

February 25th: The "Geddes Axe", as it is being called, which recommends the chopping of a massive £87 million off public spending programmes, has fallen particular heavily on the airfields of Kent. There are now just 11 active bases in south-east England and many of those are in some jeopardy. Manston, Eastchurch, Grain and Hawkinge remain in East Kent along with Lympne which will shortly become a cross-Channel airport. The Government has been asked to approve a report prepared by Sir Eric Geddes and his committee which also calls for pay cuts for civil servants, the armed forces, the police and teachers.

March 18th: Mahatma Ghandhi, the Indian nationalist leader, has been sentenced to six years' imprisonment for sedition.

March 22nd: Queen Mary today opened Waterloo Station .

May 22nd: The highest May temperature for 50 years — 88F — is recorded at Bromley.

May: George Miller of Wested Farm, Crockenhill is now known

The easiest method of making home deliveries for G.H.Coe, the baker and confectioner of Canterbury is by bicycle. Here is one of the team in St Peter's Grove.

across the country as the "peppermint king" and for a very good reason — this year he has 420 acres of the herb Mentha x piperita under cultivation at Crockenhill and Chelsfield. He fulfils British demand and exports to Europe.

June 12th: A British Everest expedition, led by George Leigh Mallory, has succeeded in reaching 26,800 feet without the aid of oxygen.

June 22nd: Field Marshal Sir Henry Wilson, the former Chief of the Imperial General Staff and a frequent visitor to Port Lympne,

was gunned down yesterday as he walked to his home in Belgravia. His killers, two Irishmen, were captured after a chase.

Enid Blyton, a 25-year-old, who has been both a school teacher and a governess is now making quite a reputation as a short story writer — various articles appearing in such prestigious journals as *Nash's Magazine* and the *Westminster Review*. She has also published a book of poems which is called *Child Whispers*.

July 18th: Lord Louis Mountbatten today married

Edwina Ashley. The Prince of Wales was best man.

The Duke of Windsor has unveiled the Naval war memorial at Chatham which stands on the Great Lines east of the Naval Recreation Ground. It consists of a rectangular column of Portland stone about 100 feet high and is crowned by a large copper sphere supported by four emblematical figures representing the four winds. On the base and buttresses are bronze panels representing those who fell in the Great War including members of the RN, RNAS, RNVR, RNR, MMR and civilians of Chatham command.

August 22nd: Michael Collins, Irish politician who led the fight for independence, died today during an ambush in his native Cork. Collins was commander-in-chief of the Irish army and chairman of the Irish Free State.

October 19th: The Coalition Government is dead. David Lloyd George has been ousted as Prime Minister, the Tories have disowned Austen Chamberlain as party leader and the King has asked Andrew Bonar Law to form a new Government. Both the Tories and Liberals are in disarray.

November 16th: The Tories rule Britain again tonight for the first time since they lost power in 1906. The Liberal, Winston Churchill, is one of the casualties.

The Dartford engineering company, J and E Hall have recently installed lifts and escalators in a number of prestigious venues including Harrods, Selfridges, Bentalls and the Paris Metro. The company is also now making more than 50 per cent of the world's refrigerated cargo installations.

Marie Lloyd, the lovable Kentish-born music hall star has died at the age of 52.

GREAT HITS OF 1922

Limehouse Blues
I wish I could shimmy like my sister Kate

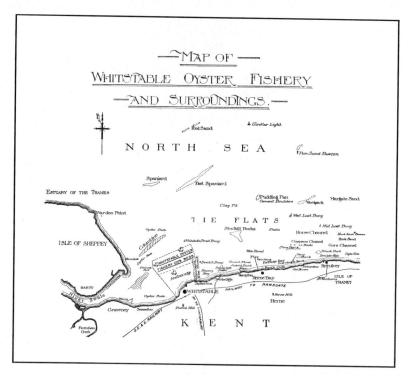

MAP OF
WHITSTABLE OYSTER FISHERY
AND SURROUNDINGS.

Sad days in 'Oysterville': pollution is blamed

May: Whitstable's major industry and one which provides a living for much of the town's population is in danger of collapsing following the death of millions of oysters. Experts believe that pollution may be responsible.

This devastating news comes just a year after a sharp frost killed off a large proportion of the stocks. For the Whitstable Oyster Company of Free Fishers and Dredgers it means that their livelihood is seriously affected and they may have to import oysters from elsewhere for resale.

Whitstable has long been renowned for the quality of its oysters which are cultivated and dredged up from the coast. The "Royal Natives', so called because the company has a royal charter from George III, are exported all over the world. It is the foremost oyster town in the country despite the fact that the grounds are only a few square miles in extent. In fact before the war the Company regularly supplied more than half of the national oyster catch — something in the region of 19 million oysters out of 33 million landed in England and Wales.

Oyster fishing in Whitstable has changed dramatically since the turn of the century. Previously the beds were worked solely by the Free Fishers and Dredgers and the company was restricted entirely to sons of freemen who shared the profits equally amongst themselves. However they were forced to change their constitution into a normal shareholding company, each member — some 600 in number — receiving twenty £10 shares. Control passed from the fishermen to a board of directors, the men were paid a flat wage and the whole tone of fishing in Whitstable changed.

Pollution of the sea has not been positively proved but it is the final nail in the coffin. The Happy Fishing Grounds, as they are known, will soon be renamed. These are sad times in 'Oysterville'.

A dredger prepares for rough weather.

More mobile Tories sweep the board

November 17th: Reflecting the national trend, the Conservative party has swept to power in Kent with Labour and Liberal trailing almost neck and neck. It means that the Tories rule Britain on their own again tonight for the first time since they lost in the General Election of 1906.

Once again the greatest excitement was in Maidstone where two recounts were necessary before the Conservative candidate, Commander Carlyon Bellairs, was declared the winner — by 33 votes. Second was Mr Foster Clark, the Independent and just behind him was Mr Hugh Dalton, Labour. All three polled more than 8,000 votes each.

The Conservative victory is due entirely to an ample supply of motor cars in which their supporters were ferried to the polling stations. The Labour candidate Mr Dalton had no such luxuries and he feels this contributed largely to his defeat. In a speech after the result was declared he said: "In Kent Toryism is seen in its worst, most offensive, most arrogant, most ignorant and most blatant shape and to have made such a fight in such a place against such an enemy so strongly entrenched and so equipped with wealth, with cars and with the power of lying was a very fine thing."

In the Chatham division of Rochester, the former flying pioneer, Col J.T.Moore-Brabazon won the seat for the Conservatives against Liberal's Sir Alfred Callaghan who had been warned that Liberalism was "more or less dead", and set out to prove otherwise. The Chatham division also returned a Tory and so did Canterbury, Mr Ronald McNeil winning a majority of more than 8,000.

There was a greater Tory majority in Dover where the popular figure of Major the Hon J.J.Astor beat another Conservative candidate, Sir Thomas Polson. Again the crucial factor was motor cars and the fact that the Major had more than 150 at his disposal clearly helped him to amass a 10,000 plus majority.

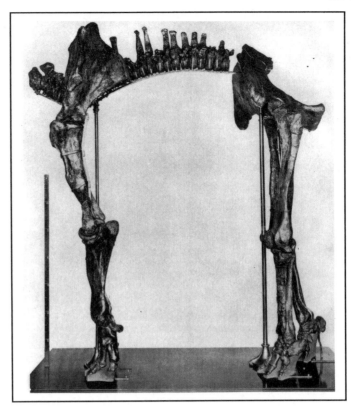

The Upnor Elephant, 12 feet seven inches high, painstakingly pieced together by Charles Andrews and now on display at the Natural History Museum.

Proved at last: elephants once roamed the Medway valley

February: After puzzling over a giant jigsaw for 12 years, the bones of a monstrous animal found in the Kent marshes at Upnor in the Medway Valley have finally been pieced together — and the result is now on display at the Natural History Museum.

The animal is an elephant, of an exceptionally large size, proving that they roamed in Kent in pre-historic times. It is believed to be 50,000 years old and archaeologists say it is the most important and certainly the biggest skeleton ever found beneath an English field.

It was in 1911 that the Royal Engineers while engaged in trench-digging practice on the banks of the Medway at Upnor, opposite Chatham Dockyard, cut through a number of large bones, some of which, together with a tusk, were completely destroyed. Operations were suspended and no further notice was taken of the discovery until Mr S.Turner, searching for flints, picked up some pieces of bone which he sent to the British Museum for identification.

Excitement was immense. It was recognised as being the carpal bone of an elephant and a careful examination of the locality was carried out. Under the supervision of Mr L.E.Parsons, the bones, many riddled with roots of trees were carefully lifted from the earth by laying strips of canvas dipped in plaster of Paris, first on the exposed side, then on the under side. Once in the museum the wrappings were undone and the bones hardened with shellac.

The Upnor Elephant today stands 12 feet seven inches high and towers above every other animal on display at Kensington. Upnor's oldest inhabitant is proving to be quite a celebrity.

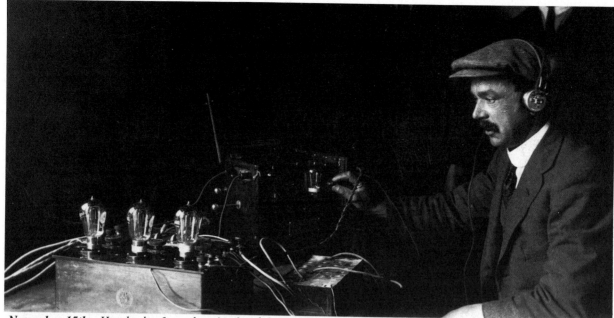

November 15th: Hundreds of people using headphones yesterday heard the first regular news broadcast. It came at 6 o'clock from Marconi House in the Strand and was read by Arthur Burrows, with material supplied by Reuters News Agency. In the more affluent areas of Kent, loudspeakers in the drawing room made it possible for the whole families to listen. Photograph shows some of the first wireless enthusiasts in Tenterden. It was in 1920 that Dame Nellie Melba made the first broadcast which was heard all over Europe. The British Broadcasting Company plans to broadcast daily with concerts and news at 6 o'clock in the evening.

Northcliffe, pioneer of popular newspapers, dies

August 14th: Lord Northcliffe, who founded the *Daily Mail*, the *Daily Mirror* and rescued *The Times,* died yesterday aged 57. He was the pioneer of popular newspapers and his passing is a great loss to the Isle of Thanet, where expressions of sympathy have gone to his wife, Lady Northcliffe and his nephew, the Hon E.C.Harmsworth, the Member for Thanet.

Since Alfred Harmsworth chose St Peter's as his place of residence he had shown a deep interest in the welfare of the district. His newspapers were always at the service of Thanet and there is no doubt that he helped to make this corner of the land both desirable and prosperous.

Ramsgate had offered to confer the Freedom of the Borough on Lord Northcliffe but the hand of death has tragically intervened to deprive the town of that opportunity.

Lord Northcliffe's accomplishments with newspaper production were greater than that of any other journalist. The *Daily Mail* was the first half-penny morning paper to give the world news in a popular form and during the war his power was used to stimulate the determination of the country to greater efforts to achieve victory.

His younger brother Harold, created Viscount Rothermere in 1919, from Hempsted, Benenden, has taken charge of Associated Newspapers. Rothermere, who lost his eldest two sons in the war, has always had the greater financial expertise.

Twelve die in road and rail accidents

August 26th: Kent, for many years, has been exceptionally free from serious road and railway accidents but this week there have been two tragedies, claiming the lives of several men. The first was on Saturday (August 19th) when eight men belonging to an excursion party were killed when their charabanc overturned into a dyke at Brookland, Romney Marsh. The second was at Milton Halt, near Gravesend on Monday when three London men, crossing the railway line, were hit by a light engine. Seconds later a passenger train ran into the engine and there was another fatality.

At the Brookland's inquest the Coroner said charabancs should not use roads to which they are obviously unsuited. In this case the road was 14 feet wide with neither fence nor hedge to separate it from the ditch. The men, returning from Hastings to Ashford, stood no chance when the vehicle toppled over.

The railway accident was due entirely to fog. Several people were crossing the line and apart from the three deaths there were many injuries.

May 4th: *An honorary degree has been conferred on Miss Ellen Terry, the actress who lives at Smallhythe Place, near Tenterden. She is seen here in her robes on the occasion of the installation of Earl Haig as Chancellor and Mr J.M.Barrie, the Scottish playwright, as Rector of St Andrew's University. Miss Terry took the leading role in Mr Barrie's play Alice Sit-By-The-Fire in 1905.*

May 25th: A phenomenal storm, which travelled over the valley of the Weald, hit the Tunbridge Wells and Southborough district today with such violence that it will remain crystalline in the memory. Hailstones, the size of tangerines, smashed shop windows and brought down roof tiles, foliage was scattered everywhere and stock in the area of The Pantiles has been badly damaged. Hundreds of tons of replacement glass has been ordered and glaziers will be busy for weeks. At Sheringham Hall, Speldhurst, a few miles away, 1,200 panes of glass were smashed. Photograph shows workmen removing hailstones from the main street in Southborough.

New home near Westerham for Winston Churchill

December: Winston Churchill, who lost his seat at Dundee in November's general election, is now out of hospital following an appendix operation and looking for a new house in the country. It is the first time in 20 years he has been out of Parliament and only recently he said wryly: "In the twinkling of an eye, I found myself without an office, without a seat, without a party and without an appendix".

He may soon have a new home. He has seen many properties but the favourite appears to be a large country house near Westerham called Chartwell Manor which has come onto the market following the death of its owner Mr William Erskine Campbell-Colquhoun. Chartwell is a lonely spot, approached down a narrow, overgrown country lane with a poor surface. The house is covered in creepers and badly neglected but Mr Churchill has said he loves the undulating countryside of the Weald, the oasthouse next door and the great lake in the grounds with an entrancing islet.

If Mr Churchill does buy Chartwell he will need to renovate the house and put in a new drainage system. He will also want a temporary home in the area so that he can supervise the rebuilding work.

'The outskirts of Bromstead are a maze of exploitation, roads that lead nowhere, that end in tarred fences....in trespass boards that use vehement language' — H.G.Wells in *The New Machiavelli*

1923

January 27th: The National Socialist party began its first public congress in Munich, a city where the Party enjoys great support. Its leader, a former corporal in the army is Herr Adolf Hitler. He is calling for a repeal of the Treaty of Versailles which most Germans consider too harsh.

Kent and Sussex Farmers Ltd have obtained from Lord Sackville, the ancient market rights in the centre of Sevenoaks. They are now looking for a more suitable site for a cattle market than the town centre which is a busy shopping area.

March 2nd: The second reading of the Matrimonial Clauses Bill, passed in the Commons today, gives more equality to the sexes by allowing a wife to petition for divorce for a husband's adultery. At the moment only the reverse is possible.

March 9th: Vladimir Lenin, Soviet leader since the Bolsheviks seized power in Russia, is paralysed after a massive stroke which has deprived him also of the power of speech. In a recent letter Lenin criticised the Communist Party's General Secretary, Joseph Stalin who he says is too rude and should be removed from his post.

April 19th: A new report from the National Birthrate Commission says that sex education should be taught in schools and homes. The report also recommends a better diet, better recreation facilities and more sunshine, particularly for children who live in cities.

April: The racecourse at Tonbridge has been purchased from Mr William Abrey and converted into one of the finest sports grounds in south-east England.

April 28th: The FA Cup Final between Bolton Wanderers and West Ham United was played for the first time at Wembley today and there was almost a terrible disaster. More than 126,000 football fans were allowed in the stadium and another 75,000 scaled the inadequate walls to gain free admission to the terraces. The crowd spilled onto the playing

John Astor takes over The Times

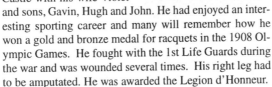

The Hon John Jacob Astor, younger son of the first Viscount and the Conservative Member of Parliament for Dover, has acquired 90 per cent of the controlling shares in *The Times* newspaper and, as co-proprietor, is responsible for the editorial policy of the newspaper. *The Times*, popularly known as *The Thunderer* is well established as the main national forum for information.

John Astor lives at Hever Castle with his wife Violet and sons, Gavin, Hugh and John. He had enjoyed an interesting sporting career and many will remember how he won a gold and bronze medal for racquets in the 1908 Olympic Games. He fought with the 1st Life Guards during the war and was wounded several times. His right leg had to be amputated. He was awarded the Legion d'Honneur.

area and a policeman on a white horse patiently coaxed the fans off so that the game could continue. Bolton won 2-1.

May 15th: Another massive mine has been washed ashore at Ramsgate. The beach was cleared as soldiers defused the monster.

May 21st: The Prime Minister Andrew Bonar Law has resigned following the news that he has incurable cancer of the throat. As he made no recommendation to the King about a successor it was assumed that Lord Curzon, the Foreign Secretary would take the job, but the Tories have chosen instead the Chancellor, Mr Stanley Baldwin.

July 13th: Lady Astor's Liquor Bill which bans the sale of alcohol to young people under the age of 18 has been passed in the Commons.

August 6th: American swimmer Henry Sullivan has swum the Channel from Dover to Cap Griz Nez in 28 hours.

August 21st: The dock strike has ended after seven weeks

September 10th: The Co-operative Stores at Sheerness have been destroyed by fire. Damage caused is in excess of £30,000 worth.

October 8th: Sir Edward Hulton has sold a number of his newspaper titles, including the *Daily Sketch,* the *Evening Standard* and the *Daily Herald* to the Lords Rothermere and Beaverbrook, for £6,000,000.

A cross has been erected on a road junction between Lympne and Hythe to mark the traditional meeting place of the Barons of the Cinque Ports. Shepway Cross erected earlier this year has now been opened by Lord Beauchamp, Lord Warden of the Cinque Ports. From this symbolic site most of the marsh villages can be seen, in good weather.

December 14th: Almost 75,000 animals — many in Kent farms —have been slaughtered following the epidemic of foot and mouth disease.

December 17th: The Imperial Air Transport Company has been formed.(IATA)

An American entrepreneur, Charles Ganahl has bought a sizeable acreage of marshland at Wallend, near Grain and opened an oil refinery.

Vita Sackville-West, the daughter of Lord and Lady Sackville, who returned to Knole in such triumph in 1910, has published a history book — *Knole and the Sackvilles.* Vita, the wife of Harold Nicholson, lives at Long Barn, Sevenoaks Weald.

GREAT HITS OF 1923

Who's sorry now

Farewell Blues

Leysdown-on-Sea is best known as the birthplace of flying in the Navy. If a proposal to rename the place is accepted it will become more famous as one of the most desirable holiday resorts in the country. The suggested name is Leysdown Super Mare. This small town has no claims to beauty but it is already popular with the masses thanks to the Sheppey Light Railway which transports hundreds of holidaymakers. Already holiday camps, camping sites, hotels and little red-box houses are being built and London business people see even more potential in Leysdown. It certainly enjoys brisk and bracing air on the eastern edge of the Isle of Sheppey.

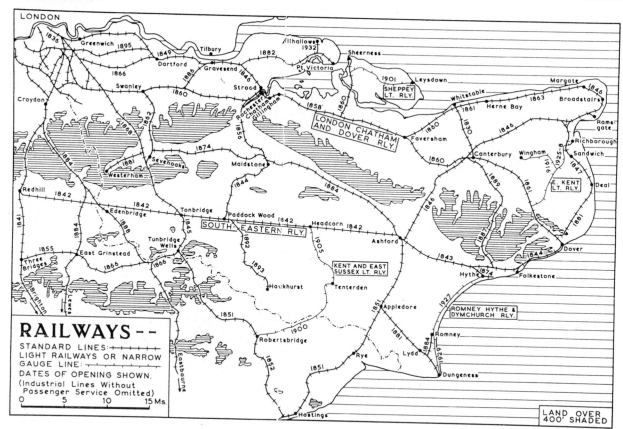

RAILWAYS --
STANDARD LINES: +++++++
LIGHT RAILWAYS OR NARROW
GAUGE LINE: +—+—+—
DATES OF OPENING SHOWN.
(Industrial Lines Without
  Passenger Service Omitted)
0   5   10   15 Ms.

LAND OVER
400' SHADED

New rail company believes in electrification

January 1st: A new company is born today which will affect the lives of every person living in Kent. The SR (Southern Railway) is one of four group companies to be given royal assent and has been created from the Railway Act of 1921. It will operate the largest rail commuter network in the world, improve communication with remote holiday spots in Devon and Cornwall and take the rich and famous from London to Paris on bigger and better boat trains.

Sir Eric Geddes, Minister of Transport, is the sponsor of the Act. SR is the smallest of the four companies and the only one committed to electrification — which is Sir Eric's great dream.

Under the Act, the Southern will absorb five constituent companies including The South Eastern Railway Company and The London Chatham and Dover Railway Company which never completely merged and have been plagued by more than 30 years of mutual antagonism.

As people in Kent know only too well the rolling stock has been frequently criticised for its poor quality; lavatories have, until recently, only been provided for first-class passengers.

Last year The South East Chatham Railway

introduced a few gangwayed, side corridor vehicles with panelling for continental services and improved its locomotive stock. There are now plans to introduce more up-to-date rolling stock with fine new coaches, to strengthen all the bridges and build some handsome new stations. The chief mechanical engineer is Mr Richard Maunsell and he will be based at Ashford.

An engine pulling three coaches at Tubs Hill station, Sevenoaks.

CIDENT TO FERRY BRIDGE. NO 4
ILWAY PASSENGERS CROSSING IN BOATS.

February: *The old bridge is damaged and railway passengers now have to queue patiently while motor boats take them across the Swale to the Isle of Sheppey — and back.*

Urgent plea to rebuild Kingsferry Bridge

November: Ambitious plans to rebuild the Kingsferry Bridge, which was damaged in an accident some months ago, is receiving massive support in the neighbourhood, especially from those whose livelihood depends on good communication by river, road or rail.

For some months now, a motor boat ferry across the Swale has been in operation but it is far from satisfactory, especially when the ferry men strike. This occurred last week and meant a complete suspension of the Sittingbourne to Sheppey rail service.

It is suggested that the new bridge should be built to the east of the existing one which would be demolished. This would involve the building of a new road and railway track, the former running directly into Queenborough, while the latter would rejoin the old line at Kingsferry and be approximately six miles in length. With this plan trains would continue through Sittingbourne to the Isle of Sheppey and not be compelled to reverse as is the case now.

The traders on the mainland side of the Swale are urging the removal of the obstruction caused by the present bridge to the navigation in the waterway. Mr Miller, secretary to Mr Edward Lloyd, owner of Sittingbourne Paper Mills, employing about 1,600 men, said the total tonnage carried by water was 450,000 tons per annum and there would be no difficulty for boats of 10,000 tons cargo reaching Ridham Docks if the new bridge were built on modern lines. A large part of their raw material, he said, came from Canada. It was just not possible to use small boats for the Atlantic trade.

People from Sheppey have made it clear that they want a free bridge. By an Act of Parliament there has been a toll on the old Kingsferry Bridge for 50 years and the revenue from this tax was exceeding more than £1,000 a year.

With talks continuing the railway company responsible for the damaged bridge is currently carrying out repairs, but with great difficulty.

Photograph shows members of Ightham village club. Cricket is now even more popular than it was before the Great War. All over Kent the game is being played more widely — by schools, factories, towns and villages. Cricket personalities and Test matches are national news and, thanks mainly to the popularity of Warwick Armstrong's Australian tourists in the summer of 1921, even soccer is now eclipsed as "the national game". With so many key players missing it was thought that Kent would struggle to achieve the standards of the pre-war years but they have finished in the top five every year and the future looks even more promising with such distinguished players as Frank Woolley and 'Tich' Freeman achieving such remarkable feats. The latter burst onto the scene at the age of 26

and, with his right arm leg spin and googlies, is returning phenomenal bowling figures. In fact, in 1921, Freeman and Woolley took 336 wickets between them while the rest of their colleagues managed just 145.

'Tich' Freeman as he is called by his colleagues is winning many matches for Kent but he is not alone. Last year Harold Hardinge set a new record for Kent with an unbeaten 249 and wicketkeeper Hubble claimed six victims in an innings to equal the record set by Huish in 1911. In the villages, more and more clubs are being formed, or reformed and schoolboys in Kent are passionately collecting cigarette cards with pictures of their heroes. Little wonder that the most popular cigarettes among dads in the county are Wills, Capstan or Players.

1923

Surprise, surprise — Sevenoaks goes Liberal

December 11th: With constituency results all in there is another hung parliament which means that the Tories will almost certainly be thrown out of office. The final tally is Conservative 258, Labour 191 and Liberal 159. It is assumed that the King will soon invite Ramsay MacDonald, as leader of the second biggest party, to form Britain's first Labour Government, less than 24 years after the party was formed.

In Kent there have been few surprises, except at Sevenoaks. This traditional Tory seat has, for the first time, returned a Liberal member, Major Ronald Williams of Brasted Hall who has defeated Sir Thomas Bennett. Considering the Liberals have been in some disarray for years it is a most surprising reversal.

What is more upsetting to the people of Sevenoaks is the prospect of a Labour Government. The *Sevenoaks Chronicle* is already receiving letters of a quite hysterical nature claiming that the Liberal action in enabling Labour to take power is putting the country into the hands of the Bolsheviks.

Richmal and William are Bromley's heroes

October: Miss Richmal Crompton Lamburn, classics mistress at Bromley High School, has been struck down with polio but hopes to continue with her teaching when her health improves. Her colleagues and friends at Bromley are wishing her a speedy recovery, hoping that she will be able to devote more time to her writing. Last year, under the name of Richmal Crompton, she published a delightful book called *Just William*

and it is already a national best seller.

The story revolves round William Brown, an irrepressibly scruffy 11-year-old schoolboy hero, who leads a gang called the Outlaws and slips away from his middle-class parents whenever he can. Gang members include Henry, Douglas, Ginger — and Violet Elizabeth Bott, who is really an intruder and despised by the boys. Violet's father is very wealthy having made a fortune out of Bott's Digestive Sauce.

Mrs Lamburn, who has been teaching at Bromley since 1917, was born in 1890 and now lives at Bromley Common. She loves her town and the countryside and has said that the area will feature prominently in all her future books. Letters are pouring into her home from well-wishers all over the country urging her to get better quickly and then write more adventures of *Just William*. The people of Bromley certainly echo those sentiments.

All time greats at the Winter Gardens

October: The Winter Gardens at Margate have been more popular than ever and the entertainment provided is no longer limited to the summer season. Alongside concerts, tea dances, cinema and exhibitions, this year's programme has included a number of international stars. Among the favourites have been Claude Hulbert with the Cigarettes Concert Company, the Imperial Russian Ballet, Miss Sybil Thorndyke, Will Evans and the most famous of all — Anna Pavlova (pictured left), the finest dancer of the 20th century who delighted hundreds of people on July 31st this year.

'The railroads are not run for the benefit of the dear public.......they are built for men who invest their money and expect to get a fair percentage on the same' — W.H.Vanderbilt in 1882.

January 21st: Vladimir Lenin, the father of the Russian Revolution, died today after a long illness. He was 54. Following the civil war and famine that gripped Russia after 1917, Lenin helped to create the Soviet state, but leaves behind bitter rivalries in the Politburo.

January 22nd: Ramsay MacDonald has become Britain's first Labour Prime Minister. He was appointed today by the King and takes power, depending on the goodwill of the Liberal Party for survival. The new minority government is not expected to last long.

February 3rd: Woodrow Wilson, former President of the United States, died today. He helped to create the League of Nations to "make the world safe for democracy" and was shattered by the US Senate's rejection of US membership.

February 16th: The eight-day railway strike is over but now a dock strike has paralysed every port in the country including Chatham. Immediately the price of bread has been increased by ½d to 8½d a loaf.

March 31st: Britain has its own national airline at last. Imperial Airways has been formed by the merger of four companies and has a fleet of 13 aircraft flying from Croydon.

The aeroplane manufacturers, Shorts of Rochester, have built their first all-metal aircraft. The first is a flying boat known as the Cockle and is fitted with two Blackburne motor cycle engines. The second is a landplane which has been entered in the Lympne flying competition.

April 1st: Adolf Hitler, leader of the Nazi party in Germany, has been sentenced to five years' imprisonment for high treason.

Rochester has welcomed an exciting new paddle steamer to the river. She has been christened the *Medway Queen*.

July 30th: The eighth Olympic Games held in Paris were

October 29th: Dover's War Memorial is unveiled.

memorable for the performance of two Britons on the track. Eric Liddell, the Scottish Rugby international switched to 400 metres to avoid competing on a Sunday and set a new record. Harold Abrahams, the Cambridge law student, triumphed in the 100 metres to beome the first European to win the Olympic title.

The ancient Hemsted estate at Benenden has been sold in lots. The house, renovated by Lord Rothermere, will become a girls' school. Sadly, the massive Hemsted oak, one of the largest in Britain has been felled. The trunk — 5 ft 6inches at the base will be exhibited in the British Empire Exhibition.

August 20th: Agreement has

been reached in London to allow 3,000 UK citizens to emigrate to Canada and live on farms. It is believed that many of the applicants live in Kent.

November 6th: After yet another General Election, the Tories are

back in power with a massive majority. Stanley Baldwin is Prime Minister once again and he has named Winston Churchill as his Chancellor of the Exchequer.

The Fort Clarence archway across the Borstal Road at Rochester has been demolished.

November 19th: The new Watling Street by-pass from Dartford to Strood has been opened by the Prince of Wales.

There is uproar in Sevenoaks as the ancient Market House in the High Street is converted into public lavatories. No-one, it seems likes the idea, but no-one can produce a workable alternative scheme.

December 24th: Eight people died today in Britain's worst air crash when an Imperial Airways aircraft plummeted to earth just seconds after taking off from Croydon aerodrome.

The children's writer E.Nesbit — better known in the Romney Marsh area where she lives as Mrs Bland Tucker has died aged 66. She spent the last years of her life with her second husband Captain Tucker at The Long Boat in St Mary's Bay where she looked out "between the marsh and the sky upon the lovely little hills of Kent". She is buried at St Mary-in-the-Marsh.

GREAT HITS OF 1924

It had to be you

Fascinating rhythm

August: There have been more setbacks for the East Kent Light Railway Company. The great dream, envisaged years earlier of railway connections between Shepherdswell, Sandwich, Richborough, Eastry, Wingham, Eythorne, Guilford and Tilmanstone, has still not materialised — and now seems unlikely to do so.

The main reason for this sad state of affairs is that one of the major companies has opposed all applications to provide lines to their collieries because, they say, they can build their own. In addition the coalfield has not developed as the EKLR had originally anticipated and a rail network does seems unnecessary.

A tragedy that has rocked the nation

February 19th: The Slade Green Filling Factory, situated midway between Erith and Dartford on Crayford Marshes, was the scene of a terrible disaster yesterday in which eleven girls and a foreman lost their lives.

Between 8.45 and 9 o'clock the girls were at their work breaking open Verey light cartridges and extracting powder. Suddenly there was a flash and in a moment that building — of brick and corrugated iron — was an inferno of smoke and fire. As the fire reached the cartridges they exploded, appearing like stars among the smoke.

Eleven of the 18 girls were trapped by the fire. Miss Charlotte Coshall, the forewoman and seven of the remaining girls managed to get out of the building, some with their clothes alight. The awful suddenness of the catastrophe and the smoke and fumes prevented any possible chance of rescue.

The Slade Green Filling Factory was originally munition works under Government control but more recently has been used by Messrs W.B.Gilbert Ltd for the breaking down of munitions. The factory consists of a number of buildings, all separate from each other and reached from Slade Green by a narrow winding road over the marshes. Close to it on the Erith side are the Thames Ammunition works.

Some of those who escaped turned back at once but, finding it impossible to reach the unfortunate girls inside, rushed towards the gates of the works screaming for help.

One eye witness said the foreman who died had tried to lift a girl through the window but the heat and smoke were too great and he fell back.

When help eventually arrived only one girl was alive,

THE DAILY MIRROR, Tuesday, February 19, 1924.

STRIKE INQUIRY: CABINET'S FOOD PRICES WARNING

The Daily Mirror

NET SALE MUCH THE LARGEST OF ANY DAILY PICTURE NEWSPAPER

No. 6,330.   TUESDAY, FEBRUARY 19, 1924.   One Penny.

GIRL VICTIMS OF FIRE IN AMMUNITION WORKS

Miss Edna Allen, and she was terribly burned. She was taken to Erith Cottage Hospital but died during the night.

The inquest will be opened at Crayford tomorrow (Wednesday) and a memorial service will be planned later.

A happy smiling picture of the girls who worked for W.B.Gilbert — a few weeks later eleven of them were dead.

Leeds Castle for sale — Randolf Hearst interested?

Death duties have forced the family of the late Mr Cornwallis Wykeham-Martin to put his lovely moated home, Leeds Castle, on the market — and already interest has been shown by the great American newspaper tycoon, William Randolf Hearst.

Apparently, some months ago, Mr Hearst sent a telegram to his English agent which tersely stated: "Want to buy an English castle — please find which ones available". His agent has now inspected Leeds and replied with the news that it is unique as an antiquity but it will need quite an expenditure to make it habitable.

Leeds Castle was first built in stone as a formidable fortress by a Norman baron in the reign of Henry Ist. It came into the possession of the Crown and was a royal palace for six of England's mediaeval queens, passing eventually into the hands of famous English families including the St Legers, the Culpepers and the Fairfaxes and then the Wykeham-Martins.

It is unlikely that Mr Hearst will want Leeds Castle. There is no proper bathroom, the place is still lit by oil lamps and the servants quarters are in the dungeons.

Two Roman homes discovered at Folkestone

May: Excitement in Folkestone reached fever pitch this week as archaeologist Mr S.E. Winbolt and his loyal band of helpers finally brought to light the remains of two Roman houses, complete with bathrooms on the East Cliff, high above the town.

Some months ago a landslip revealed part of a Roman house and the end of a drain was seen with a Roman tile projecting from it. Mr Winbolt, who lives nearby, found 20 men to help him clear the site and after much hard work they discovered the two houses — one built before the year AD 100 and the other some time later. It is believed that each house was inhabited until about AD 350.

The excavation team have found the remains of more than 20 rooms, a corridor and a courtyard with a mosaic floor. There is also a kitchen with two fireplaces and, quite amazingly, the remains of food, several open hearths with the earthenware nozzles of the bellows used to blow the fires. Coins, hairpins, brooches, silver and bronze and a chain and a bronze screw with perfect thread have also been found lying there.

Now there is great speculation as to the owner of such an impressive home. Some say that Carausius lived there but Mr Winbolt thinks it more likely to have been the home of the Admiral of the Saxon Shore.

1924

The Gravesend and District Bus Company Fleet — no serious competition here.

It looks like war on the bus routes

March: Since 1909 the Tunbridge Wells-based bus company, Autocar has enjoyed a monopoly on the traditional bus routes around the town and nearby villages. Since the war, however, competition has appeared in the form of small Chevrolets owned by independent coach companies which have been little more than an irritation to the wealthy, well-established Autocar Company with its fleet of 14 comfortable Leyland saloons.

A new competitor has now appeared on the scene offering a more efficient service and cheaper fares. The company is called Redcar and it is operating on all the Autocar routes from nearby Tonbridge with a number of fast new small saloons.

The rivalry between the two bus companies is fascinating; in fact many passengers believe they are on course for a price war. That will be good news for the customers who will be the beneficiaries.

New Watling Street has cost a million pounds

November 19th: The Prince of Wales today opened the new road from the Crayford boundary of Dartford, over ancient Watling Street to Strood — an occasion that marks an epoch in the history of inland transport. It is one of the most important new roads in England. Apart from its historic interest, it forms one of the main arteries by which commerce, the life blood of the nation, may pass from London to the coast and so to the limits of the Empire and to all parts of the globe.

The new road has been built to provide work for the large numbers of unemployed ex-servicemen in the London County Council area and to create an easier and better route for

The Prince of Wales inspects the 5th Battalion (RWK) Regiment before opening the new road at Dartford.

through traffic than the congested London-Dover Road which passes through Dartford, Greenhithe, Northfleet and Gravesend. The cost is estimated at £1,000,000 and a total number of 550,000 days' work has been provided over a period of 2½ years.

The new road begins at the Brent, Dartford and follows the line of the old Roman Watling Street, through Swanscombe Park, Springhead, crossing the Gravesend-Wrotham Road and by-passing Singlewell, traversing Cobham Park and by-passing Three Crutches village to Strood Hill. The total length is 11½ miles and during the progress of the works many examples of Roman pottery have been found.

In passing through Cobham woods every care has been taken to preserve their natural attraction and many new points of sylvan beauty have been revealed.

SUBSCRIBERS

The following kindly gave their support to this book.

Mrs I C Rhodes
Les & Lin Maskrey
Chris Powis
Mrs W J Baigent
Mrs Iris Watkins
Mr A G Priestley
J H Warner
Ron Yates
D F & S Dunton
D S & B M Baron
Leonard Egan
Mr & Mrs R Woodgate
John F Dorling
A P Currant
Malcolm Round
Maureen Humphrey
J T Armstrong
Pam Nye
J Wilmhurst
Lucy Peatfield
Ian Martin
K L Hayes
D E Nowers
Mark Heselden
B L & J F Matthews
Bob Holness
Bill Morton
Michael J Tong

Mrs E Palmer
Mrs C L Jones
Leslie Fettis
George Hughes
Mr Frederick Bywater-Holmes
A J Ladd
Mrs Alice Kathleen Butcher
Trevor Robbie
J J Butcher
H W M James
Anne Davis
Muriel E Harker
C H Fox
Mrs Jean Crisfield
Robert A Barham
Briars Family
Elsa Robinson
F H A Williams
George Winton
John Edward Wratten
Violet Brand
Kathryn Phillips
Mrs Emerald Frampton
Agnes Todd Morgan
Margaret & Alan Wilkinson
Mrs Janet Chambers
Leslie John Wood
William Frank Wood
Ann Buckett
G R Boxall

Paul Rason
Pat Brown
P R Rogers
L L Pett
John London
Nigel Riley
Simon Baldwin
Muriel Neal
Betty J Church
John Dawson
Mr & Mrs B G Harber
Doris Bellringer
Maurice Stocker
Eric Keys
Tessa & Mike Sheeres
Doris M Brown
Mrs M Kessel
Alan Deares
Centre for Kentish Studies
Bexley Library Service
Dorothy Hamlyn
Stan Stringer
Edwin Thompson
C J Huke
James Paterson
Bruce Walker
Florence W Clarke
Evelyn M Evans
Peter J Kiff
Marie Wicks & Robin Butson
James McQuillan

Mrs Paula Bugg
Hugh William Taylor
Sidney Edward Taylor
Valerie Thatcher
Ben Hammock
Miss M V Borner
C W Rumley
Joyce Cook
B J Bowles
Brian A Holyland
C J Wood
Richard Cross
Aubrey John Stockford
Colin Butcher
Mrs Pat Wright
Mrs E M Tucker
Mrs M E Potter
Alan Smith
Guy Hitchings
A Brett-Harris
Maria J Jarvis
Frederick G Neville
David Thomas Hobbs
C A Miles
Paul Thompson
David Witherspoon
Roy Rofe
Iain H Anderson
Freda Stevenson
Maurice Short

Charmian A Amos
Peter T Summers
Dawn Crouch
Wendy Brazier
Chris Wyer
Gillian & Chris Whittingham
Bill & Vera Roberts
Rev M G Hewett
Lionel J Wood
Kathryn Phillips
Betty Marsh
Denis Fentiman
Eunice Towersey
Hugh R. Pryke
Bryan Richardson
Jim Davis
Jack Hayton
Peter Ellison
Eric Edgehill
K.W.Hammerton
Doreen Allibone
Mrs W.M.Cuthbert
Robin Carden
Dorothy K.Elliott
A.Davidson
Mrs Amanda Young
Len Squires
Kent County Council Arts & Libraries
KE Taylor
Christiane P Foster
Roy Cleveley
John Pluckrose

BIBLIOGRAPHY

In writing this book I have referred to a variety of pamphlets, newspaper articles and miscellaneous documents kept in the Centre for Kentish Studies at Maidstone and various libraries throughout the county. Prominent among these is the monthly journal Bygone Kent published by Meresborough Books. I also referred to a vast number of books including the following: Kent, *Arthur Mee;* Kent, *Pennethorne Hughes*; Kent, *Dorothy Gardiner*; Kent, *Frank Victor Dawes*; Hidden Kent, *Alan Major*; Kent A Hundred Years Ago, *Aylwin Guilmant*; Tales of Old Tonbridge, *Frank Chapman;* Rudyard Kipling, *Martin Seymour-Smith*; Romney Marsh, *Anne Roper;* Lady Sackville, *Susan Mary Alsop;* History of Southern Railway, *Michael R.Bonavia;* The Pleasant Town of Sevenoaks, *John Dunlop;* H.G.Wells (An Anthology) *W.Warren Wagar;* History of Gravesend, *Robert Hiscock;* Portrait of the Medway, *Roger Penn*; History of Fire Fighting in Kent, *Harry Klopper;* Kent Headlines, *Alan Bignell;* Action Stations 9, *Chris Ashworth;* Grandfather's Biggin Hill, *John Nelson;* History of Maidstone, *Peter Clark* and *Lyn Murfin;* The Astor Family, *Gavin Astor;* Sittingbourne in Old Photographs, *Eric R.Swain;* Hythe Haven, *Duncan Forbes;* The Story of the Queen's Own Buffs, *Gregory Blaxland;* Brain Waves, *P.W.Boreham;* Kent Transport, *Eric Baldock*, Memories of Kent Cinemas, *Martin Tapsell;* Dover, A Pictorial History, *Ivan Green;* The First World War, *Martin Gilbert,* The Boer War, *Thomas Packenham;* Chronicle of the Century*, ed Derrik Mercer;* The Dover Patrol, *Admiral Reginald Bacon*; Life in Kent at the Turn of the Century, *Michael Winstanley;* David Copperfield, *Charles Dickens;* Guinness Book of Records; Biggin on The Bump, *Bob Ogley;* Kent Weather Book, *Bob Ogley;* Queen's Own Royal West Kent Regiment, *C.T.Atkinson;* Kent Murders, *Alan Bignell,* Dartford Country, *Geoffrey Porteus;* Portrait of Canterbury, *John Boyle;* Kent Crimes and Disasters, *Bill Bishop;* The Book of Orpington, *Dorothy Cox*; Knole and the Sackvilles, *Vita Sackville-West*; Kent Women, *Bowen Pearse,* Hopping Down in Kent, *Alan Bignell.*

THE AUTHOR

Bob Ogley was born in Sevenoaks, has lived all his life in the county and is proud to be a Kentish Man. An author of more than a dozen books he has travelled extensively in pursuit of information and photographs and has discovered a surprise supplementary career as a speaker to clubs and organisations. He is also a regular broadcaster on BBC Radio Kent.

Bob is a former editor of the Sevenoaks Chronicle and the author of *In The Wake of The Hurricane* — the book on the great storm of 1987 which went into the top ten bestseller list and stayed there for seven successive months. He has also written *Kent at War, Biggin on The Bump, Doodlebugs and Rockets, the Story of Robson and Jerome* and co-written a series of books on the history of the weather. His books have raised more than £95,000 for various charities.

Information for subscribers

The second volume of this *Kent Chronicle of the Century* series will be published in October 1997 and will cover the years between 1925 and 1949. It will be identical in format to this book. The great difference will be that it reaches into the age of nostalgia — for many — rather than history.

Many readers will recall the great achievements such as Lindbergh's solo crossing of the Atlantic and Campbell's land speed record but perhaps be unaware of their respective Kentish connections. Others will remember with affection the arrival of the Jazz Age and the Charleston and the golden age of the silver screen when Garbo and Fairbanks and Crawford lured us all to the Odeon and the Plaza. There will be memories of political turbulence — the great strike, the alarming rise of the Third Reich. And then, of course the death of George V, the abdication and the second world war.

If you would like to subscribe to the next volume please write (or telephone) as soon as possible to the address below for details. There will be a substantial reduction for subscribers and their names will be printed in the book. We will, of course, require a deposit followed by the balance just prior to publication. Signed copies will be available on request.

**FROGLETS PUBLICATIONS, BRASTED CHART,
WESTERHAM, KENT TN16 1LY.
TEL: 01959 562972. FAX 01959 565365**